White Tie and Dagger

ALSO BY ANDREW TULLY

WHITE TIE
AND DAGGER

by Andrew Tully

William Morrow & Company, Inc.   New York 1967

To My Son John
With Love

Contents

White Tie and Dagger

Skulduggery
with Champagne

1

Lyndon Johnson, Fox

MANY MONTHS after the free election of a constituent assembly in South Vietnam in September, 1966, the pundits were still wondering why the Communist Viet Cong made such a perfunctory effort to sabotage the election. The turnout of up to eighty-five percent of the five million registered voters was at least a propaganda victory for democracy in Southeast Asia, if only because of its revelation that a majority of the South's adult population was interested in participaing in Saigon's version of the democratic process. Moreover, it gave the Saigon regime of General Nguyen Cao Ky a flavor of legitimacy which the Communists had always vigorously denied it.

Yet, except for sporadic flurries of almost offhand terrorism, the Communists showed a strange lack of interest in the election. It was almost as if—as the then Under Secretary of State George W. Ball told a reporter—"the Commies didn't give a damn about it."

As Ball and a handful of other top United States officials knew, that was not the full explanation. To be sure, the Communists acted as if they didn't give a damn, but they acted so because they had been lured into a trap conceived by a politician named Lyndon Baines Johnson and sprung by some bright young men in the State Department's Bureau of Intelligence and Research. The springing of that trap was a classic example of a government employing diplomats accredited to it to serve its own ends. Among other things, the ploy illustrated the truism that in the suspicious world of international politics, a government almost always gives special credence to information obtained through stealth or deviousness.

The story began on a sultry evening in late June, 1966, when President Johnson was conducting a private and unannounced strategy meeting with some of his closest defense and diplomatic advisers. The subject was the upcoming September election in South Vietnam, and those attending the meeting were concerned about the danger that the Viet Cong would launch a massive campaign of terror that might succeed in keeping large numbers of South Vietnamese from venturing to the polling booths. It was vital to American policy as well as to the political stability of South Vietnam that there be as big a turnout as possible. Saigon and Washington both wanted to show the world that the Vietnamese under the Ky regime would react enthusiastically to an opportunity to take the first step toward representative government.

There was agreement on the need for increased security measures, but for obvious reasons it was necessary that the Americans defer to the Ky government in this regard. United States forces, of course, could and would try to keep the Viet Cong guerrillas in the country-side so occupied that their opportunities for terrorist incursions against the hamlets would be considerably reduced. There would be an increase in tactical bombing of Viet Cong installations. Yet it was generally agreed that the guerrillas, and the daytime-honest Vietnamese citizens in cities such as Saigon and Da Nang, who turned Viet Cong at night, could be a serious problem.

"I wish our friends the Communists weren't aware of how much we're depending on this election," Johnson remarked. "We'd be better off if we hadn't had to make a federal case out of it. Now we stand or fall on that election, and the Communists know it. It's in their interest to sabotage it if they can."

Someone mentioned that until recently Hanoi had ignored the election, and that even now its only comment had been an objection to a Saigon suggestion that the election be witnessed by observers from the United Nations. Johnson replied sharply that the United States couldn't bank on Hanoi continuing a hands-off policy. "They'll be jumping in with both feet when the time is ripe," he said. "But I'd give my right arm if we could somehow get them to ignore the election right up to the opening of the polls."

Johnson's mouth turned up in what an observer later described as a "fiendish grin." As he spoke, the President leaned forward almost eagerly. "We've all been too emotional in public about this election," he said. "Perhaps we should have been more detached. Maybe we should have been more critical of General Ky and his regime, as though we didn't quite approve of holding an election just yet. It's too bad we can't somehow get across to Hanoi and the Viet Cong that we really don't like the election worth a damn and that we've privately washed our hands of it." Johnson paused, thinking. Then, "Yes, I wish we could make them think we knew it was going to be a flop and planned to blame the flop on the terrorist campaign waged by the Communists. That might give them pause."

There were smiles around the room, including the President's. This, everyone seemed to be saying, was the stuff of which dreams were made. Dreams, but at this late date hardly practical policy. The discussion continued.

But the next morning, "someone" at the White House awoke convinced the Johnson idea was worth pursuing. Since even in a White House so completely dominated by Lyndon Johnson a right hand occasionally refuses to confide in a left hand, this "someone" got on the telephone to another "someone" at the State Department. During the morning, there were a number of conversations among officials of the State and Defense Departments, the Central Intelligence Agency and some police-type advisers. It was decided that whatever was done would be done by State, and that officially the real big shots would wash their hands of it.

The details of the planning are still unknown except to a few persons, but before nightfall several bright young men had been assigned to see what they could do to spread confusion in the Hanoi camp. "It's your baby," they were told. "Don't come to anyone else if you get in trouble. If there's a fuss, you may all wind up in the Agriculture Department."

But the bright young men were enthusiastic. They believed not only that it was worth trying, but that they might be able to carry it off. It was agreed that to have any chance of success the piece of flummery would have to be leaked to Hanoi by a diplomat with impeccable credentials as a loyal, credible, and effective vassal of Communism's Wave of the Future. They scrutinized a list of their social contacts in the tight little colony of European Communist diplomats. Any one of the diplomats on the list would have served as a transmission belt to North Vietnam, but the question arose as to how much faith Hanoi would place in information obtained in Washington by an Iron Curtain operative. Not enough, it was decided. Moscow was suspect in the

Peking-Hanoi camp as not above feeding its "friends" false intelligence for its own purposes. No, it would have to be a neutral, who deep inside was actually a bleeding-heart Communist untarnished by the exigencies of his own nationalism.

They had just the man. He was a passionate, rather tedious fellow from a neutral Asian nation who was known around Foggy Bottom and along Embassy Row as a kind of walking pipeline to both Hanoi and Peking. His own rather ambivalently nonaligned embassy knew of his activities, but kept him on for reasons peculiar to the complexities of a certain variety of "neutral" diplomacy. But he could not be approached directly. Although two of State's men occasionally joined him for lunch and a cordial couple of hours, he would smell a large rat if either of them tried to feed him any kind of a story, let alone this one.

For two days the little task force pored over names. At the end, it had to settle on another neutral diplomat who represented a calculated risk. State's men had excellent reasons to believe that this individual, a junior staffer at a West European embassy, occasionally passed on information to the fellow-travelling Asian diplomat, for a price. He also was in the occasional employ of three or four other embassies. Moreover, the State men had only accidentally stumbled on knowledge of his activities, and thus the European had no reason to believe that any American would regard him as anything more than a loyal servant of a loyal American ally. In short, he should have no suspicion that the American was trying to plant a bogus story with him. Instead, he probably would be flattered at being let in on some juicy inside stuff.

The calculated risk involved actually was twofold. No one was absolutely sure that the European had done business before with the Asian, and it was not certain whether the Asian would swallow anything put on his plate by the European. But both parts of the risk were worth taking. The two men were friendly and had been seen in frequent casual conversations at Washington parties. The story was one the European logically would pass on to a friend of Hanoi and Peking. As for the Asian's degree of confidence in a colleague with a reputation as a dilettante, it had to be chanced. As a schemer himself, the Asian would know that other schemers often donned a bogus personality as a cover. Besides, the story would be coming from an individual known to travel in respectable Western circles.

They went with the European, hereinafter to be referred to by the pseudonym Gregory, simply because it bears no resemblance to his real name. A member of the task force who periodically did some pub-crawling with the man telephoned him and arranged to meet him for drinks at the Georgetown Inn, a rather precious establishment on Wisconsin Avenue in that determinedly social neighborhood. On that occasion nothing passed between the two except the usual exchange of information about new girls in town and some rather casual conversation on the De Gaulle mentality. But when they met a week later in the bar of the Mayflower Hotel on Connecticut Avenue, the State Department man almost off-handedly unfolded the story in bits and pieces. Since Gregory knew his companion only as a toiler on the Southeast Asia desk and not as an intelligence type, he seemed impressed by the tale of what a nuisance the election had become to the American policy makers.

The tipoff was Gregory's own casualness. "I'm not surprised," he said, when told that both the State Department and the White House privately wished they had never heard of the election. "It's a very spurious business. Ky is not to be trusted. I think your government will be sorry it got mixed up in this allegedly free election."

So far, so good. The next step was to put a twenty-four-hour-a-day tail on Gregory, an effort that required only thirty-seven hours of work. As the surveillance went into its thirty-eighth hour, Gregory was found sitting across from the Asian neutral in the Genghis Khan, a restaurant specializing in curried dishes. It took the two of them four hours to eat dinner that night, and when they left the restaurant they seemed to be on excellent terms.

In late July, when the Saigon government announced that more than five million citizens had registered to vote, the Communist propaganda line took on a noisier and more violent note. There were also some two hundred acts of terrorism between July 25 and August 31. But it was obvious the Communists were operating well below their capacity to obstruct the election. Hanoi, in fact, was in the throes of indecision.

It was learned later from unimpeachable sources that the Asian dutifully had reported his conversation with Gregory to both Hanoi and Peking. In both capitals it was greeted by politicians who had long suspected the sincerity of Washington's alliance with General Ky and its willingness to throw all its support to an election that was suspect in so many other quarters of the Free World. In short, Peking and Hanoi both had feared that Washington was engaged in some form of trickery, that it was using the election as a means not of cementing democracy in South Vietnam but of exposing the obstructive efforts of the Communist partners.

The report from the Asian diplomat seemed to verify these suspicions. More, it was evidence that the United States had no faith in Ky's ability to get out the vote and was making plans to cover its own confusion once the election was exposed as a failure. Hanoi, with Peking's approval, decided to keep its hands off the election, to let it proceed unmolested, in order that afterwards it might say to the world: "You see, we stood aside and let them have their election, and it was a farce. Now will you believe us when we tell you that the Ky regime is rejected by the common people of the South?"

Meanwhile, little by little, sly criticisms of Ky, which were attributed to high American officials, began to appear in the press in the United States. The word was passed to various respected diplomats that Washington was not too happy with the Ky regime or with its post-election plans. In capitals all over the world, politicians reached the false conclusion that Washington hoped to get out from under its commitment to Ky. Notable among them all, Hanoi lapped it up.

Twenty-four hours before the election, it became clear that Hanoi was getting nervous. Ky's statements seemed too confident; there were too many reports of enthusiasm for the election among the peasants and other plain citizens. Almost as an afterthought, the Viet Cong turned on the terror on election eve and launched 166 acts of violence which resulted in the death of thirty civilians and soldiers and the wounding of 167 others.

As one American diplomat put it: "At that point the Communists must have suspected they had been hornswoggled. So they tried to do the job cheaply, just in case their suspicions were unfounded. At that point, too, they probably thought it was too late to intimidate the voters. They probably realized that even if there wasn't an American plot afoot, the Saigon regime would count the vote twice and would inevitably claim a victory."

One other circumstance figured significantly, however. According to United States intelligence reports from Vietnam, the lower-level Viet Cong operatives had been ordered early in the game to do nothing to obstruct the election. When this order was countermanded, these ward heelers refused to change signals. They were afraid of losing the popular support in the hamlets they were counting on against the day when the United States "abandoned" the Ky government.

At any rate, the trap conceived by Lyndon Johnson was almost spectacularly successful. It kept the Viet Cong terrorists at arm's length long enough for General Ky to stage a reasonably free election that added greatly to the political stability of the country, while demonstrating that the Saigon regime controlled a majority of the South—that it was accepted, if not exactly loved. Moreover, although similar cloak-and-dagger tactics perhaps should never be introduced into any handbooks for Eagle Scouts, it is hard to find fault with such adventures in skulduggery by the American government. State Department officials have always been certain that both Peking and Moscow benefit from intelligence passed on to them from staffers in the Indian, Indonesian and French embassies, and in recent years Washington has contrived to plant false information in these quarters, both to confuse the enemy and to expose our friends.

There is involved in all these cases the handy excuse called "reasons of national security." Surely, national security was a valid concern in the Vietnam elections, since American troops were fighting in that country. There is also an element of national security involved in finding out what both our friends and enemies are saying about each other, and occasionally in leading them astray. And since various means must be used to keep informed, the United States frequently has eavesdropped on a number of embassies with electronic devices.

Franklin D. Roosevelt initiated the policy of permitting the FBI to engage in wiretapping and bugging, with specific authority from the Attorney General, during the years preceding World War II. For a time, the FBI had several microphones concealed in the Japanese Embassy, and also tapped the embassy's phones, but little was learned for the simple reason that on both the telephone and in conversations within the embassy, the Japanese spoke code when they discussed military or security matters. However, wiretaps of the German Embassy's telephones gave the State Department its first inkling of the Nazi-Soviet pact in 1939, which precipitated the war. One of the key sentences intercepted was a reference, in a conversation between the German Foreign Office and the embassy, that "Stalin has agreed to sign." At the time of Pearl Harbor, wiretaps and bugs in both German and Japanese embassies produced only a kind of static, apparently caused by some type of "scrambler" installed in the embassies.

In State Department corridors, it is an open secret that at various times telephones have been tapped and bugs installed in the Indian, Pakistan, Cambodian, Burmese and Egyptian embassies—among others. It is understood that some interesting bits of information were obtained from the Burmese tap in 1965 concerning domestic troubles within Communist China, including indications that Mao Tze-tung was having difficulty controlling some elements within the regime who were plumping for an accommodation with the United States. Unbelievers at the time were red-faced when full-scale fighting on a revolutionary scale broke out a year later.

During 1966, it was also revealed that telephone wires of the Dominican Embassy were tapped during at least the previous three administrations, with the knowledge and approval of Presidents Truman, Eisenhower and Kennedy. This came to light during pretrial hearings in the case of Bobby Baker, former secretary of the Senate Democratic majority, charged with tax evasion, theft and conspiracy to defraud the government. When the judge impounded some of the conversations the Justice Department admitted had been obtained by electronic eavesdropping on Baker, it developed that both sides had agreed that since they involved calls by Baker to the Dominican Embassy, the national interest was involved.

In the more recent past, it was learned, the wiretaps were installed to obtain information on the situation in the Dominican Republic after the assassination of the dictator Rafael Leonidas Trujillo Molina in 1961. The State Department was especially interested in the prospects of Joaquin Balaguer, then provisional president, becoming permanent president. Balaguer returned to the presidency in 1966 after defeating the left-wing candidate, Juan Bosch, in an election which followed settlement of a civil war.

At any rate, the wiretaps were especially useful to American policy makers during the Dominican civil war. They learned, for example, that of all the politicians jockeying for position, the only one who had been blackballed by the Communists was the right-to-center Balaguer, who up to that time had been regarded by some thinkers in State as a wishy-washy politician likely to do business with the Reds if expedience dictated. From that point, Balaguer's stock started going up in Foggy Bottom.

Bugging and wiretapping, of course, remain a two-way street in the diplomatic dodge. The various organizations of lawmen assigned to the protection of American internal security are aware of the constant efforts of certain foreign diplomats to tune in on United States government establishments. Indeed, Washington shops report that the bulk of their sales of electronic listening devices are made to "foreigners." Thus there was no great surprise displayed among those on the inside when the FBI exposed an attempt by two Czech diplomats in 1966 to bug the State Department office of Raymond Lisle, Director of the Office of Eastern European Affairs.

Clearly, this was a carefully conceived espionage ploy which originated in 1961, when the Czech diplomats sought out a State Department employee to use as an intermediary. Their ultimate objective, according to the FBI, was to bug the office of the then Under Secretary of State, George W. Ball.

Eventually, the Czechs settled on Frank J. Mrkva, a general services officer and passport courier with State, whose duties included messenger runs to the Czech Embassy with visa applications. Zdenek Pisk, a second secretary in the Czech Embassy, struck up an acquaintance with Mrkva and arranged for Mrkva to receive invitations to embassy functions. Mrkva, as alert as State would like all its employees to be, notified his superiors, and thenceforth his contacts with the Czechs were with the full knowledge and guidance of his own department and the FBI. Pisk and Jiri Opatrny, an embassy attaché, made their first approach to Mrkva on November 30, 1961, when the three had dinner in a Washington restaurant, and the Czechs asked Mrkva about his family background, his relatives in Czechoslovakia and his duties at the State Department.

Mrkva was surprised when the two Czechs mentioned the amount of his mortgage payments and the fact his daughter required an operation. He was first offered one hundred dollars for information, but as the plot unfolded the price was gradually raised, and offers also were made to assume the mortgage payments and pay for the daughter's operation. In all, Mrkva had forty-eight meetings with one or the other of the Czechs from November, 1961, to July, 1966—eleven with Pisk and thirty-seven with Opatrny after the latter took over upon Pisk's recall to Czechoslovakia in May, 1963. The Czechs paid Mrkva a total of $3440, all of which was turned over to the FBI and eventually deposited in the general fund of the United States Treasury, as required by law.

In return for this money, Mrkva supplied the Czechs with assorted generally available and unclassified documents such as the State Department telephone book, press releases and administrative reports. But as time passed, the Czechs became more specific in their demands. They asked for a blank United States passport of a new series, information about the physical layout of various State Department offices, and a map of the office of the Director of Eastern European Affairs. Mrkva dutifully supplied a General Services Administration catalog of government furniture, which was to be used in designing a device that could be put in an unobtrusive place.

A few weeks later, Opatrny delivered to Mrkva a listening device, made in Czechoslovakia, which he ordered Mrkva to install in the base of a bookcase in Director Lisle's office. The bug was contained in a rectangular wooden case about thirteen inches long, one and one-eighth inches wide and one-half inch thick. The case looked like one of those wooden blocks used to support a bookcase or other piece of furniture. There was an opening on the side of the case for a small microphone, capable of picking up all conversations in the room. Inside the case was a miniature radio transmitter which could be turned on by remote control with an electronic signal from outside.

Power for the transmitter was supplied by seven American-built dry-cell batteries, which gave the transmitter the capability of sending very-high-frequency radio signals to the Czech Embassy on Massachusetts Avenue, about a half-mile north of the State Department building.

Mrkva brought the transmitter to the State Department on May 29, 1966, and turned it over to FBI agents. The FBI men put the transmitter in place, and soon thereafter Opatrny conducted a twenty-minute check which he told Mrkva showed that the transmitter was operating successfully. But several days later, Opatrny summoned Mrkva to a meeting at which he complained that the bug was no longer working, and wanted to know why. Mrkva explained that he had dropped the transmitter and that perhaps it had been damaged.

"Get it back," Opatrny ordered. "We'll have to send it back to Prague to be repaired."

Mrkva balked. He said it would be dangerous for him to go prowling about Lisle's office. There was a heated discussion, in which Opatrny revealed that he had learned a few American cuss words. He had promised Mrkva a thousand dollars for installing the transmitter, but now refused to hand over the full payment until the device had been returned. "We want to put it in Ball's office later," he told Mrkva. Then he gave the American five hundred dollars.

Mrkva, who had not even told his wife about his secret role, stalled Opatrny for another few weeks, promising that he would retrieve the transmitter from Lisle's office as soon as he found a good opportunity to do so. The FBI, of course, wanted to delay public exposure while it sought to discover if any other persons—Czechs or Americans or both—were involved in this or any other plot. But the lawmen finally had to step in when Opatrny told Mrkva he planned a holiday in Czechoslovakia. Opatrny got his holiday sooner than he had planned. When the story broke, he was given the usual three days by the State Department to get out of the country. At the same time, the department informed United Nations General Secretary U Thant that Pisk, who had returned to the United States as first secretary of the Czech UN mission, also was *persona non grata*.

The American government must be constantly on guard against the espionage activities of not only Communist but neutral diplomats who may be giving or selling information to its enemies. Although they are furiously and constantly active, the Communist embassies actually are of less concern; the FBI keeps them under twenty-four-hour-a-day surveillance and for the most part manages to control the movements of their occupants, as the frequent headlines about the involvement of Communist diplomats in spy plots suggest. But neutral and allied diplomats pose a peculiar problem, first because they are not automatically suspect and thus are not usually subjected to surveillance, and second because there just isn't enough counter-intelligence manpower to shadow all of them.

Moreover, in the Cold War era as in the era of World War II, the neutral diplomat is much sought after by both sides. Colonel Stig Wennerstrom, the Swedish air attaché who served the Soviet Union as a spy in both his native country and along Washington's Embassy Row for fifteen years, told his interrogators that in the diplomatic social swim only the neutrals were able to move freely among both their Communist and democratic colleagues, and thus were able to pick up much valuable information. Some of this they traded to other diplomats for payment in kind, some they sold to the warring sides. All neutrals want to be known as good sources of information, for only by gaining such a reputation can they acquire the bits and pieces of intelligence their own countries want.

Officially, a military, air or naval attaché is an "observer." By the terms of international protocol, he is supposed to confine himself to obtaining information by overt means in order to report to his country on the power and progress of the armed forces of the government to which he is accredited. Actually, as Wennerstrom did as a spy for Moscow and as others do to inform their own countries, these attachés acquire their intelligence in any way they can, legal or illegal. Thus, although great courtesy is extended them by the Pentagon, there are foreign attachés the American military brass wouldn't trust for sixty seconds with the cafeteria silver.

An example of this type was Pawel Monat, military attaché at the Polish Embassy from 1955 to 1958, who defected to the West by seeking asylum in the American Embassy in Warsaw in 1959. Four or five times a year, Monat received from his intelligence bosses in Warsaw requests for specific classified information which filled twenty-five or more typewritten pages. His work load was so heavy that a year after his arrival in Washington his staff was increased from five to eight—all but two of them, Monat told the FBI, members of the Polish secret police. Every year, Monat was required to answer thousands of questions about new American weapons and equipment, the character and abilities of military leaders, and even changes in the curriculum at West Point and Annapolis. In 1957, he was able to inform his bosses that the new U-2 American reconaissance planes flew at too high an altitude to be shot down over Poland before they crossed the Soviet border.

Diplomatic spies of the Wennerstrom stripe are also useful in providing information in depth concerning American foreign policy. During the Suez crisis of 1956, Wennerstrom used his contacts at the Pentagon to obtain secret information on the movements of American air and naval units in the Mediterranean. He sent this intelligence to Moscow, and a few weeks later he was congratulated for having successfully predicted the movements three days before they took place.

Sometimes, too, a diplomat in the pay of a country other than his own can, unwittingly, contribute to the cause of peace, or at least to a calming of tensions. Wennerstrom did this one day in 1954, when his Soviet contact in Washington arranged a meeting and showed up in an excited state.

The Russian told Wennerstrom that the Soviet Embassy had received a high-priority message from Moscow ordering him to check on a report that the United States was planning a "surprise attack" against the Soviet Union. Wennerstrom told his Swedish police inter-rogators that he couldn't believe the United States was capable of such a strike, but he did the obvious thing. He drove across the Potomac to the Pentagon to see whether there was any frantic activity among the brass. He did this by calling on the aides of several high-ranking officers and asking for appointments with their bosses in the next few days. When the appointments were made without any trouble, he concluded that the Moscow report was false and so reported to his Soviet contact. Thereafter, Wennerstrom's standing with Russian in-telligence went up a notch or two.

That part of official Washington which deals with foreign relations and national security not only frets and worries about the possibility that Embassy Row shelters false friends; it must also concern itself with the vagaries of a diplomatic colony which must be constantly assured, in terms of varying emphasis, that this nation's policies seek to become all things to all peoples. It is a far cry from the good old days immediately following World War II when the United States and Great Britain sat down and decided what was good for everybody. Today, many other countries have fixed positions which must be con-sidered by the White House, the State Department and the Pentagon. Thus, the bombing of North Vietnam might be greeted with applause in Australia and Korea, while France and Britain throw up their hands in horror and pious India calls upon Uncle Sam to renounce materialism and force.

When the French Foreign Minister, Couve de Murville, visited Pres-ident Johnson in October, 1966, one of the tribal chieftains in the amiable jungle known as the State Department summed up their dis-cussions in language redolent of the pool hall.

"The guy wanted Johnson to appoint De Gaulle referee in Viet-nam," he reported. "Couve was a kind of Gallic Billy Graham bring-ing the gospel from on high, to wit that De Gaulle wanted Johnson to take his chances that a peace conference might result in the Saigon government falling under Communist control."

But even without visitations from foreign capitals, any American President is surrounded by special pleaders operating out of Embassy Row. Their job is to handle this rich and powerful uncle in order at once to share in his financial largesse and to have their political way with him. In the world of diplomacy, the British frantically seek to maintain their special status of junior partner, while De Gaulle's France tries to supplant the boss and the Soviet Union wants only to dictate the world's future without being distracted by a lot of tedious twaddle from the children.

This is heady wine for the President. It is verification that, while these foreigners may sneer behind Washington's back and call us *nouveaux riches,* they yet acknowledge that only Washington can give them what they want. A France which talks big remains pretty small potatoes in the international hierachy, even with its erector-set nuclear establishment. As for most of the rest, the United States moves warily, sometimes with an amused—or bemused—smile on its official face. The Latin Americans almost always feel neglected and must be tossed a bag of goodies from time to time. The Nationalist Chinese must be reassured that we still love them despite the high cost of supporting them. The neutral nations get the wheedling attention required to prevent them from becoming too neutral on Communism's side.

"Thank God for the Soviet Union," Dean Acheson once told a reporter, when he was Secretary of State in the Truman Administration. "I always know what to expect from those characters on Sixteenth Street. I wish I could say the same about our friends."

2

Embassy Row Versus LBJ

IN ONE SENSE, at least, Dean Acheson's wry appreciation of the Embassy of the Union of Socialist Soviet Republics was a shrewd observation. In a city whose diplomatic panjandrums become apoplectic over the slightest deviation in the rules of protocol, the Russians have never cared about the trappings or petty courtesies of the trade. Nowadays, from Ambassador Dobrynin down, they are interested only in doing practical business. They stand on their diplomatic prerogatives only when there is something in it for the home office.

Perhaps because they have more time on their hands, members of other embassy staffs are sensitive to any seeming snub by the Colossus of the West. In matters of protocol, they insist that Washington follow the book, and especially the book's fine print. Thus Secretary Rusk was predictably concerned shortly after the elections of November, 1964, when Dr. Guillermo Sevilla-Sacasa, the portly and amiable Ambassador of Nicaragua, requested an appointment "on a matter of the utmost urgency."

There are, of course, few matters of any degree of urgency involving Nicaragua, but Rusk arranged a meeting with Sevilla-Sacasa at the earliest possible moment. For Sevilla-Sacasa was not merely the representative of his government but also the representative of the Washington diplomatic colony. Having presented his credentials to President Franklin D. Roosevelt on July 30, 1943, Sevilla-Sacasa was dean of the diplomatic corps and therefore a man of considerable importance. If he wanted to see Rusk, the chances were the diplomats were unhappy.

They were. Seated comfortably in Rusk's office, Sevilla-Sacasa solemnly reported that the diplomatic colony was "on the verge of revolt." Its members, he said, were solely vexed by President Johnson's attitude toward them. The President kept ambassadors waiting for as long as two hours, frequently declined to see them privately, and usually so monopolized the conversation that they were given no opportunity to bring up matters of serious business. Unless there was a change, said Sevilla-Sacasa, he was sorely afraid that some representatives of foreign governments would refuse to have anything more to do with the President.

Shortly thereafter, President Johnson—as one diplomat put it—"saw the light." Within a few months, Johnson had had more than one hundred private conversations with ambassadors. Some were invited to his Texas ranch. Others were bundled up and taken on cruises down the Potomac on the Presidential yacht or invited to small White House lunches. After a year-long Cool War between the White House and the diplomatic colony, Lyndon Johnson had accepted Secretary Rusk's thesis that the ambassadors were the President's "international constituents."

It was quite a constituency. Including the 114 ambassadors and ministers, Washington counted more than 2,500 diplomats in its own colony, plus another 3,200 stationed at the United Nations in New York either as members of national missions or of the UN Secretariat. In addition, another several hundred were scattered about the country in the various foreign consulates. For comparison, only four foreign countries maintained missions in the infant United States in 1800.

Things had been rough during Lyndon Johnson's Cool War. Although the protocol incorporated into the rules promulgated by the Congress of Vienna in 1815 provides for the reception of ambassadors by the Chief of State, Johnson seemingly couldn't be bothered with them. He kept foreign diplomats waiting for weeks before accepting their credentials and thus condemned them to a kind of social twilight zone in which they were forced to pass up dinner invitations and quasi-official engagements lest they violate that section of protocol which says they are not bona fide representatives of their government until they have been received by the Chief of State. Often, they were herded to the White House in bunches, like delegations from the Iowa State Flower Society, given a casual handshake by the President, had their pictures taken and then hustled back to their embassies.

Nor did Johnson surrender easily. Pressed by Rusk to reform, he snapped that "These characters are your responsibility, not mine. Take care of them." The President urgently desired to save time by delegating to someone else the chore of receiving ambassadors, and when Rusk pointed out that he was trying to buck protocol, Johnson ordered the Secretary to have a memo prepared describing "in plain English" what the Congress of Vienna had to say about the matter.

Johnson got no comfort from the memo, dated December 4, 1964, and titled: "Presentation of Credentials." Its opening sentence read: "In response to a query from the White House on presentation of credentials to a person other than the Chief of State . . ."

The memo went on: "For several centuries it has been the norm in international relations for the Chief of State of a host country to receive, or grant an audience to, a high-ranking diplomatic representative of another country for the purpose of receiving the latter's credentials. This practice has not been customary for diplomatic representatives of low rank, e.g. chargés d'affaires, but in recent decades it has been almost universally followed as the norm for ambassadors and ministers.

"The procedures and ceremonies prescribed for the reception of newly arrived diplomatic representatives (often very elaborate) frequently vary according to the rank of the diplomat being received, but there is no variation in the reception of diplomats of equal rank (e.g. ambassadors) no matter how great the difference may be in the size, population, or importance of the states they represent."

A man who never fights City Hall, even when it's located in Vienna, Johnson bowed to what he called "the monkey-suit bunch." Henceforth, he decreed, ambassadors were to get all the trimmings, including a detachment of troops presenting arms in the White House driveway and a private chat with the President. But he was annoyed when an aide kept referring to the *Règlement de Vienne.* "If you mean those Vienna rules, say so," growled Texas' Number One citizen.

Moreover, Johnson kept his prerogative of giving envoys the rough side of his tongue whenever the governments they represented did not behave in a manner the President believed to be conducive to furthering the interests of the United States, which he usually managed to equate with those of the world. Beneath the leathery armor of his personality, Lyndon Johnson basically is a courteous and hospitable man. As he is fond of saying, he wants "folks to be at home with me."

But he also regards any meeting with a foreign official as an opportunity to get some things off his chest. He feels that any complaint or new emphasis on policy has greater impact when an ambassador can report it to his government as coming from the horse's—or Presidential —mouth.

Thus Johnson had one of his favorites, Soviet Ambassador Anatoly Dobrynin, on the carpet almost before Dobrynin had a chance to get settled in his chair one afternoon in February, 1967. "I wrote your Premier Kosygin a letter last month suggesting that the American and Soviet governments get together and discuss how we can limit the arms race," complained the President. "I'm still waiting for an answer. I don't think that's very polite, Mr. Ambassador. All this horsing around is the sort of thing that makes Americans get mad at you Russians. You never seem to be able to do anything in a straightforward way. All I want to do is talk; I haven't asked Mr. Kosygin to make any concessions."

Presumably, Dobrynin returned to the Soviet Embassy and dispatched a verbatim cable covering Johnson's remarks. And, as a State Department type remarked, "If there's anything a Russian hates it's to be accused of being impolite." At any rate, Johnson was able to announce on March 2 that the Soviet Union had agreed to open discussions with American Ambassador Llewellyn Thompson about the deployment of a Soviet anti-ballistic missile system.

Johnson can be just as blunt and petulant with representatives of allied governments. Although by April, 1965, he was warming up to the chore of greeting ambassadors, the President made a point then of suddenly discovering he hadn't the time to receive individually the new ambassadors of Chile, Denmark and Great Britain. Instead, he had them in together. Speaking directly to British Ambassador Sir Patrick Dean but making it plain his remarks concerned all three governments, Johnson delivered a tongue-lashing on the subject of our allies' unwillingness to make common cause with Washington on the war in Vietnam.

"I don't understand you people," complained Johnson. "You seem to be more concerned with the blood shed by Communists than by that shed by Americans. When an American bomb kills a North Vietnam civilian, it's an accident, but the Viet Cong set out deliberately to kill and maim civilians in South Vietnam."

The President told Dean, "You British are too damned pragmatic.

You're always worried about your precious trade. Well, you won't have any trade if you let the Communists take over the rest of the world. I should think that by now you'd have learned the lesson of Munich."

On an earlier occasion, Johnson told the then British Ambassador, Sir David Ormsby-Gore, that in Cyprus "the British are following their old practice of ducking their responsibilities." Ormsby-Gore had informed Secretary Rusk that London no longer could spare the money and troops to keep peace in Cyprus and that either the United States or the United Nations would have to step in. "An alliance is a share-and-share-alike partnership," Johnson told the British envoy. "Hasn't it ever occurred to you British that the American people already have been forced to take more than their share of trouble?"

In fact, Lyndon Johnson has a fundamental admiration and respect for the British people, and is fond of citing history to show that the British "always come through when the chips are down." But he feels there are times when he should talk tough in order to force the British government into a quid pro quo for American help. There was a method in his irritable reaction to a proposal in 1964 by Prime Minister Harold Wilson that he visit Washington. He told Ormsby-Gore that "Wilson wants to come over here to pick up some votes at home. I don't see why I should let him do his electioneering in the United States." Wilson had to cancel his visit, but Johnson volunteered "all our help" for Britain's monetary campaign to save the pound, and it was no coincidence that Wilson stood firm on his government's passive support of the American role in Vietnam.

Johnson's relationship with two French Ambassadors—Hervé Alphand and Charles Lucet—has been proper and polite, but hardly cordial. It stems from the President's determination to do nothing to nourish what he feels is President Charles de Gaulle's antagonism toward the United States. "De Gaulle is an old man," Johnson once told an interviewer. "He can't live forever, although he himself may think so, and when he passes I expect there'll be some changes." Johnson has issued strict orders that De Gaulle be treated with the utmost courtesy, "Call him General and always say thank you," Johnson commanded.

Nevertheless, Johnson occasionally has been sharp with Ambassador Lucet. During the period when Vietnam peace feelers were sprouting all over the globe in the winter of 1966-67, Johnson told Lucet the

French government's peace efforts were aimed at "stirring up trouble" among our allies on the Vietnam question. He remarked that De Gaulle was not in possession of all the facts and thus could be excused for "monkeying" with the problem, but he concluded sadly that "Your government isn't helping matters any."

Secretary Rusk shares Johnson's impatience with many of the ambassadors from European countries. He feels they represent governments which have not faced up to the reality that Asia is part of the world and which are too involved in petty efforts to build their economies and advance their nationalist ambitions. Rusk is fond of Lucet, but he has concluded sadly that Lucet fulfills no important function because De Gaulle not only calls all the plays but usually neglects to keep his own ambassador informed of the various switches in signals.

Rusk has had some exasperating sessions with Lucet, a man of charm and casual culture. At one of these meetings, during the fall of 1966, Rusk attempted to wring some comment from Lucet on the Vietnam situation. He reviewed the war in detail, then looked to Lucet inquiringly. Lucet was silent. Still trying, Rusk asked whether a Paris newspaper story which reported Paris had demanded the withdrawal of American troops was factual. Lucet replied that he could not describe it as "inaccurate."

"Can you give me a definite outline of France's position?" asked Rusk.

"I'm afraid I cannot," replied Lucet.

In contrast to the blank stares official Washington encounters from Charles de Gaulle's personal diplomats, the Russians since about mid-1966 have been much easier to do business with. That is to say, communications have been easier and, often, surprisingly effective.

Thus when President Johnson launched his step-up of the military campaign in North Vietnam in the late winter of 1967, he did so with an act of careful diplomacy aimed directly at the Kremlin. In effect, it could be safely said that the decision to mine North Vietnam's rivers was taken with the implicit approval of the Soviet Union as a step toward increasing the pressure on Hanoi to agree to peace negotiations.

When the decision to mine the rivers was reached, the President instructed Secretary Rusk to summon Soviet Ambassador Dobrynin "for a chat about Vietnam." In the course of that chat, on February 23, Rusk informed Dobrynin of the decision, and it was emphasized that mining the rivers was merely another step in efforts to force Hanoi to the peace table. The United States, Rusk told Dobrynin, appreciated Moscow's efforts to launch peace talks and so wished to explain the decision in advance. Rusk also pointed out that the mining of the waterways was no threat to Soviet shipping using the principal harbor of Haiphong and other ports.

Dobrynin passed along this information to Premier Kosygin, and the reaction from Moscow was the most Washington could have hoped for. That is, no objection was raised to the step-up. Kosygin did not say the Soviet Union approved of the escalation, but Washington was informed that his silence should be construed as indicating that Moscow would not "at this time" make a Kremlin case out of it. The impression the State Department got from this exchange was that the Russians finally had been convinced that the U.S. was sincere in its peace-seeking campaign and that only Hanoi's intransigence stood in the way of negotiations.

At the outset of the Egyptian-Israeli crisis of May, 1967, Johnson carried his penchant for personal diplomacy directly to Soviet Premier Alexei Kosygin. In several conversations with Kosygin on the "hot line" between the White House and the Kremlin, Johnson pressed the Soviet leader to issue a public statement saying that Russia would not intervene militarily. Kosygin refused to do so, but he gave Johnson "personal assurance" that the Soviets would "do everything within our diplomatic power" to prevent outbreak of a war. Russia, Kosygin told the President, would regard any full-scale outbreak of hostilities as an "international disaster" and would use its influence with Egypt's President Nasser to submit the quarrel to outside arbitration.

Johnson freely acknowledged to Kosygin the Soviet Union's continuing rise in influence in the Middle East since the 1950 tripartite pact signed by the United States, Great Britain and France in which the three nations implied they would intervene in the event of any attempt to change the Egyptian-Israeli status quo. Since Russia had become a world power, Johnson told Kosygin, it would be "unrealistic" if the three Western nations undertook joint action to preserve peace in the Middle East without Soviet cooperation.

For the most part, Johnson's clashes with the diplomatic corps involve matters of political substance, but some of the stickiness has resulted from gossip reaching Johnson's ears that certain members of the colony and their wives are wont to poke fun at both the President and the First Lady. Among those so accused are French Ambassador and Madame Lucet, former French Ambassador and Madame Alphand, Spain's Merry del Val and Kuwait's Al-Ghoussein. Usually, members of the so-called "Kennedy Government in Exile" also are involved. Johnson tries to take reports of these slurs philosophically. As a politician, he realizes it is always open season for his critics. But his anger is white hot when he hears that Mrs. Johnson has been ridiculed. "I can take the heat," he once told a visitor, "but when they start picking on my wife they're looking for trouble from me. Aside from the outrageous taste involved, Mrs Johnson has done more for her country than any other First Lady, including Eleanor Roosevelt."

Both Rusk and Johnson have been furious at our allies' insistence on trading with the North Vietnam and Cuban regimes, but they have made little progress in stopping it. Possibly, however, they have derived some satisfaction from venting their feelings to the various ambassadors of these countries.

Johnson frequently has upbraided Spanish Ambassador The Marquis Merry del Val about Fascist Spain's trade with Communist Cuba, and once commented bitterly to the Marquis that it was hard to understand governments which seemed to have no basic principles to guide their international relations. Merry del Val, who probably has less leeway than Charles Lucet in expounding policy, smiled wanly and said he hoped the President's remark was not an accusation against Spain. Johnson said nothing. Later, Johnson complained to an aide, "Those birds are always accusing Americans of being materialistic. Hell, their own countries don't think of *anything* but money."

Rusk had a stiff session with British Ambassador Dean in January, 1967 after the British government had announced a five-year credit to the Castro regime for construction of a thirty-nine million dollar fertilizer plant by a British firm. Rusk told Dean he found it passing strange that Britain could "play footsie" with Communist Cuba at a time when the United States was going out of its way to enforce British-sponsored sanctions against Rhodesia. Rusk got little satisfaction. Dean replied rather haughtily that there was a difference. He pointed out that the Rhodesian sanctions had the backing of the United Nations, while the American boycott of Cuba did not. Frustrated, Rusk could remark only that there was "such a thing" as a moral issue.

A man with a great deal of rugged Georgia boy behind his Foggy Bottom facade, Rusk has frequently lost patience with United Nations

Secretary General U Thant—to the point, at times, where he doubted Thant's credentials as an honest broker between the United States and North Vietnam. U Thant was asked in a letter from the U.S. Ambassador to the UN, Arthur Goldberg, on December 19, 1966, to use his "good offices" to bring about discussions between the two governments, but Rusk has not always been happy with Thant's approach. He has told intimates and an occasional visitor that Thant has been inclined to become emotionally and politically involved in the case for North Vietnam.

Rusk has been particularly irritated by Thant's contention that the National Liberation Front, political arm of the Viet Cong, should not be regarded as merely as stooge of Hanoi and that the conflict was a purely civil war between opposing South Vietnamese factions. It has always been the U.S. position, of course, that the war was instigated by the North Vietnam regime and that the Viet Cong was organized by Hanoi politicians.

At their infrequent meetings, Rusk has argued to Thant that the latter's viewpoint is at variance with the written record. During a visit to Thant in New York in the fall of 1966, the Secretary of State submitted to Thant copies of captured documents in the possession of the International Control Commission which stated flatly that the National Liberation Front was created by the North Vietnamese Communist Party both to deceive the West and to "liberate" the South by force.

Rusk also told Thant he was "dismayed" by Thant's continuing calls for an unconditional halt to U.S. bombing of North Vietnam, while voicing no criticism of Hanoi for refusing to comply with the second point of Thant's peace program providing for mutual de-escalation of military activities in the South.

"Have you no indignation left for Hanoi?" Rusk asked Thant.

He also went into a burn when Thant insisted that North Vietnam was "motivated by questions of principle." It was the Georgia boy speaking when Rusk inquired of Thant, "What principle is involved in the kidnapping and murder by the Viet Cong of 26,000 civilians in the South during the past thirty-two months?" Later, remarking on what he called Thant's "tears for the North Vietnamese civilians," Rusk asked the UN Secretary General why "you have never addressed yourself to the fact that while the South is overrun with refugees, no one runs to the North to escape persecution or torture?"

Back in Washington, Rusk gave a nutshell briefing to an aide. "We can deal with our enemies," he said dryly, "but God save us from neutrals like Thant."

Both Rusk and President Johnson were furious at U Thant for his hasty accession to Egyptian President Nasser's demand that United Nations troops be withdrawn from the Egyptian-Israeli frontier in May, 1967. They could see little excuse for an action which brought the world to the brink of war, and were particularly incensed that Thant had not even consulted the member nations of the UN before taking that action. It was their contention that Thant not only had revealed his incapacity for avoiding those actions which lead to the occasion of war, but had flouted the rule of law.

Specifically, Thant was accused of violating the General Assembly's Resolution 1121 (XI) under whose terms the Nasser regime agreed that the UN force should remain "until its task was completed." The resolution made it plain that, while the initial entry of the troops required the approval of the host government, it was not intended that the force remain at the sufferance of the host.

One reason advanced for Thant's surrender to Nasser may have been his almost paranoiac frustration over his failure to settle the Vietnam war. In some American eyes, Thant had taken the position that if the world would just listen to him, and to him alone, he would bring it peace. Unfortunately, peace is like any other commodity in the market-place—it is attainable only if both sides get something out of the deal. And Thant had insisted that the United States surrender, by requiring initial concessions only from Washington. There was a feeling, too, that Thant viewed Nasser as a qualified candidate as the leader of a Third Force to balance the conflicting interests of Communism and the Free World. Foggy Bottom officials wondered why it never occurred to Thant that such a force requires leadership dedicated to avoiding war, not starting it.

President Johnson is noted for his thin skin, of course, but it is unfair to state as law that his sensitivity is responsible for his impatience in some of these diplomatic contretemps. The President had a sound point in April, 1965, when he complained to Canadian Ambassador Charles Ritchie about a speech Canadian Prime Minister Mike Pearson made in Baltimore in which he criticized the American bombing of North Vietnam. Johnson told Ritchie, "You shouldn't let that fellow come to the States to make such speeches. He can make them at home if he wants to, but it's not polite to make them as this country's guest."

A myth has grown up that Lyndon Johnson is the only President ever to sound off to a foreign diplomat. It is a myth that ignores the record. Harry S Truman often delivered scoldings to ambassadors, and once told the then Prime Minister Clement Attlee of Great Britain that the British "ought to be ashamed of themselves" for trading with Communist China. Truman also blistered Spanish Ambassador Jose Felix de Lequerica for "lobbying in the people's Congress" for a foreign aid loan. "I ought to have you recalled," Truman told the ambassador. "Tell Franco what I said." Calvin Coolidge was forever sarcastically asking European ambassadors when their governments were going to pay their World War I debts. Dwight D. Eisenhower roared a rebuke replete with barracks language during a meeting with French Ambassador Alphand at the height of the Suez crisis of 1956, and suggested that Alphand should start worrying about "what you'll say to your Creator." And John F. Kennedy, who had an unusual rapport with foreigners, called Soviet Ambassador Dobrynin a liar during the Cuban crisis of 1962, when Dobrynin insisted he knew nothing of the Soviet missiles installed on the island.

And yet, despite these occupational hazards, the diplomatic corps remains the world's most privileged official class. However an ambassador may suffer from the rough side of a President's—or monarch's—tongue, he is in a sense untouchable because he is not answerable to the laws, the customs or the morals of the host country. His special status goes back to Biblical times when, to make negotiations possible between nations, certain conventions had to be observed as a means of protecting the visiting envoys. For example, although the exporting of female slaves was prohibited in most ancient regimes, there were mutual agreements excluding foreign diplomats from the prohibition; a monarch could never tell when he himself might want to sample the wares of another country.

Indeed, the word *diplomacy* connotes a status above and beyond ordinary laws of behavior. It comes from the French, who borrowed it from the Greek word *diploma,* meaning a folded paper conferring on an individual a privilege or license. Diplomats naturally insist that they strictly observe the primary definition of the English word *license* —which confers authority or liberty to do or forbear any act—and not the later meaning noted by Webster as denoting an excess of liberty, licentiousness.

The ancient Medes and Persians, Greeks and Romans used ambassadors, or envoys, to conduct their affairs with foreign countries, but there was no generally recognized diplomatic machinery until Venice set up permanent missions in the latter part of the fifteenth century. Shortly thereafter the Italian prince, Niccolo Machiavelli, would give his name to a particularly unscrupulous brand of diplomacy which has since been a monkey on the back of even the most honest and straight-forward Italian statesmen. Actually, rulers who had never heard of Machiavelli looked upon diplomacy with great suspicion; Ferdinand of Spain remarked that diplomats were little better than spies, perhaps because he employed his own envoys in that capacity. But diplomats were needed in an era when the great powers had established the first permanent standing armies. If one nation had the stronger army, another would attempt to wheedle concessions through negotiation until its own forces were ready to go to war.

In diplomacy's early days, as today, the term ambassador designated the monarch's or government's highest representative; the Vatican has always called its envoys nuncios or legates. To save money, a lesser class, the minister, is sent to the less important countries, and when full diplomatic representation is not possible, an agent known as a chargé d'affaires becomes the envoy. Originally, the language of diplomacy was Latin, since it was the international language of medieval Europe. French superseded Latin in the seventeenth century, although the British characteristically reserved the right to use English in their diplomatic communications. Then at the Paris conference of 1919, the newly-recognized influence of the United States resulted in an agreement providing for what the conferees called "the perfect equality of English with French."

Talleyrand, among other stiff-necked European statesmen, undoubtedly tossed in his comfortable grave and perhaps even considered recrossing the Styx to set things right when he heard from a French newcomer of this concession to perfidious Albion and its American colony. "English!" Talleyrand once snarled during a Paris ball at which he had sought unsuccessfully to sell a bill of romantic goods to a beautiful but icily detached London matron. "One cannot make love in English, or negotiate a treaty, because its coarseness corrupts one's meaning." Bismarck dismissed the language as that "spoken by Englishmen and the backwoods barbarians of New York."

However, failure to resolve conflicts is rarely due to the differences in diplomatic language. Rather, compromise is prevented by intense feelings over the real issues. Sometimes, despite a warlike stance, one side will at some point offer to negotiate, usually through a third party. Thus, over the years, governments often have used diplomats of other governments to transmit messages which, for a variety of reasons, they hesitated to communicate directly to a regime with which they were having difficulties. Frequently, the neutral government entrusts the message to an international dignitary with a reputation for unchallenged credibility in order to make certain it receives the proper attention.

Thus, in early 1967, President Charles de Gaulle of France arranged to have his Foreign Office transmit through Senator Bobby Kennedy a North Vietnam "peace" proposal for President Johnson's consideration. At the French Embassy in Washington, it was freely acknowledged that Kennedy was chosen to carry the message in order to get President Johnson to take French mediation efforts seriously. The theory was that Johnson would be forced to give weight to a French signal carried to Washington by a man who had become a symbol of his martyred brother's New Frontier.

There were denials down the line that any peace offer had been made, but the French leaked its details all over the world. They included: (a) direct discussions of U.S.-North Vietnamese relations; (b) Hanoi's readiness to discuss the future U.S. role in South Vietnam; (c) negotiations aimed at an overall settlement in Vietnam.

It was no secret that De Gaulle was furious that Johnson had dismissed other peace feelers from Paris as "French speculation." De Gaulle was obsessed by the idea that Johnson objected to "interference" in the Vietnam war by Paris, and was determined not to let France get credit for any settlement that might be achieved. So De Gaulle decided to put some political pressure on Johnson by bringing Kennedy into the act. After Kennedy was given the message, the French promptly arranged to let several journalists in on the secret, so that the world would know the message not only had been received but had been carried to Washington by a politician of considerable prestige.

Kennedy, of course, had always been very much "in" with the French. He is close to Ambassador Charles Lucet and to former Ambassador Hervé Alphand, who was an intimate of President Kennedy during his tenure in Washington. And the French hoped that Bobby Kennedy would not permit the White House or State Department to dismiss their latest overture, but would discuss it on the floor of the Senate and otherwise give it the public relations treatment. The French also knew that Kennedy's association with a "peace overture" would not damage his Presidential ambitions.

The Hanoi-to-De Gaulle-to-Kennedy-to-Johnson maneuver was unusual for its intricacy. Actually, most diplomatic exchanges are not so circuitous, complicated, or carefully planned.

A belief prevalent in the provinces is that an ambassador's life is a merry one of dancing till dawn, whispering sweet nothings to nubile charmers, nibbling on caviar and sipping champagne, and sleeping untroubled until noon. The fact is that the ambassadors from the more important countries—or those of real or fancied importance to the United States—work harder than the average stevedore, and are beset by problems a hundred times more complex. Certain Latin-American and African envoys, to be sure, spend most of their waking hours at play, but that is attributable both to their carefree personalities and to the fact that their official chores are of scant interest to anyone of importance in Washington. The swingers swing because they have nothing else to do.

But Soviet Ambassador Dobrynin, for example, rises at six o'clock every morning, is at his desk by eight, and seldom calls it a day before midnight. British Ambassador Dean and French Ambassador Lucet work a ten-hour day, and Spanish Ambassador Merry del Val drives himself almost as strenuously. The late Polish Ambassador, Edward Drozniak, a favorite in the diplomatic colony, put in a regular work day and in addition often toiled from three to six A.M. on his paper work so he wouldn't be disturbed. Drozniak once pinpointed another of the ambassador's burdens: "I always have to be dressed up, as you Americans put it, fit to kill," he complained. "I can never work comfortably in an old sweater, at least during the daytime, in case someone should come to see me." German Ambassador Heinrich Knappstein runs a tight shop with militaristic overtones. All but the top-ranking members of his staff sign in and out, morning and night, and the staffer who is more than four minutes late receives a stiff memo from the boss. Knappstein also cracked down on long lunches, and is in the habit of phoning various offices at seven P.M. to learn how many of his subordinates are putting in "voluntary" overtime. It is Knappstein's boast—a thorn in the side of his staff—that he has worked a seven-day week ever since he arrived in Washington in September 1962.

There is, of course, no such thing as a "typical" ambassador, and therefore any attempt to describe a "typical" day in an ambassador's life is fraught with peril. Moscow's Dobrynin, for example, is all political business despite his considerable wit and charm, whereas the strenuous work schedule of Spain's Merry del Val is devoted largely to cultural and tourist matters and the burnishing of Generalissimo Francisco Franco's somewhat shopworn image. Because he is one of the swingers, Algeria's Cherif Guellal has a reputation as a playboy. However, insiders know his is one of the finest minds on Embassy Row, and he has earned respect as a sharp negotiator. Yet there is a certain pattern to all ambassadorial days, whether the chores involve arrangements for the showing of a Michelangelo painting or a NATO crisis. Thus it is permissible to take a look at twenty-four hours in the life of French Ambassador Lucet and to suggest that it represents the routine if not the diplomatic preoccupations of his colleagues.

Arriving in his office in the gray stone, Tudor-style Embassy on Kalorama Road, at 9 A.M. Lucet gives his attention first to the cables which have arrived from Paris during the night. On an average day, there will be at least a dozen of these, some of them night-action cables which already have been seen and initialed by a responsible Embassy officer.

The cables cover a variety of subjects. There may be one from the Foreign Secretary telling Lucet to have a few words with Secretary Rusk about a speech delivered by Defense Secretary Robert McNamara which seemed to accuse France of reneging on certain commitments to the West. If the cable notes, "The General has inquired . . ." Lucet forthwith arranges the conversation; Charles de Gaulle is impatient as well as imperious.

Another cable might ask Lucet to sound out certain members of Congress on the latest Vietnam peace proposals put out unofficially by the French government. There might be a suggestion that Lucet summarize American public opinion on revisions in the Selective Service system, and instructions to extend all courtesies to a visiting member of the Chamber of Deputies—but to keep him away from Embassy files on NATO discussions.

Some of these cables will be signed by De Gaulle, and they are often larded with sarcastic criticisms of the Ambassador. The general often occupies himself with details which would seem trivial to another head of state; he once complained to Lucet that a dinner party the Ambassador had given in honor of Secretary Rusk was "too grand." On another occasion, at the height of one of the many French-American misunderstandings on a possible *détente* with the Soviet Union, De Gaulle questioned the intelligence of a member of Lucet's staff and wound up calling him a *lourdon.* This was tough on the staffer; *lourdon* means a sottish lout.

Most of the cables from Paris, however, are signed by the officer in charge—that is, the Foreign Office official in charge of France's relations with the United States. For most business, he is Lucet's contact with the French government. Lucet tells the officer in charge everything he knows about what is going on in official Washington, including reports of a rift between President Johnson and one of the Presidential aides and gossip that the Joint Chiefs of Staff are headed for a showdown with Secretary McNamara over escalation in Vietnam. He presses for a reply on the State Department's request for a revision of certain trade agreements between the two countries. Lucet also transmits a request from Rusk that the French government give its support to the nomination of an Italian diplomat to a high-ranking job at the United Nations.

Since diplomacy is simply politics on an international scale, Lucet also must keep in touch with American political trends. Before Senator Bobby Kennedy was entrusted with a North Vietnam "peace" feeler in February, 1967, Lucet commissioned a private poll to measure Kennedy's popularity. He is under continuing instructions to make periodic reports on the influence and chances of the Republican candidates for President. In January, 1967, Lucet reported that Michigan's Governor George Romney was outdistancing the pack, but two months later he was also advising Paris to keep its eye on Dick Nixon and Senator Charles Percy of Illinois.

Meanwhile, Ambassador Lucet makes his daily rounds. He confers often, both personally and by telephone, with Under Secretary of State Nicholas deB. Katzenbach and an assortment of French specialists at the State Department. He sees American newspapermen alone and in groups, planting a story here, sending up a trial balloon there, and always making it a point to *seem* to speak frankly. He confers with members of Congress, mostly senators, and finds time for Franco-American groups planning exchange programs or dinner dances to help cement relations between the two countries. He is on determined good terms with White House aide Walt Rostow, who is the President's most influential adviser on national security affairs, and Marvin Watson, one of the President's chief political and patronage advisers.

Since an embassy is a microcosm of its government, Lucet is responsible for every matter which has, or might have, any impact on that
government. He directs the 75-man foreign service staff that mans the
administrative, economic and political sections. He commands the activities of scientists, and specialists in fisheries, minerals, aviation, petroleum, labor and trade. He also supervises French consulates across the
United States, which deal in such mundane matters as the issuing of
passports and visas, the gathering of trade statistics and the protection
of French citizens. Lucet personifies France to the American people
and theoretically is supposed to mix with all classes of citizens; actually,
this charming diplomat probably wouldn't recognize an Appalachian
coal miner if he saw one. Like most diplomats, Lucet is forced by circumstance—and probably inclination—to travel with the elegant pack.

But excursions in folksiness are of little importance, since an ambassador's principal job is to attempt to work his government's will on
the government of the country to which he is accredited. That job
involves efforts to influence American foreign and domestic policies, to
sell his country's wares at the best possible prices, to represent citizens
of his country temporarily residing in a strange land, to get a share of
American foreign aid, and to obtain information through official
channels. The diplomat also must do his best to find out things official
Washington doesn't want him to know. In a less polite milieu, some of
the things he does or condones would be called spying, an activity
engaged in by our enemies and allies alike—and, of course, by American diplomats stationed in both friendly and unfriendly countries.
Thus, while Lucet reads his cables, his military attaché may be buying
information about a new missile analysis system developed at the Pentagon, although the chances are Lucet knows nothing about the deal
because some ambassadors are kept in the dark about such skulldug-
gery to protect their status. In the language of diplomacy, this is called
obtaining information by covert means, a form of espionage necessary
even between allies, not only because today's ally may be tomorrow's
enemy but because even allies don't always come clean with one another.

Meanwhile, Charles Lucet must see to it that the United States is
constantly made aware of France's importance, an assignment which
includes getting things done for France. He must assiduously seek
American support for his government in its relations with, say, Al-

geria. He must work for concessions in both international relations and in the export of French wines. And, as a very real servant of Charles de Gaulle, he must constantly seek to persuade the White House, the State Department, the Congress—and even those beautiful official wives who help decorate his Embassy parties—that Le Grand Charles knows best.

For these assorted duties, Lucet is paid $100,000 a year in salary and housekeeping and entertaining allowances. British Ambassador Dean gets $95,000 and German Ambassador Knappstein $78,500. Congress is much more niggardly with American ambassadors; our envoy to the Court of St. James draws only $79,000 a year, which means he must make up shortages out of his own pocket. Indeed, in the early days of the Republic, Congress was so offended by the splendor that surrounded an ambassador that until 1893 the United States was represented abroad by ministers in charge of legations.

Due to the exigencies of the Cold War, all ambassadors are not first-class diplomatic citizens. In retaliation for restrictions on the movements of American diplomatic personnel in Communist countries, the State Department bans travel by Iron Curtain diplomats to certain sections of the United States. In effect, the Reds are limited to a corridor along the East Coast which encompasses Baltimore, Philadelphia and New York as well as Washington, and they are banned from most Atlantic Ocean beaches for what the State Department and the FBI feel is an obvious reason. Because the Russians are tougher on American diplomats in their country, Russian diplomats in the United States are more closely restricted than those of the satellite embassies.

Otherwise, the diplomatic corps is still the little colony of equals among equals conceived by the *Règlement de Vienne*. Every ambassador, for example, has the right to demand a private meeting with the President. However, a kind of caste system prevails on the social scene. At any official function, it doesn't matter how intelligent or witty or distinguished an ambassador may be or how powerful is his country. Precedence goes to the ambassador who has been longest in the United States—in the spring of 1967 this honor was still the due of Nicaragua's Sevilla-Sacasa.

In all this, the ambassador's duty remains constant. It was once summed up succinctly by Hervé Alphand when he was French Ambassador to Washington. "Be sure that you are noticed," advised Alphand, and every ambassador or minister theoretically seeks in his own way to achieve that end. After all, he's a travelling salesman for his country. President Kennedy once remarked of a certain eager and ineffable diplomat, "He not only represents his country—he peddles it door-to-door." Although few ambassadors approach that measure of indefatigability, none would object to being thus characterized. It is, in fact, the image most ambassadors are pleased to assume for themselves in their cables to the boss back home.

3

The Innocent Americans

OVER A BOURBON and branch water with a few reporters one day, the always refreshingly candid Harry Truman remarked on the growth of the State Department since he came to Washington as a senator in 1935. "It's a big place now," he said. "It has to be, to keep an eye on all those foreign spies who pose as diplomats."

Truman was not overstating the case by very much, if at all. Although the State Department has not been increased to its present size merely to watch over embassy staffs, certain of its personnel are responsible for keeping tabs on those foreign diplomats suspected of trying to find out more about America's policies and its defense posture than Washington wants them to know. And of course all diplomats everywhere, including the American variety, occasionally resort to covert means to pick up information. State does not—officially, anyway— assign any of its employees to shadow the riper prospects among the spy suspects in striped pants; it merely encourages its staffers to maintain regular and close contact with them.

This would be a big job even if all foreign diplomats were as pure as the driven snow and constitutionally incapable of stealing a state secret. For with so many foreign missions in Washington, it requires an enormous number of man-hours merely to keep track of who's in town at a given moment and to handle the routine housekeeping chores of day-by-day diplomacy. Yet, although State has about 7500 American employees in the United States and an equal number stationed abroad, plus about ten thousand foreign nationals employed at overseas posts, it nevertheless is the second smallest of the executive departments. Only the Department of Labor has fewer bodies on the payroll.

A State Department man's relationship with a foreign diplomat naturally varies according to the relationship between the United States and the country represented by that diplomat. That is to say, the State man is not quite so trusting of a diplomat from the Soviet Union or Hungary as he might be with a member of the Swedish or Italian mission. This does not mean that an American lunching with a diplomat whose country has just sworn eternal allegiance to United States policies takes down all his hair. He knows, as all American diplomats should know, that even allied embassies are not without sin in the field of espionage; that the Englishman, say, is under the same pressure from his government for more information as is the American stationed in London. Moreover, there is always the chance that even a diplomat from an allied country could be working secretly for another government, such as the Soviet Union. The most notable recent example of everybody's Western friend was Colonel Stig Wennerstrom, an air attaché at the irreproachable Swedish Embassy, who was sentenced to life imprisonment for spying for Russia in both Sweden and the United States. Since the Wennerstrom case, every employee of the State Department who deals with foreign diplomats undoubtedly has had a refresher course in the little tricks and casual devices employed by any diplomat, anywhere, who is worth his salt—and has been warned again of the danger of taking anyone for granted. Nor has the *modus operandi* of the diplomat at large in America changed.

The man from State knows that all Iron Curtain diplomats— and many more from allied and neutral embassies than is generally suspected—perform a set routine whenever they check into a hotel in an American city. They usually manage to pick up a couple of extra registration cards. Upon their return to Washington, these cards are dispatched via sealed diplomatic pouch to the intelligence headquarters of the country represented by the diplomat, and there stored with thousands of pieces of similar material against the day when the spy shop may have to "prove" that on a given date another of its agents was in, say, Rochester, New York. To the Iron Curtain countries, and, for that matter to most other foreign governments, it would not matter that the hotel itself showed no record of that particular guest; the Communists would charge an imperialist plot, and the allied or neutral country would mumble something diplomatic about a slip-up in the hotel's record-keeping.

Items such as hotel registration cards and hotel stationery are among the raw materials collected by most travelling diplomats for use in phony cover stories. They also pick up material of a more direct military and intelligence value, such as the wide variety of road maps available at gasoline service stations, and all sorts of literature offered by chambers of commerce, especially that dealing with business and industry. None of this information is valuable in itself, but when pieced together with similar material from other cities in the United States it helps to give an intelligence agency a broad and detailed picture of American commerce plus the location of such strategic installations as defense factories and railroad sidings, and the layouts of airports and other port facilities.

A foreign diplomat is not permitted, except under special circumstances, to enter the missile base at Cape Kennedy, Florida. But any member of the Polish or Czech Embassy may drive up to the perimeter, check on the location of the gates and the "No Trespassing" signs, the degree of security imposed, and how and where power and telephone lines are run into and out of the base. Such information is the bread and butter of sabotage teams.

In Fayetteville, North Carolina, site of the prestigious Fort Bragg, home of the celebrated 82nd Airborne Division, Communist diplomats wander through the stores stocking up on shoulder patches, unit insignia, and military uniforms. These eventually find their way to intelligence costume departments in Warsaw, Moscow and Budapest. For a price, neutral diplomats will see that such items reach Peking. Most Iron Curtain embassies subscribe to military base newspapers, which are a fund of information and gossip about maneuvers, promotions, and transfers. Moscow especially, and other Red governments to a lesser degree, maintains a filing system of folders on every known United States military officer from the rank of colonel and Navy captain on up. The folder contains not only information on the officer's unit and his career, but stray pieces of gossip about his personal habits, his wife and family, and his girl friends, if any. After all, the evaluation of a military unit depends partially upon knowledge of the officer who commands it. Assorted bartenders and waitresses in officers' clubs are listed by name in other folders, and so are maids in officers' homes; some day one of them might be a source of intelligence information. If a Negro officer or enlisted man is involved in a courtmartial, or files charges of discrimination, his name goes into a special Communist "civil rights" file. Names of white servicemen who get into trouble go into another. A grudge-holder can be of considerable assistance to foreign intelligence, often unwittingly.

Pawel Monat, a military attaché at the Polish Embassy in the 1950's who successfully spied on the United States for several years before defecting, told the FBI he was able quite legally to get his hands on millions of words of information about the American military establishment and strategic facilities merely by spending a few dollars on unclassified publications. Often, he said, he could collect valuable "secrets" for Z-2, the intelligence branch of the Polish armed forces, without leaving his desk in the Embassy.

Two of Monat's favorite sources were the magazine *Aviation Week* and *Missiles and Rockets,* a publication specializing in information about the new science of astronautics. From one issue of *Aviation Week,* in February, 1957, he got a whole bagful of goodies:

The first squadron of twelve F8U Crusader planes will soon be put into service in the U.S. Navy.

The Convair F-102A jet interceptor has a wingspan of 32 feet 2 inches, is 68 feet and 3 inches long, 21 feet and 3 inches high, has a speed of Mach 1, is powered by the J-57, and carries a Falcon missile produced by Hughes which is 6 feet long, 6 inches in diameter, has a wingspan of 2 feet, weighs 100 pounds and is guided to its target by a radar homing device.

The British have a Saunders Roe SR/53 rocket-jet interceptor . . . ready for testing.

Italy has three brigades of fighter-bombers, each outfitted with F-84's and F-84F's, and an all-weather fighter brigade equipped with F-86-K's.

The Saab Aircraft Company in Sweden has completed the maiden flight of its all-weather J-32-B night fighter, which differs from the A-32 in that it has a more powerful Rolls-Royce engine, an enlarged afterburner, new armament, a new navigation system, and new fire-control equipment.

Monat noted that very little of this information was of a classified nature; any foreign government could have dug it up from other sources. But such digging would have cost thousands of dollars, and the accuracy of its product would always have been suspect. *"Aviation Week* and *Missiles and Rockets,"* Monat told the FBI, "gave us this stuff on a silver platter."

Monat also struck a rich vein in the monumental Government Printing Office. One day in 1957 he received from Warsaw what he was sure was an impossible assignment—to obtain detailed and technical descriptions of all major United States seaports, Warsaw sent him a list of 150 questions it wanted answered about harbor depths, the width and depth of the channels, location of railroad sidings and repair shops, tide tables. He figured that even if he found an agent with all this information at hand it would cost the Polish government at least fifty thousand dollars to buy it; in the meantime, he discovered, it would take a staff of twenty-five to thirty operatives at least a year to dig it up, with no guarantee of success.

Then, on a trip to the Government Printing Office to pick up a collection of bland pamphlets, Monat asked casually if there was any material available on the port of Baltimore. After a short wait, he was handed a fat book published by the U.S. Army Engineers describing the Baltimore port to the last rivet. He also bought a catalog listing similar reports on other American ports, and in the course of the next few weeks he and his assistants picked up the complete set of eighteen volumes. The cost was twenty-five dollars and change. Later, he bought by mail from a California firm a complete set of aviation maps of the United States, including facts and figures on the length and width of runways, the best approaches for landing, and the location and frequency of radio directional beams. Monat took a calculated risk in swinging this deal by using an assumed name, a ruse which would have got him into trouble with the State Department had he been found out.

One of the best sources of information for diplomat-spies is the Pentagon, which is open to anybody able to walk. To be sure, the areas housing the Joint Chiefs of Staffs and other high officers, the intelligence staffs and policy planners, are closely guarded, but most of the rest of the huge building is as accessible as the Smithsonian Institution. Embassy attachés wander through the long, cavernous corridors and loiter in the snack bars and shops of the concourse, picking up information by keeping their ears washed and open. They concentrate on eavesdropping on officers, who in the military tradition tend to gossip with their pals about the secrets they share. The name of a brigadier general who had just been assigned to the Pentagon and was greeting old friends in a snack bar is shipped off to Moscow, where the files show he is an expert on nonpoisonous gases. Put together with other information acquired elsewhere, this tips off the Soviets that a new chemical warfare project is in the planning stage. A Rumanian diplomat hears that an Army division is getting special nuclear training, or learns about a new weapon which his intelligence branch had yet to discover. Monat claimed that an assistant of his first heard about the B-70 plane from a conversation between two colonels in Brentano's Pentagon bookshop.

Colonel Wennerstrom, whose fifteen years of espionage activities in behalf of the Soviet Union included five years of spying in the United States, told his interrogators after his arrest that the "possibilities" of obtaining valuable information at the Pentagon were "almost fantastic." As air attaché at the Swedish Embassy he had entree everywhere, and American officials greeted him enthusiastically, even affectionately, when he arrived to take up his post in April, 1952. He not only represented a friendly neutral, but he was "known" to be pro-American. He also had a reputation as an expert on the Soviet Union as a result of his service at the Swedish Embassy in Moscow, and shortly after his arrival a group of Pentagon intelligence officers arranged to pick his brain for assorted tidbits of information on Russian military power.

Summing up his meetings with these elegant spooks, Wennerstrom told his interrogators simply that "I told them what they wanted to hear," namely that American military power had a big edge on Soviet power. He also fed his new American friends bits of unimportant intelligence furnished to him by his Soviet superior in Moscow, always managing to make it sound like secret information.

Obviously, the Pentagon's cooperation with a foreign military attaché is in direct ratio to the official American attitude toward his country, and Wennerstrom thus found it much easier to obtain information than Monat did, or any other Iron Curtain diplomats. Moreover, Wennerstrom also was head of the United States Purchasing Commission for the Swedish Air Force and he was welcomed with open arms by top officials of aircraft and munitions plants. His Soviet masters had instructed him to concentrate on getting information on the latest American developments in bombers, fighters, bombsights, radar, high-frequency radio and guided missiles; he did this simply by requesting it in writing from the Defense Department. Indeed, his Pentagon friends sent him much more material than he needed, and the most time-consuming part of his job was in separating the wheat from the chaff.

Wennerstrom's position vis-à-vis defense plant officials was ideal; he wanted to buy, and they wanted to sell. He was interested in all kinds of equipment and materiel, including many items he knew Sweden

couldn't possibly be interested in purchasing, and American businessmen told him all he wanted to know. Top officials of defense plants
were forever inviting him to country weekends, and such attentions
made a deep impression on subordinates from whom Wennerstrom
was seeking information. "Give this man all the help you can!" was
the word passed down the line from company presidents and board
chairmen who had succumbed to Wennerstrom's charm and business-
like approach. Occasionally, Wennerstrom reported, he had to resort
to bribery and he found this no problem. His statements are sprinkled
with comments such as "I was able to gradually get this information . . .
and I think I paid one thousand dollars for it. It was sent to the
Soviet Union."

There is always something faintly ridiculous in the mechanics of
espionage, and Wennerstrom was amused by Moscow's instructions for
making contact with its man in Washington—Major General Viktor
Kuvinov, air attaché at the Soviet Embassy. Kuvinov, Wennerstrom
was told, would tell him that an acquaintance in Moscow had asked to
be remembered to Wennerstrom—a man named Nikolai Vasilyevich.
"And in reply I would thank him and say that I knew the person very
well and that I remembered having met him several times at a place in
Moscow called Spiridonovka." After two meetings at which Wennerstrom and Kuvinov exchanged polite banalities, Kuvinov finally
uttered the password at a third meeting in the Soviet Embassy, gave
Wennerstrom five thousand dollars in working capital to get him
started in the spying business, and provided him with a schedule of
meeting places in various Washington neighborhoods.

Under orders, Wennerstrom employed the usual hackneyed means
of handing over material to Kuvinov and other Soviet contacts. If only
a small envelope or package was involved, he would do so by shaking
hands with the contact on the street, in a department store or at a
diplomatic reception. He practiced these maneuvers with Kuvinov and
his other contacts and concluded that Kuvinov was a bit of a dolt
because the Russian was always messing up the performance. Nevertheless, he once managed to transfer some film to Kuvinov during an
official meeting in the Pentagon, a revelation that still has the Defense
brass shaking its collective head in shame. Sometimes Wennerstrom
would make the transfers at parties at the Soviet Embassy. He left the
film in a pocket of his topcoat and then at some point during the

reception whispered the number of his cloakroom check to his Russian contact. The contact would thereupon go to the cloak room and remove the film.

Whenever Wennerstrom and a Soviet contact met on the street or in a public park, they had a set of signals used to indicate whether one or the other suspected he was being followed by an FBI operative. If there was no danger, the left hand was out in the open, moving back and forth when walking. If either felt he was being followed, he put his left hand into the pocket of his jacket or topcoat or trousers. The material to be passed was always carried in the right hand.

Since Kuvinov liked to fish, Wennerstrom occasionally met him beside some bucolic stream outside of Washington for a picnic lunch. "Kuvinov was most scrupulous," Wennerstrom said. "He always had his fishing license with him."

Almost always, the Russians employed a complex maneuver to shake off possible shadows. Wennerstrom's police interrogators said he told them that if an embassy man was to meet Wennerstrom, Kuvinov would order two men to leave the embassy, the second about three hours after the first. The function of these men was to attract FBI agents or other security shadows and keep them occupied. Once it was felt these decoys had soaked up all the shadows available, a third man would go out to meet Wennerstrom.

Wennerstrom used a Leica camera, mounted on a stand, to photograph documents in his office on weekends and in the evenings. He used two types of film—a conventional type for those documents he felt could not be traced back to him, and a special "secret" film provided by the Soviet Embassy for papers too many people knew he had seen. This film could be developed only in Moscow with a special chemical; ordinary developing fluids would ruin it. Wennerstrom guarded against being interrupted during his photography by installing a red light outside the door of his office and ordering his secretary not to enter or allow anyone else to enter while the light was on "because I would be photographing classified material for transmission to Sweden."

Meanwhile, Wennerstrom managed to pick up two thousand-dollar-fees from America's own Central Intelligence Agency for doing a little spying on his Russian bosses. One day he was introduced to a CIA representative at a luncheon at the Pentagon, and after a hearty meal the CIA man took him aside and said he had something he thought would interest Wennerstrom, if the latter had time that afternoon for a little discussion.

"I was first afraid that they had detected some of my activity in the United States," Wennerstrom said later. But, "I accepted his invitation . . . We went in his private car to an out-of-the-way office in Washington with no door plates . . . The person in question . . . asked me whether I was willing to help them over some difficulties they had. My reaction was one of relief . . . and I answered yes. He explained that there was material in the Soviet Embassy that had to be gotten out of there. He then asked me to what extent I was invited to the Soviet Embassy and apparently found my answer satisfactory."

In any event, Wennerstrom twice received a package from a Russian-speaking contact at a Soviet Embassy reception and dutifully turned both packages over to a CIA contact. He did not of course report this bit of double agentry to that Slavic Izaak Walton, General Kuvinov.

Wennerstrom, whose take-home pay from the Swedish government was $1500 a month, made about $750 a month as a Soviet spy, out of which he claimed he had to pay substantial expenses. For this relative pittance, he handed over to Moscow more than one hundred thousand photographs of classified documents relating to nuclear weapons, bombsights, the air-to-ground HM 55 missile, the ground-to-air Bomarc missile, and the performance of numerous war planes and tactical weapons. He also received, when he left Washington in June of 1957, an American decoration, the Order of the Legion of Merit, for diplomatic services to the country he betrayed.

In contrast to Wennerstrom's suave and almost effortless operation, the Polish military attaché, Monat, was forced to work much harder and at times to descend to the crudities of physical theft. There were two obvious reasons for this. First, Monat had no entree of any significance to official Washington, and second, he was under almost constant surveillance by the FBI. Consequently, he was forced to pick up his more important information wherever he could find it—or stumble upon it—as in the case of the American aerodynamics scientist.

Monat told the FBI he met the scientist on a train from Washington to Chicago, which he had boarded with a colleague, Captain Tadeusz Wisniewski. Monat and the scientist exchanged a few pleasantries in the corridor of their car and the scientist invited him to come into his compartment and sit down. There, the American confided to

Monat that he did research in aerodynamics for the government and was presently involved in plans for a wind tunnel to be used to test new aircraft designs.

The American picked up a brief case bulging with papers. "Look at this," he told Monat. "This is the project I'm working on."

Monat thrilled with excitement and delight. Warsaw and Moscow were vitally interested in new United States aircraft designs so that Communist engineers could devise means of shooting them down. It was, he told the FBI, the chance in a spy's lifetime.

When the American invited Monat to join him for dinner, Monat accepted, but when they started down the corridor he told the scientist to go ahead to the diner while he went back to wash his hands. Monat, of course, rushed back to his own compartment, where he told Wisniewski to get out his photocopy equipment and photograph every paper in the American's briefcase while he, Monat, and the American were eating dinner.

Monat kept the American at the dinner table for more than two hours by insisting on dessert and then plying him with three brandies. He had told Wisniewski to do the photocopying in their compartment and then return the briefcase to the scientist's room. He also told Wisniewski that when he and the American returned from dinner, he would knock on Wisniewski's door. If Wisniewski hadn't finished the copying job, he was to hide the briefcase in their own compartment. Monat decided if the scientist found the briefcase missing, he would convince him it had been left in the diner. Then, while the American went to get it, Monat would retrieve it from Wisniewski, and stash it under the scientist's berth. When the scientist returned, Monat would pretend he "found" it and would explain that the porter must have put it under the scientist's bed.

After dinner, Monat knocked softly on Wisniewski's door, then suggested that his friend must have gone to sleep. He proceeded along the corridor with the scientist and stood there while the latter peered into his own compartment. The scientist breathed a sigh of relief. "I'd forgotten until now about my briefcase," he said. "I'm glad to see it's still here. Think of all that work I'd have to do over if someone had taken it."

Ordinarily, however, Monat's days were filled with the dull routine of reading *Aviation Week, The New York Times* and other newspapers, and checking the proceedings on Capitol Hill in the *Congres-*

sional Record. In perusing the latter publication, a drab gray blob of eight-point type, Monat found himself profoundly grateful to those Congressmen and Senators who specialized in asking penetrating questions about defense matters and thus provided a poor Polish military attaché with reams of intelligence he otherwise could not have obtained.

Monat offered the FBI an example of how questions at a Congressional hearing exposed American defense secrets to the knowledgable Communist spy. He recalled a 1957 hearing at which the principal witness was Brigadier General Chester De Gavre, Director of Development in the Army's Office of Research and Development. The General was showing committee members some slides of new weapons, and was being peppered with questions by Representative Daniel Flood of Pennsylvania.

General De Gavre pointed to a slide of the new M-56 assault gun and remarked, "We have named it the Scorpion because it cannot stand up and slug with tanks. The crew is entirely on the outside of the vehicle . . . It gives the Airborne Division the first capability of antitank defense."

Flood interrupted. "You are going to send that against tanks?" he asked incredulously.

"Yes sir." replied the general. "This is the only thing that can be delivered by air. The present status is that they are now being procured for the Airborne Division."

Flood cleared his throat. "It would be a suicide operation against tanks."

Monat also learned to reach conclusions from the occasional insistence of Defense Department witnesses on going "off the record." If there was a secret discussion about a new plane or a tank or a gun, Monat could learn by the comments of Congressmen when the discussion went back on the record whether the developers were having trouble with the new item. If these comments were caustic or petulant, he concluded that the Congressmen were dissatisfied with what they had heard. If the congressmen seemed pleased, the new item was something Warsaw and Moscow would have to start worrying about.

Indeed, one of a military attaché's biggest problems is to convince his Iron Curtain bosses of the reliability of their reports. Military establishments in Communist dictatorships are even more obtuse than their democratic counterparts; they form their own opinions of an adversary's capabilities from information obtained from their own special sources, and they don't like to be contradicted. Thus, it once took a Soviet military attaché, Colonel Philip Bachinsky, two weeks of argument to convince Moscow that in May of 1956 the United States Air Force had a B-47 bomber capable of what the military called "over-the-shoulder bombing."

Colonel Bachinsky had attended a demonstration of the B-47 at Elgin Air Force Base in Florida and had observed the feat and taken pictures of it. In the maneuver, the plane rolled over backward, releasing a bomb as it started the roll. The effect was that of a plane throwing a bomb over its shoulder while flying off in the opposite direction.

Bachinsky cabled a report of the spectacular demonstration to his chiefs in Moscow and received an incredulous reply. Such a thing was impossible, said Russian intelligence; the B-47 was too heavy for such a maneuver. It was not until he sent over his pictures together with a more detailed report that Moscow was convinced. Understandably, the Soviets couldn't understand why the United States would show an audience of foreign military attachés something about which they had been completely ignorant.

Monat operated from the Polish Embassy Annex, a three-story brick house at 2224 Wyoming Avenue, which was outfitted in the fashion of a military command post. Any diplomatic building is part of the country represented and thus is outside the jurisdiction of American authorities. But Monat told the FBI he had never been completely satisfied with his headquarters.

"We were right in the middle of a little Communist complex," he complained. What he meant was that within a few blocks were the office of the Soviet military attaché at 2552 Belmont Road, the Czech Embassy at 2349 Massachusetts Avenue, and the Rumanian legation at 1601 23rd Street. "It made it too easy for you people to watch us," Monat said.

Nevertheless, Warsaw had seen to it that the annex was as FBI-proof as possible. Monat worked in a second-floor office, with his two assistants in two other rooms on the same floor. Adjacent to Monat's office was a large closet which was converted into a vault. Its walls were lined with heavy steel sheets. The safe was an American model from which the original combination lock had been removed and replaced with a key lock brought over from Poland. The lock had been installed by Polish workmen who travelled from Warsaw just for this one job. These workers, working mostly at night, also installed Polish locks in the rest of the building. When each member of the staff went home at night, he was required to lock his own door and then seal it with wax which, if broken, would betray any overnight attempt to break in.

The annex was guarded twenty-four hours a day by a Polish secret policeman, who worked during the daytime as a doorman. At night, he and his wife slept in a third-floor bedroom closed off from the rest of the house by a locked iron door stretched across the stairway. Near the guard's bed, a system of lights and bells would signal an alarm if anyone tried to open a downstairs door or even tapped on one of the outside walls.

Also on the third floor was a photographic laboratory, a locked closet crammed with documents and American maps and military manuals, and a shortwave radio. Monat claimed he and his colleagues faithfully observed the reciprocal diplomatic prohibition against transmitting messages, but the set was used to receive secret instructions from Warsaw.

Other communications from Warsaw to the Embassy on Sixteenth Street were received via the ubiquitous diplomatic pouch delivered once a month by two couriers from Warsaw. There were always two couriers, Monat told the FBI, so one could watch the other. Both of course were secret policemen. All pouches were locked and sealed with wax before leaving Poland and were never opened until they were safely inside the Embassy. On their arrival at the airport, the couriers were met by an Embassy car with diplomatic tags for obvious reasons. The diplomatic plates gave the car's passengers *and contents* diplomatic immunity, and if the car were in an accident—real or contrived —the pouches were safe from prying democratic eyes so long as they remained inside the car. If the car broke down en route to the Embassy, everyone and everything stayed put until another car with DPL tags was dispatched to the scene. So far as is known, no agency of American authority has framed an accident in order to permit its agents to get their hands on the diplomatic pouches during such a transfer.

All messages from Warsaw were in code and were decoded at the embassy by a special corps of code clerks, all members of the Polish secret police, who lived in the embassy under heavy guard against any attempt to kidnap them. However, even these elite cops never saw the dispatches addressed to the military attaché's office. These were separately wrapped, and upon arrival were delivered by embassy car to the annex, where Monat did the decoding. This remains the case in all Iron Curtain embassies and in many others, for a quite simple reason. It is that most countries don't want their ambassadors to know what their military attachés are up to, lest they be embarrassed by some piece of bungling which arouses the wrath of the host country. Thus, whether truthfully or not, the British, French and Israeli representatives all protested they had no advance notice of the Suez invasion of 1956, when summoned by an irate Secretary of State John Foster Dulles.

Shortly after he was sentenced to life imprisonment in 1964, Sweden's Stig Wennerstrom suggested seriously that the nations of the world try to find some means within the rules and regulations of diplomacy to keep closer tab on military attachés assigned to an embassy. "It was not quite realistic," remarked Wennerstrom, "that I should have carried an identity card signed by the Secretary of State of the United States which urged American officials to extend to me every courtesy and assistance in stealing their country's secrets."

Such a proposal might evoke a wistful reaction in many chancelleries whose spies in diplomatic clothing have not shown a substantial enough profit, but it hasn't a chance of serious consideration. Nothing has happened since Jehovah ordered Moses to send agents "to spy out the land of Canaan" to reduce the dependence of nations on the second oldest profession—espionage—about which the professionals admit ruefully that it does not always measure up to the more exacting standards of the first.

4

Kremlin, U.S.A.

OVER THE CENTURIES, the woman scorned has played an important part in certain diplomatic developments which temporarily discompose the orderly footnotes to history. Thus, a security officer in the State Department dutifully if not enthusiastically gave audience one day in October, 1962, to a young woman who had informed his secretary that she "knew something" about the War Minister of Great Britain, a call girl, and a naval attaché of the Soviet Embassy in London.

Miss X turned out to be an American secretary at a Latin-American embassy, and she told her story swiftly, articulately and with a nice appreciation for the relevant details. She had been dating a second secretary at the Soviet Embassy in Washington whom she knew only as "Yuri." During a succession of bibulous evenings with this young man, he had boasted to her of having a powerful friend in London, one Captain Ivanov, who was "making a fool" out of War Minister John Profumo. It seemed, according to Miss X, that Captain Ivanov and Profumo both were romancing the same girl, whose name he did not confide to Miss X. Her Russian beau implied rather strongly that Ivanov hoped to pick up some valuable information from the girl whose favors he shared with Profumo, and had encouraged her to pursue her relationship with the War Minister.

Succinctly, Miss X explained why she had decided to unburden herself of this tale. "Yuri" had jilted her, and gone off to Moscow without leaving her so much as a farewell note.

A few days later, the security officer confronted Miss X with the intelligence, obtained from the Soviet Embassy, that there had not been an employee at the embassy bearing the first name "Yuri" for the past two years.

"I don't care if his real name was Oscar," said Miss X. "He was a second secretary because I went to a party at the embassy with him once. He claimed he couldn't tell me his last name because he was on a special assignment and it was better for me not to know. I didn't care. I fell for the creep."

Thereupon, she furnished the security officer with what must rank among history's most accurate and comprehensive descriptions of a human male; at times her interrogator could feel a blush suffusing his face. Several hours later, "Yuri" was identified as a second secretary with another name who had recently been called home.

Both State Department Intelligence and the Central Intelligence Agency went to work. Less than a month later, their combined efforts dredged up enough information to confirm Miss X's story. Profumo was seeing a girl named Christine Keeler, a member of what might loosely be called London's Bohemian set, who had also played boy-meets-girl with Captain Yevgeny Ivanov, assistant naval attaché at the Soviet Embassy in London.

Naturally, this intelligence was passed on to British authorities with the suggestion that it was at least unusual that a British official should be patronizing the same female favored by Captain Ivanov. From the British there was only a long silence. Then in January, 1963, the Americans were told politely to mind their own business. It was not until March, 1963, that this information—fattened by material from the FBI's dossier on Ivanov and "Yuri"—forced a showdown which brought about the resignation of Profumo and the involvement of Christine Keeler and Dr. Stephen Ward in a series of legal actions pertaining to moral turpitude. Then it developed that Dr. Ward was known as a "society osteopath" and sometime artist, who numbered Winston Churchill among his patients; and Prince Philip, husband of Queen Elizabeth, Princess Margaret, and her husband, Lord Snowden, among patrons of his art.

At the denouement, what surprised old hands at the State Department was not that a British minister was susceptible to a young girl's charms, but that the Soviet staffer, Ivanov, was able to pursue a private life of romance and all-around high jinks. In State's annals, the only other Russian diplomat who so enjoyed himself was Valentin Gubitchev, convicted with Judith Coplon of conspiring to steal American secrets, but Gubitchev, a member of the Soviet delegation to the United Nations, was courting Miss Coplon under orders from on high.

Russian diplomats ordinarily lead a rigidly circumvented private life. They avoid not only pretty foreign girls but even other diplomats, and rarely see a member of the press. In a real sense, they are prisoners even when they go home at night, for those employees of the Embassy who are members of the Soviet secret police maintain a close watch over their colleagues' activities—even while they themselves are under similar surveillance.

In no other embassy in Washington is the privilege of diplomatic inviolability more zealously guarded than by the Russian Ambassador and his staff and embassy employees. The Russians operate in the letter of the international diplomatic code, which says an embassy is a transplanted chunk of the country it represents. Wherever embassy personnel are assigned, they live as it were in their own land, behind a frontier of secrecy. In a town where diplomatic gregariousness is the rule, the Russians have isolated themselves as completely as if they were still in Moscow.

The barred door to their prison is the rule laid down by the Kremlin which prohibits Soviet diplomats in democratic countries from mixing with the population beyond a certain fixed limit. A Soviet Embassy staffer's day follows a rigid, unchanging routine—he leaves home, goes directly to the embassy and returns straight to his residence again after his day's work is done. He rarely steps into an American home and before he and his wife may attend a movie or a concert he must get permission from his superior. He may attend diplomatic functions where protocol demands his presence or at which his superior believes he may be able to pick up some information. Otherwise his social life is limited to parties in the embassies of Soviet satellites or at the homes of satellite diplomats.

Years ago, the author was on fairly cordial terms with Alexander Zinchuk, then one of the first secretaries of the Soviet Embassy. He was available a few times a year for lunch at Duke Zeibert's or the Mayflower Hotel—but not the National Press Club— and it was comparatively easy to see him at the embassy. Then he was called home. When he returned to Washington a few years later as Minster Counselor— the number two man to Ambassador Antoly Dobrynin—every effort to see him, or even to speak with him on the telephone proved fruitless. Members of the embassy staff who previously met reporters suddenly were "not in"—ever—when called.

The regimentation of Soviet diplomats reaches proportions that are ridiculous to an American. One day in the summer of 1966, a fashionable physician in Washington received a call from a man who identified himself as an attaché at the Soviet Embassy. The caller, who had refused to talk to the doctor's secretary, asked for an appointment to undergo a physical examination, and a date was set for two weeks later.

Then as the doctor was about to hang up, the Russian cleared his throat and said he'd like to ask a few questions about the physican's educational and professional background. Good-naturedly, the doctor listed the schools he'd attended and the graduate work he'd done. "Oh, and of course I'm a good capitalist," he added facetiously.

The caller laughed in a hollow way and hung up.

The day the Russian was due for his appointment he phoned again. This time he deigned to talk to the doctor's secretary.

"I am very sorry," he said, "but I cannot come. I cannot keep my appointment." The secretary said that was too bad, and asked if he wanted to set another date for his physical examination.

"No, no, I'm sorry," said the Russian. "I cannot come—ever. The doctor has not been approved by my superiors."

No one will ever know whether the physician was turned down because he said he was a capitalist, although even a humorless Communist bureaucrat would hardly expect to find a bomb-throwing anarchist in the healing business in America. Possibly Moscow reasoned that anyone who could joke about his political beliefs was too frivolous a man to practice medicine—especially on a good proletarian.

At any rate, it is too bad the Russians are so standoffish. They are convivial souls, intelligent and with curiosities, articulate and trenchant in their conversations. With his guard down, the average Russian diplomat is most likeable in a rough-hewn way; the late Secretary of State John Foster Dulles once described the Russian personality as "Texan with overtones of the Elks Club."

For a long time after the Vietnam War heated up, Soviet diplomats even seemed to be avoiding high-level meetings with their American opposites in the State Department. Ambassador Dobrynin was available for conversations only with Secretary of State Dean Rusk or the then

Under Secretary, George Ball; he could, not, of course, avoid either man without offending protocol. Just below the ambassadorial level, the Russians were reluctant to discuss the war with State's Russian desk people or Assistant Secretaries of State. Their standard response was "Talk to Hanoi." Then in September, 1966, they began to go out of their way to "explore American thinking," as they put it. The reason for this switch, as advanced by Kremlinologists in State, was that Moscow believed its influence in Hanoi, after a long period of sterility, was on the rise. The Kremlin wanted in on peace discussions, both to consolidate its influence and to take advantage of the ideological upheaval in Communist China.

But the State Department has learned over the years that the Russians blow hot and cold, depending on the vagaries of their foreign policy. During the early fifties, when the saturnine Georgi Nikolaeyvich Zaroubin presided over the Soviet Embassy, the atmosphere had all the cordiality of a wing of Moscow's notorious Lubyanka Prison. Zaroubin, a short, thickset man with satyrlike eyebrows and a heavy, suspicious air, came to Washington with a background unlikely to inspire trust. A graduate of the Moscow Textile Institute, he became a diplomat in 1940 and later was linked to two of the most notorious espionage cases of our time. Zaroubin was ambassador to Canada in 1945 when an elaborate Communist spy ring was broken up, and was envoy to Great Britain when Klaus Fuchs confessed passing on vital atomic-energy secrets to the Kremlin. In the first six months of Zaroubin's tour in Washington, three of his attachés were expelled for spying.

But although Zaroubin was a persistent and disagreeable obstructionist in his sessions with American diplomats, he seemed eager to ingratiate himself with the ideologically unwashed American public, before which he performed like the Mephistophelian hero of a Dale Carnegie book. When he went to the White House in 1952 to present his credentials to President Truman, he told reporters that his heart's desire was to see an American baseball game "and get to know your great working class." For a while he attended every diplomatic party in town, where he buttonholed lower-echelon Western diplomats and poured on his ponderous Slavic charm. This diplay of camaraderie once prompted a reporter to confront Zaroubin at a party and ask him if he was really enjoying himself. Zaroubin beamed at the journalist like a fading matinee idol conning a producer. "I am always happiest," he replied, "when I am with Americans." That year, he asked a radio commentator to transmit his Christmas greetings to the American people. Dead pan, the commentator complied.

Then there was "Smilin' Mike," Mikhail Menshikov, who took over from Zaroubin as ambassador in 1957. When Menshikov presented *his* credentials to President Eisenhower, a reporter asked him, "What should we call you?" Menshikov smiled a tapioca smile. "Just call me Mike."

Smilin' Mike had a head of distinguished gray hair and the carriage of a subaltern in a fashionable British regiment. The ladies loved his looks and his manners and even his fractured English, which he used with a prodigality that was sometimes somewhat bewildering and, on at least one occasion, embarrassing to his audience.

That was the night Mike was entertaining at the Russian Embassy and, after ingesting several glasses of champagne, rose to propose a toast to Mrs. Robert Alfonso Taft, whose wit was masked behind a façade of royal dignity. "Up your bottom!" ordered Mike genially.

Despite his unconscious affinity for Mrs. Malaprop, Menshikov for several gay months remained a favorite on the canape circuit. As Russell Baker of *The New York Times* wrote, "Menshikov hit Washington with a TV announcer's grin and a hearty handclasp. To everyone's astonishment, he seemed no more like the run-of-the-mine Russian ambassador than George Babbitt was like Fyodor Pavlovitch Karamasov . . . For a few giddy months that coincided with one of Moscow's smiling moods, he was the sensation of Washington." Eventually, of course, the Kremlin found that some domestic consideration dictated that it was time to zig instead of zag, and Menshikov faded into the sober inscrutability of the conventional Russian diplomat.

Yet, it was a measure of Menshikov's brief impact on Washington that for a time he was compared by old timers with Maksim Maksimovich Litvinov, whose popularity stood the test of more than twenty-five years of Soviet zigging and zagging. Litvinov served for two years as Moscow's World War II ambassador to the United States, and he and his British-born wife were lionized not only by Washington but by large segments of the American population. It helped, of course, that the Soviet Union was our ally against Hitler and that organized Russian lovers staged frequent and orgiastic rites to emphasize our great good luck. But Litvinov, a pudgy little man with steel-rimmed glasses, had both a warm personality and a good record when he arrived in the

United States on December 7, 1941. (Japanese bombs began falling on Pearl Harbor twelve hours after Litvinov's plane left Honolulu on the last leg of its Pacific route to America).

It was Litvinov who played a major role in the conduct of negotiations for establishing diplomatic relations between the Soviet Union and the United States in 1934, and American diplomats had found him a pleasant man to work with. Throughout the thirties, as Commissar for Foreign Affairs, he urged a Western coalition against Hitler, and in 1938, when Germany was pressing Czechoslovakia to cede the Sudeten territories, Litvinov announced that Russia would go to the Czechs' aid if France would do likewise. Indeed, it was his opposition to German ambitions that cost him his job just before the sneak Soviet-Nazi pact in 1939. He was appointed to the Washington post shortly after the Germans invaded Russia.

Litvinov, a Pole whose real name was Meir Walach, lived in England for a number of years prior to World War I as a revolutionary exile. There he married Ivy Low, daughter of the British historian, Sir Sidney Low.

When the couple arrived in Washington, they found hundreds of letters and telegrams of welcome from all over America. There was also a flood of invitations to speak at assorted Russian front meetings to raise money for the Russian War Relief Fund. In his letters to his children in Russia, Litvinov related with what now seems a kind of gleeful greed that "I went with Mama" to one of those meetings "and she had great success. Twenty-five thousand dollars were collected! I have spoken only once—to a meeting of the press . . . My statement was printed in full in the biggest newspapers. It was useful."

By that time Litvinov was sixty-five and he found his new job most wearying. "I have much work," he wrote his children. "I must make many visits and receive many people. I cannot just take a walk, or relax. In the evening I am completely worn out, but I don't have time to sleep. Our ambassador in Washington has twice as much work than in any other capital."

Litvinov's heavy work load was understandable. During this time he was trying to get huge Lend-Lease grants for the Soviet Union, while simultaneously agitating for a "second front" in Western Europe to take the pressure off the Russian army in the east. He got along famously with President Roosevelt, who agreed with him on most of the things Litvinov wanted; in one of his letters to Joseph

Stalin, Roosevelt referred to the Ambassador as "my good friend."

Meanwhile, Litvinov was fascinated by the personal interest Americans showed in him and his wife. "Mama began to limp a little because of a blister, and the telephone began to ring," he wrote his children. " 'How is her excellency's blister?' the newspapers asked. Yesterday, some newspapers reported that I bought suspenders in a store. As a result of her innoculation, Mama developed a rash, and the newspapers treated it as a serious illness. This is a strange country and a strange people." (On December 18, 1941, the Washington *Star* headlined a brief news story: "Mme. Litvinov Improving from Illness.")

Physically, Washington impressed Litvinov. "We have a good apartment in the embassy," he wrote. "The city is big and extremely well-organized. The streets are long, and a large part are numerated and alphabetized, so it is very easy to become oriented . . . Some local customs. As I was standing in the street, some strangers came up to me and said 'Are you Mr. L?' They shook my hand, slapped me on the shoulder and with a big smile left. Some newspaper reported that at my press conference I drank orange juice. Several days later, some farmer in Florida sent me a basket of the finest oranges with a clipping from the paper. Mama has taken up writing and drawing. She gives music lessons to a well-known Senator who diligently arrives every morning (he's a beginner)."

Like most foreign diplomats before air-conditioning came into general use, Litvinov suffered from the heat and humidity of Washington's summers. He reported to his children, "We have not gone to a dacha, although we should. As punishment, we are suffering here from heat and humidity. Shirts stick to your skin . . . We've put an air-conditioner in our bedroom, but it lowers the temperature only a few degrees. Several times a day, you must lie in the bath, and then walk stark naked into the room to cool off. The most unpleasant of all is the humidity."

In a relatively short period following the end of World War II, the Litvinov Era ended in Washington and was succeeded by the Cold War Era. Then, figuratively, the lights went out all over the Russian Embassy while suspicion and espionage crept in. The headquarters for this darkly brooding, almost paranoic diplomatic colony is an ornate four-story mansion of stone and beige-colored brick at 1125 Sixteenth Street, located up the street from the Statler Hotel and only three blocks from the White House. The mansion was built in 1910 by Mrs.

George M. Pullman, widow of the sleeping-car magnate, but she never occupied it. The Russian Czarist government acquired it shortly before World War I and used it as an embassy until the 1917 revolution. It was vacated during the period of United States nonrecognition of Communist Russia and then reoccupied in 1934, after diplomatic relations were reestablished.

The house has thirty rooms, some of them thirty-five and forty feet long, and contains a gold room, a green room, a rose room, and a winter garden which is painted a bluish green. It is decorated in old-world style, reminiscent of the Vienna of Metternich rather than the Moscow of the Politburo. The reception room on the first floor, for example, is tastily furnished in the style made famous by that old People's Commissar, Louis XV. A flight of marble stairs leads to the great ballroom, where is hung prominently a portrait of the current Number One Russian—in 1967, Premier Kosygin.

A distinguishing characteristic noted by most visitors is that the embassy probably is the most overheated building since that famous cow shed of the Chicago fire. During the winter thermostats are set to deliver a temperature of eighty degrees, and all the windows are kept tightly closed no matter how balmy the weather may be. Thus its Russian inmates are in a constant sweat physically as well as ideologically. The entire embassy is now air-conditioned, but up until 1958 there were only two air-conditioning units in the house—in the ambassador's office and in his bedroom. Irreverent journalists submitted this was an ironic commentary on a regime purportedly dedicated to the equality of mankind.

Members of the Russian diplomatic staff are permitted to have their own individual homes, most of which are located in the middle-class areas of the respectable-to-fashionable Northwest section of the capital. But the lives of the embassy's forty-odd clerks, stenographers, chauffeurs and domestic servants are severely restricted. About a dozen families live together in a communal household in two untidy, connecting red-brick houses in a beatnik neighborhood just off Dupont Circle. There the wives of the employees and unmarried female workers take turns doing the cooking, ironing and housekeeping.

A few blocks away, embassy children attend a special, rigidly Communistic elementary school, complete with Russian teachers and textbooks. None of the children is more than ten years old. Besides Russian, the children learn French—but they are taught no English until they return to Russia. Occasionally they play with American children, but never enter an American home or invite the American moppets to enter theirs. Children over ten are required to return to Russia to pursue their studies in ideological safety.

And yet when the Russians do go out into the world they are usually greeted warmly. Salespeople in Washington shops have grown rather fond of their Soviet customers, though they acknowledge that Russian men are apt to be a trifle imperious in their demands and that both men and the women are fussy shoppers. But they are pleased with the Russians' courtesy and their enthusiasm for anything that strikes their fancy. One counterman in a food store tells of the time he discouraged a Russian housewife from buying one cut of roast beef and sold her another that was more tasty. "She came back the next day, all smiles, and shoved a package at me," he recalled. "It was a little jar of Russian caviar. She really seemed to appreciate me steering her right." A Russian male was so pleased with a pair of shoes which pampered his bunions that he sent the salesman a dozen roses.

Russian food shoppers show a great fondness for steaks and lamb chops, understandable to any American who has ever sampled the grilled dry beef and withered lamb served in Moscow restaurants. The Russians also like American bacon and hamburger—they buy mostly the ready-ground meat. They don't care for American bread, American cheese or American sausage, but they are still fascinated by frozen foods. Reports from supermarkets indicate the frozen french fried potato must be the Russians' national dish away from home.

For the most part, like other diplomats, the Russians get their liquors and wines through the embassy at special, tax-free prices. But they occasionally visit a liquor store to buy Scotch, Rhine wines and American beer. They complain that bourbon is too harsh, and that gin is "too English." They get most of their clothes from Russia, but they do make occasional purchases in Washington stores. The men prefer double-breasted suits in dark shades, and like their trouser legs longer than the American style—so that the cuffs fold deeply on the shoetops. They have always complained that American trousers are cut too narrow. A saleslady in one shop said she's tried unsuccessfully to get a couple of Russian women customers to buy their bras and dresses large enough. "I think they like to bulge," she noted.

Those Americans who have Russian diplomats or embassy employees for neighbors say they are quiet and courteous. All the Russians

seem to have television sets. Among the shows they have told neighbors
they enjoy are "I Spy," the "Ed Sullivan Show" and Lawrence Welk.
The men are fascinated by professional football games and the women
by variety shows, but American gags often elude them. And all complain that there isn't enough "culture" on American television, that
there should be more classical concerts and readings from "good
books." Practicing what they preach, they spend a great deal of time at
the National Gallery of Art—a gift of that celebrated capitalist, Andrew Mellon—and are regulars at the concerts at Constitution Hall. A
box is always reserved by the embassy for the current ambassador.

Periodically, various groups of Americans are invited to attend the
showing of a Soviet film at the embassy. Usually the picture is pure
political propaganda, but occasionally the feature is what the Russians
describe as a "romance." The effect on the viewer of these epics is
something akin to a sudden encounter with an overripe mackeral.
Largely, the fault lies in the structure of Soviet actresses, who are inclined to dumpiness and who dress like bales of cotton. Their male
counterparts are a little neater, but they alternate tediously between
the vacant stare and the overdone dramatic flourish. Most of the love
scenes are wooden and uninspiring, as in the movie about the triumphant return of the Soviet Army at the close of World War II. In
one scene, showing the reunion of a soldier with his wife after five
years, the soldier kissed his wife tentatively and then opined, with eyes
bright, "How high the wheat is already! Our Soviet agricultural
planners have done well." It does seem that whenever Soviet lovers
find themselves alone in some bucolic dell, they speak not of the
tender passion but deliver themselves of such phrases as "I put the
wheels on three tractors today" and "The Soviet peoples must be on
guard against the cosmopolitan deviationist criminals!"

Presumably, Russian film lovers talk like that because they—and the
script writers—know what's good for them. Should an actress dare to
collapse in her hero's arms and declaim "I'm yours, Boris Borisovitch
O'Molotov," a swarm of secret police probably would descend on her
snarling, "Like hell you are, baby, you're the State's!" At any rate,
Western diplomats resign themselves to an evening of shattering boredom when a Soviet invitation lists a film showing *before* the drinks.

The greater part of the elegant Soviet Embassy is off limits to non-
Russians most of the year. Even diplomats from the satellite countries
go there only when summoned. The outside world's main opportunity

to peek inside comes at the Russians' one big party of the year—the reception held every November 7 celebrating the Bolshevik Revolution of 1917. It is one of the most elaborate shindigs on the diplomatic calendar, with enough fancy food and liquor to nourish and intoxicate a Russian village for a month.

At a typical November 7 party, the Russians serve vodka, Scotch, bourbon, Manhattans, Martinis, brandy, Russian wines, Russian beers and Russian champagnes; the wines, from Soviet Georgia, are usually excellent. On the long buffet table in the upstairs ballroom are caviar —red, black and gray—duck bigarade, breast of pheasant, chicken Jeannette, fillet of beef, roast veal, chicken à la king, lobster salad, beef tongue, sturgeon, salmon, Smithfield hams, turkey, shrimp, glazed rockfish, potato salad, Russian salad, fruit salad, mixed green salad, rice pilaf and an assortment of hot and cold hors d'oeuvres. The desserts include coffee frappé, vanilla ice cream with raspberries, chocolate éclairs, napoleons, mints, bonbons and assorted chocolates. There is always a huge cake—one year it weighed two hundred pounds— which requires the muscles of two men to carry up the stairs to the ballroom.

Naturally, the Russians are the lions of the Communist social whirl in Washington. They give two big parties a year for the satellite diplomats—a New Year's Day affair for the children, and a reception in honor of the satellite ladies to celebrate International Women's Day on March 8. The Russians love children and they give them a good time at the New Year's party, providing costumes and gifts and good-naturedly supervising the games while the parents take a breather. At the reception for the women, each guest makes a speech thanking the Soviet Union for its paternal benevolence, a chore that must come hard for the Czech speaker, whose country's economy has deteriorated under Communism.

Even on such occasions, however, there is often a lack of gaiety because the relationship between Russians and satellites remains one between master and subordinate. The Russian tends to look down on the Rumanian diplomat because of the decadent Latin lineage in his background. In turn—but in private—the Czechs, Poles and Hungarians sneer at the Russians. Perhaps the most strained relationship is that between the Russians and the Czechs, who are inclined to consider themselves more Westernized—and thus more civilized—than their comrades to the east. A Czech in his cups—and in surroundings he considers ideologically safe—sooner or later will make a nasty crack about the Russians, usually about their table manners or the way they wear their clothes.

This bitterness erupted into a good-sized brawl at a party at the Polish Embassy one night. It was past midnight, and the guests had gathered in little groups, when a Russian major spilled some vodka on a Czech. As reported by a waiter for the catering company employed that evening, the Czech made a sneering remark about barbarians who become awkward when they drink too much. The Russian major swung and half a dozen guests joined in the melee that followed. It took the then Polish Ambassador, Josef Winiewicz, and several burly bodyguards to restore order. Four days later the Czech was recalled to Prague.

Much of this resentment among satellite diplomats derives from the Russian policy of using the satellites to do some of their dirty work for them. Since a Westerner quite naturally would be suspicious of any information volunteered by a Russian, the Soviets try to leak misleading tidbits through their Communist vassals. An example of this occurred in 1956, after revolts in both Poland and Hungary, when the British, French and Israelis took some of the heat of world opinion off the Russians by invading Nasser's Egypt. The Kremlin wanted to capitalize as much as possible on criticism of the Egyptian adventure and attempted to float rumors along Embassy Row that the Russians would send volunteers into Egypt if the invaders did not withdraw.

From conversations with satellite defectors, the FBI learned that even Colonel Sergei Edemsky, assistant Soviet military attaché, believed the Soviet threats were empty. Nevertheless he set about trying to sell them through leaks from the Polish Embassy. Edemsky approached the Polish Embassy spy Pawel Monat with a complaint and a request.

"No one wants to talk to us these days," he told Monat. "On the other hand, everybody seems to think you Poles and Hungarians are gallant heroes. Please try to convince the people you see and talk to that we do mean business and that we will send volunteers to Egypt. Let me know what reaction you get."

When Monat demurred, saying he didn't believe Khrushchev really intended to intervene, Edemsky laughed. "Don't concern yourself with details," he told Monat. "Of course we're not going to send volunteers to Egypt. But we want everybody to think we are."

As it turned out, Khrushchev had no intention of sending in volunteers but instead planned to use rockets against the invaders.

While the satellites may not believe and trust the Russians, the Russians trust nobody and thus their embassy is the most heavily guarded diplomatic establishment in the capital. Most of the windows are barricaded with steel shutters, and all locks are made in Russia and installed by special secret police workmen brought from the native heath. Armed secret police are on duty twenty-four hours a day, and during the working hours—from nine to four—these police are stationed at all doors and windows. Daytimes, their arms are concealed in shoulder holsters, as is the gun carried by the secret police doorman. Monat, the Polish military attaché who defected to the West, told the FBI the secret police in Iron Curtain embassies had three functions: (1) to carry out special political and economic espionage against the United States, (2) to provide security for the embassy and its annexes, and (3) to keep an eye on their own people.

In an emergency, most embassies burn their secret papers in fireplaces, stoves and backyard bonfires. The Russians use a strong chemical which can reduce a ten-inch stack of documents to soup in a matter of seconds. They dispatch only photographic films of secret papers in their diplomatic pouches, keeping the originals locked up at the embassy. The film is packed in a special container equipped with a combination lock. Should anyone not knowing the combination try to open the container a vial of acid opens automatically and destroys the film.

Naturally, every room in the embassy is bugged—to eavesdrop on staffers and other employees as well as on the enemy come to call—and so is the headquarters of the Soviet mission to the United Nations in New York. A Washington lawyer, William Dill Rogers, discovered traces of this eavesdropping equipment when he took over as head of the Center for Inter-American relations, which was moving into the old Soviet mission at 680 Park Avenue. Above the high-ceilinged dining room, workmen found a small control room from which multiple wires led under the dining room floor to the area where the dining table once stood. There were outlets at intervals roughly corresponding to the positions of the chairs at the table.

Painters and other workmen called in to ply their innocent trades get a sample of the supersecurity measures employed at the embassy. One owner of a decorating firm recalls that guards were stationed in every room in which his men worked, and before the painters were permitted to go into another room the guards went in and locked all the desks, chests and filing cabinets. If a painter wanted a glass of water, it was brought to him. If he had to go to the bathroom, a guard went with him.

Nevertheless, the Russians are bedevilled by the same human element that dogs Western diplomat-spies. In his book, "The Craft of Intelligence," Allen Dulles, former chief of the CIA, told of the Soviet intelligence officer assigned to the Soviet Embassy who sent his trousers to the cleaners without checking the pockets. In one of the pockets the presser found documents which "brought to light one of the most flagrant cases of Soviet espionage in American experience." The officer, one Gorin, was recalled to Moscow, where—Dulles suggested—"he surely must have been shot for his sloppiness." There was, too, the Russian diplomat who absent-mindedly left a pair of shoes at the cobbler's with instructions to resole them. The cobbler noticed that the heels were run down, removed them and discovered that in each was a hollow compartment containing some strips of paper covered with notes which the FBI found most interesting.

Forty-one Soviet diplomats or employees stationed at the embassy in Washington or the mission to the United Nations were declared *persona non grata* or informally ordered to leave the United States from March, 1950, to February, 1967. All were accused of some form of espionage. By contrast, only fifteen Soviet-bloc diplomats were expelled during the same period. The reason more Russians get caught is simply that there are more Russian diplomats in the United States and they do a lot more spying than any other diplomats.

In the *Diplomatic List,* a book published several times a year by the State Department, the Russians take up three and a half pages of type, compared with less than three pages for the British Embassy. There are more than one hundred names under the listing for the Embassy of the Union of Soviet Socialist Republics, but these include only the more important members of the mission. At various times there are between two hundred and two hundred and fifty Russians stationed in Washington. Over the years, the office of the Soviet military attaché has averaged a staff of forty persons. The FBI has estimated that sixty percent of all Soviet personnel engage in some kind of espionage activities.

The Russians are not only the most numerous among foreign diplomats, but the hardest working. In Moscow, Soviet intelligence headquarters soaks up every piece of information its agents can lay their hands on. More than six thousand analysts in the gloomy complex which the Russians call *Glawnoje Razwiedowatelnoje Uprawlenie* carefully sift thousands of scraps of intelligence every week. To feed this huge digesting machine the Soviet Embassy must spend hundreds of man-hours a month obtaining and transmitting bales of such curious material as the size of the President's shirts, a two thousand dollar contract for some spare electronic parts and the marital problems of a staff sergeant assigned to a general's office at Washington's Fort Mc-Nair.

An American intelligence officer explained Moscow's interest in the President's haberdashery. "They never know," he said, "when they may have to plant an agent in, say, Turkey, whose knowledge of such things must be among his credentials. Soviet agents who claim to have worked as valets for prominent American political and military figures are always popping up around the world."

In the rather formalized *laissez-faire* world of diplomacy there is little inclination among Western diplomats to regard Soviet diplomats as wicked men, personally. They love their wives, their children and their country and, like all diplomats, they peddle their government's current line. But they remain committed to the goal of Communist world conquest, and they have been carefully indoctrinated with the dogma of Lenin that because Communism itself is so pure, any means to achieve its ends is justified. In Washington, the attitude of the State Department toward the Russians is therefore wary rather than unfriendly. The late Secretary of State Cordell Hull perhaps expressed this attitude best when he said he saw no reason to be rude to the then Soviet Ambassador Litvinov.

"But," added Hull, "whenever I shake hands with him I always check to see how many fingers I've got left."

5

Wall-to-Wall Spies

IN SEPTEMBER, 1966, when the State Department ordered Soviet diplomat Valentin A. Revin expelled as a spy, it was announced that Revin was one of seven "science officers" assigned to the Soviet Embassy. The disclosure pointed up the extent of the Russian diplomatic espionage network in the United States—a network so well supplied with bodies that Moscow can afford to take some often rather silly chances of losing an occasional operative.

FBI Director J. Edgar Hoover reported in February, 1967, that there were 865 Soviet bloc personnel and more than twelve hundred persons listed as "dependents" stationed either in Washington or at the United Nations in New York City. All of them had some degree of diplomatic immunity, which means they were protected from prosecution under United States laws. Thus, if a Soviet diplomat or "dependent" is exposed as a spy, he suffers only the disgrace of expulsion, after which he can be dispatched to another country to resume his cloak-and-dagger activities. These are not casual spies. American intelligence estimates that more than ten thousand undercover agents, including diplomats, are trained every year at the Soviets' secret spy center near Kutchinsk, outside Moscow. A small percentage of these then take a kind of graduate school course at the new Aerodynamic Institute in Barkovo, which has about as much to do with airplanes as the Metropolitan Museum of Art.

Valentin Revin, who was listed officially as a third secretary, was involved in a rather inept and shoddy conspiracy which is a prime example of one of the methods Soviet diplomats use to obtain classified or secret information in America's open society. With the assistance of five other embassy officers, Revin dealt with an American citizen of Russian ancestry who had been hired to steal official secrets. In their intense chauvinism, Communist bloc diplomats and Russians in particular seem obsessed with the idea that Americans from bloc countries secretly are still loyal to their foreign fatherlands. Training manuals from the Kutchinsk spy center emphasize that such individuals "willingly cooperate if approached properly." In the Revin case, the American hireling cooperated willingly, but only with the approval and supervision of the FBI.

The American was a young (thirty-one in 1966) metals engineer named John Huminik Jr., who hornswoggled his Russian employers for five years before the FBI stepped in and threw Revin out of the country. During that period, the Russians paid Huminik more than five thousand dollars—some intelligence sources placed the amount as high as a hundred thousand dollars—for information carefully screened by American authorities to prevent transmission of any data of genuine value to the Russians. In addition, Huminik passed on some erroneous information to the Soviets, including carefully doctored matter concerning various failure analysis reports on rocket motors and space vehicles.

Curiously, one of the programs about which the Russians sought information was the Surveyor moon probe. This puzzled officials of the National Aeronatics and Space Administration because they could think of nothing about the Surveyor program that was classified. Surveyor took more than eleven thousand pictures of the moon on June 1, 1966, but all of them had been released. Moreover, NASA officials pointed out that Revin could have obtained detailed drawings of the Surveyor spacecraft merely by visiting the NASA newsroom.

Security people, however, said the Russians' interest in Surveyor probably was a blind. They pointed out that Huminik also had been told to get "personal background information" concerning key scientists at both NASA and the Department of Defense. With such information, the Russians conceivably could have blackmailed or put other pressures on these scientists to spill more important secrets. In the world of international espionage, it is not only the government employee with a guilty secret who is victimized, but also those who are in financial or marital difficulties or who have children or relatives through whom they can be intimidated.

At the time of Huminik's first contact with the Russian spies, he was vice president and senior scientist at Value Engineering Co. in Alexandria, Virginia, a firm with secret government contracts on rocket motor and space vehicle failure analysis. Later, Huminik left Value Engineering to found his own chemicals firm, Chemprox Corp., and was also employed as manager of the materials engineering department of Fairchild-Hiller Corp. in Germantown, Maryland.

Huminik's first encounter with the Soviets was both social and casual. It came at the monthly meeting of the American Society for Metals, of which Huminik was secretary of the Washington section. Two foreign visitors showed up at the meeting—Sergei N. Stupar, then the Soviet Embassy's scientific counselor, and Aleksandr N. Izvekov, then a third secretary. Izvekov asked Huminik if they hadn't met before, and Huminik recalled that he had taken some relatives on a tour of the Soviet Embassy several weeks earlier and that Izvekov had acted as their guide. Thereafter, both Russians showed up regularly at the Society's monthly meetings and once brought along a colleague, Anatoli V. Kuznetsov. Stupar even accepted Huminik's invitation to address the Society and gave a learned, detailed talk on Soviet metallurgy.

After that meeting, Stupar invited Huminik to have lunch with him at the Four Georges Restaurant in the Georgetown Inn—and popped the question. Stupar wanted some unclassified but hard-to-obtain materials. That same afternoon, Huminik got in touch with the FBI and was told to maintain the contact.

For the next two years, the Russians seemed satisfied with Huminik's role as a sort of glorified messenger boy, or—as Huminik put it—"a purchasing agent for Soviet espionage." For Huminik, the documents the Russians wanted were readily obtainable; he was, as it were, merely doing his Russian friends a favor by picking up materials they would have found inconvenient to obtain themselves. But when Huminik founded his Chemprox Corp. in 1963, Stupar apparently decided the time had come to trust him with top-priority espionage assignments.

Stupar hinted that a trade agreement with Chemprox was possible. "You help me and I'll help you," he told Huminik.

Still, the Russians seemed modest in their demands, perhaps because whoever was preparing the unclassified information made it seem more interesting that it was. At any rate, it was not until the summer of 1964 that the matter of Huminik expanding his activities was brought up again. Stupar had left for a holiday in Russia, but before doing so had introduced Huminik to Vladimir P. Butenko of the Soviet Embassy's commercial division and Vladimir M. Zorov, another third secretary.

Over hamburgers at a Virginia restaurant, Zorov suddenly volunteered that "Our country is willing to pay for certain kinds of information." Zorov said they would discuss it in further detail later on. He seemed in no hurry; perhaps he hoped that if he gave Huminik enough time to think it over, the American would become greedy and therefore anxious to do business. Meanwhile, Huminik had the two Russians to dinner at his home in Camp Springs, Maryland, and Butenko brought along a camera "to take some family snapshots."

A few months later, in the fall of 1964, Valentin Revin, third secretary, appeared on the scene. He telephoned Huminik "bringing greetings from Dr. Stupar in Moscow." At lunch in a restaurant in Hyattsville, Maryland, Revin told Huminik he was taking over negotiations for a trade deal with Chemprox. Two weeks later, Revin met with Huminik again and told him he had made a fast trip to Russia, but that "there won't be any trade agreement, I couldn't fix it up." However, Revin said, the Soviet government wanted to employ Huminik as a "consultant." Revin added, "Don't worry, John we'll pay well for it." This time, the Russians wanted top-secret information.

They dined a few nights later at the Blair Mansion Inn in Silver Spring, Maryland, and Revin gave Huminik the cash to buy an expensive camera for photographing secret data, and a miniature tape recorder which could be worn under his jacket for recording conversations with Pentagon officials. Revin also set up a system of "dead drops"—out-of-the-ways spots outside Washington where film and information could be left—and devised a code for marking certain pages of telephone books at designated phone booths, by which Huminik could inform him of the time and place for each "drop."

Huminik went along. He bought the camera and tape recorder and spent long evenings photographing doctored documents for the Russians. Huminik didn't enjoy this part of the work. "It was a hot, stinking job," he told the FBI. Meanwhile, Revin was paying Huminik large amounts of money in cash, which Huminik turned over to the FBI for transfer to the United States Treasury Department.

By this time, Kutznetsov, Butenko and Zorov had all returned to the

Soviet Union. Huminik had hoped to double-cross Revin in such a way that Revin would be forced to defect to the United States and possibly become a spy against his own country. Huminik felt this could be done by showing Revin "physical evidence" against him. In his syndicated column, Drew Pearson quoted a report from Huminik to the FBI which said such evidence would convince Revin "that embarrassment to him will be so great that his inability or unwillingness to cooperate with the United States will totally ruin his image and will embarrass his government . . . This evidence must be newspaper proofs showing his espionage activities with pictures and captions which are embarrassing to him. He must be called a blundering spy, playing into the hands of the Americans . . ."

As the story was later pieced together, the FBI went along with Huminik's scheme for several months, under some pressure from the State Department, which hoped that if Revin could be persuaded to defect there would be no Soviet retaliation against any American diplomats in Moscow. But in such cases there is always the danger that the Soviet agent, becoming suspicious, will try to cover himself and his government by exposing the attempt to force him to turn into a traitor. This has happened a number of times in recent years, and it tends to diminish the American government's case against the agent, however airtight it might be. At any rate, the FBI finally decided the scheme to make Revin into a turncoat wouldn't work. Valentin Revin was given three working days to pack his bags and leave the country. Presumably he was transferred shortly thereafter to a Soviet embassy in some other Western country.

Meanwhile, the FBI has been forced to direct more and more attention to the glass houses of the United Nations on Manhattan's East River. Of the forty-one Soviet diplomats publicly expelled for espionage from 1950 to 1967, nineteen worked either for the Russian mission to the UN or for the UN Secretariat. (It should be emphasized that there is a great difference between public and private expulsions. Most cases of diplomatic espionage never come to the public's attention because of quid pro quo arrangements between the United States and the offending government.)

Valentin Gubitchev, who was convicted with the government analyst, Judy Coplon, of trying to steal secrets from the Justice Department, was a member of the UN Secretariat. So was Ivan Egorov, who masterminded a 1962 spy plot which involved two Washington residents of Czech ancestry. Maksim Martynov, who was taken in by an FBI agent disguised as Martynov's American contact, was a member of the Soviet mission to the UN. As FBI Boss Hoover notes in practically every report on the Communist apparatus, the Soviet bloc regards the United Nations pretty much as an instrument of espionage.

For that reason, Communist bloc governments are always whining that they are underrepresented in the United Nations Secretariat, and periodically charge that the United States has more jobs in that body than it is entitled to. American overrepresentation is a myth, however. As Francis T. P. Plimpton, former Deputy American Representative to the UN, noted in an article in *The New York Times Magazine* in 1966, the U.S. actually is somewhat underrepresented according to the rough governing formula approved by the General Assembly, which takes into account population and budget assessment.

Plimpton also pointed out that, despite their complaints, Communist regimes "will never permit UN recruiting among their nationals and are slow about making recommendations to fill the vacancies constantly being caused by Communist policy against letting any comrade stay at the UN for more than three years (lest he be corrupted by capitalism or internationalism?) . . ." The Russians and their satellites do their own recruiting and never dispatch one of their nationals for duty with the Secretariat until he has made a passing grade in secret police tactics. As for the Soviet mission to the United Nations, the FBI has advanced the expert opinion that eighty percent of its personnel are members of one of the numerous branches of the Soviet security establishment.

Henry Cabot Lodge, who served as Ambassador to the UN under President Eisenhower, described the mission in earthier language. "Wall-to-wall spies," Lodge said.

It is this wholesale prostitution of the diplomat's art which periodically causes members of Congress to rise up and wonder publicly whether the United States is not inviting its own destruction by admitting so many Communist diplomats. Among others, Senators Everett Dirksen of Illinois and Karl Mundt of North Dakota expressed vigorous opposition early in 1967 to a proposed consular treaty between the United States and the Soviet Union on the grounds the treaty would permit the admission of "more spies."

Although Secretary of State Rusk pointed out that even without a treaty the Soviets could bring in more personnel, Dirksen and Mundt maintained their opposition. Since the treaty was aimed at the opening of a Soviet consular office in Chicago in return for a U.S. consular office in Leningrad, the two midwestern legislators complained this was making it "too easy" for the Kremlin's intelligence network. Curiously, both sides cited letters from FBI Boss Hoover in support of their case. Dirksen and Mundt waved a communication from Hoover to Mundt which said the treaty would increase internal security problems. But Hoover also wrote Rusk that he did not oppose the treaty, but had merely pointed out a "problem" it posed. Hoover also told Senator J. W. Fulbright, chairman of the Senate Foreign Relations Committee, in still a third letter, that "I did not imply that this problem could not be handled by the Federal Bureau of Investigation."

Meanwhile, Dirksen was visited by Igor D. Bubnov, First Secretary of the Soviet Embassy, who, Dirksen said, "lobbied me to support the consular treaty." Dirksen told reporters Bubnov's "come-on was, 'Yours is a big name in Moscow.' But I told him I only wanted to be a big name here and preferably in the state of Illinois. I said to him, 'You're always talking about cooperation, but what you want to do is hit someone on the head with a baseball bat and then say: Let's cooperate.' I suppose he didn't take a very good report back to his ambassador."

Later, with the insouciance for which he is famous, Dirksen dropped his opposition to the consular treaty and helped push it through the Senate. Mundt, however, remained opposed to the bitter end to what he called "making concessions" to a nation which was supplying war material to the North Vietnamese regime.

In the UN Secretariat, conceived of as an exclusively international civil service, personnel of various nationalities theoretically are kept honest by the Charter's Article 100, which forbids them to "seek or receive instructions from any government or from any other authority external to the Organization." To the Communist bloc, such a prohibition is arrant nonsense. As Nikita Khrushchev once told the General Assembly, "There are neutral countries, but there are no neutral men." The Soviet mission was angry, not ashamed, when the UN's Russian Under Secretary, Georgi Arkadyev, was caught passing advice via surreptitious notes to Valerian Zorin, the Russian serving at the time as president of the Security Council. During their tenures as Secretary General, Trygve Lie and Dag Hammarskjöld both admitted privately that they never took a Russian staffer completely into their confidence; there was too much leakage of confidential information to the Soviet mission.

While the United Nations is not the nest of spies and saboteurs described in the literature of the John Birch Society, it nevertheless remains the setting for some pretty ugly plots against the security and well-being of the American people. Indeed, it would be surprising if it were not. An enemy of the United States need not spend time and money trying to smuggle saboteurs into the country. All it has to do is accredit them to the United Nations. Hindsight offers a valid argument for the case that the United States, as the chief target of Communist subversion, should not have been so insistent that the UN locate within its borders. For one thing, the UN causes a great deal of trouble for the government's law enforcement and security arms and it costs the American taxpayer more money than he realizes. It takes at least nine FBI men to watch over a diplomatic suspect, plus a back-up crew of assorted experts. In some cases as many as forty FBI agents have been involved. For another thing, certain "diplomats" accredited either to UN missions or the UN Secretariat remain a clear and present danger to American lives and property. One can only shudder over the 1962 exposure of a plot by a group of Castro Cubans to blow up a great deal of Manhattan Island. Had the plot succeeded, thousands of persons would have been killed and injured, and the property damage would have run into the billions of dollars. And it is simply a fact of life that while the United Nations headquarters remains in the United States there will be other, similar plots hatched.

Among some American intelligence experts, there is a conviction that the Cuban bomb plot was masterminded by Moscow, through its ambassador to Havana, Sergei M. Kudryavtsev. There is no concrete evidence available to the outsider, simply because there are no official announcements of what American intelligence is thinking or has discovered unless it suits national policy. But the theory is not farfetched. Kudryavtsev's record suited him for the role.

Kudryavtsev started life as an agent of Soviet espionage in the Berlin office of the Soviet wire service, *Tass,* during the years Hitler ruled Germany. He headed the Russian spy ring in Canada in 1945 which provided the Soviet Union with the know-how to build the atomic bomb, and had operated a Soviet sabotage and espionage network in West Germany. There is impeccable evidence that Kudryavtsev also ran a saboteur training school outside Havana, produced a fine class of graduates and, allegedly, drew up a master plan for sabotaging New York. Kudryavtsev then departed for an assignment in West Germany, leaving the job of pulling off the operation to his successor, Alexei Alekseyev.

Shortly thereafter, Alekseyev is said to have hand-picked the leader of the sabotage team. In any event, the man chosen was a graduate of the Kudryavtsev terror school, a short, slight, curly-haired terrorist of twenty-seven named Roberto Santiesteban y Casanova. In due course, Santiesteban was named to an inconspicuous post in the Cuban mission to the United Nations and left Havana for New York on the night of October 3, 1962, in a Cubana Airlines plane which also carried Cuban President Osvaldo Dorticos and Foreign Minister Raul Roa. Santiesteban's diplomatic passport identified him as an "attaché" at the Cuban mission.

Within a few days after his arrival in New York, Santiesteban had made rendezvous with the other members of the conspiracy. They included José Gomez Abad and his wife, Elsa, both attachés at the Cuban mission; José Garcia Orellana, forty-two-year-old naturalized Cuban immigrant, who ran a costume jewelery shop which catered to the garment industry; and Marino Antonio Esteban del Carmen Sueiro y Cabrera, employed by Garcia as a salesman.

Gomez Abad, a kind of office manager for the conspiracy, had rounded up the other members of Santiesteban's team and had arranged with Garcia to store a cache of explosives, explosive equipment and weapons in the vault of Garcia's costume jewelry shop. As a teen-ager, the twenty-one-year-old Gomez Abad had fought with Castro's guerrilla forces and had marched into Havana with his leader; his wife, twenty, had made a reputation as one of the finest rifle marksmen in Castro's army. She operated a telephone switchboard at the Cuban mission, an assignment whose duties included eavesdropping on conversations to detect any would-be turncoats. Admirers of the Borgia clan would have found this couple attractive. Garcia and Sueiro both belonged to Fidel Castro's 26th of July Movement, and Garcia was president and Sueiro treasurer of the Casa Cuba Club in New York, where an abortive plot had been hatched to hijack American airliners and fly them to Cuba. They were also active in the rather curious Fair Play for Cuba Committee, which was largely notable for its reluctance to give the United States a fair shake.

Estimates of how many others were involved in the plot ranged from twenty-five to fifty people. Certainly, the saboteurs' plans were too ambitious to have been carried out successfully by the five eventually nabbed by the FBI. Over a period of several days, the timetable called for destruction of or damage to several refineries along the New Jersey shore, The Statue of Liberty, Macy's department store, several subway stations, Manhattan's main bus terminal and Grand Central Terminal. The best guess seems to be that a least a score of conspirators burrowed back into the woodwork when the FBI arrested the five principals.

At any rate, this is how the FBI reconstructed the plot and climax:

Santiesteban, Garcia and Sueiro were to meet on the night of November 17, 1962, in Garcia's shop in the sixth floor of 242 West 27th Street, in the heart of the garment district. Garcia's vault, six feet high and with five shelves, was crammed with explosives, incendiaries and hand grenades. On Garcia's desk was a booklet of instructions on the care and handling of their arsenal. Printed in both French and English, the text among other things warned against attaching detonators to incendiary bombs "while you have it on your person." Diagrams indicated where incendiaries should be placed "for maximum destruction" to oil tanks, trains, railroad stations and ships. The saboteurs' first target was to be the multimillion-dollar petroleum refining plant of the Humble Oil and Refining Company in Linden, New Jersey.

Santiesteban was walking along Riverside Drive, heading for a car with diplomatic license plates he had borrowed from a colleague, when the FBI closed in. As they did so, Santiesteban rammed a piece of paper into his mouth and began chewing furiously. Two FBI agents clawed the paper out of his mouth. It contained the formula for an explosive. Santiesteban put up a fight, but six agents were too many for him. He never had a chance to get at the revolver in his inside jacket pocket.

Sueiro was plucked out of a parked car at the corner of Third Avenue and East 24th Street. He had been sitting in the car talking with a pretty young teacher until the time came for his rendezvous with Santiesteban and Garcia. The teacher subsequently was absolved from any implication in the plot. José and Elsa Gomez Abad were taken into custody as they left their apartment in 265 West 71st Street.

That left Garcia, the costume jeweler, who was inside the vault stacking hand grenades on one of the shelves. When the door to his shop was suddenly opened, Garcia seemed surprised. "So early, Roberto?" he called.

Predictably, there was an uproar from the Cuban mission over the arrest of the Gomez Abads, and the couple was subsequently released and ordered to leave the country under the provisions of diplomatic immunity. But their guilt was plain. Among other evidence, the FBI displayed some of the packages of the explosives found in Garcia's vault which bore the address of the Cuban mission to the United Nations—155 East 44th Street. The Cubans also insisted that Santiesteban was entitled to diplomatic immunity, but Santiesteban was a victim of the creaking bureaucracy of the State Department. Although he had entered the United States on a diplomatic passport, the processing of his papers had been delayed, with the result that he could not legally claim a diplomat's right to avoid prosecution.

Santiesteban, Sueiro and Garcia were escorted to jail, where Santiesteban was held in $250,000 bail and the others in $100,000 each. They were indicted on November 21 for sabotage and conspiracy, and charged also with having acted as unauthorized agents of a foreign government. Five months later, all three were returned to Cuba in exchange for certain United States nationals who had taken part in the abortive Bay of Pigs invasion of Cuba.

Deadpan, Radio Moscow indulged itself in what a footnote to history surely must record as one of the more unwittingly ironic pronouncements of the century. It shrieked that the United States was not a safe place for "neutral diplomats" and demanded that Washington pay one million dollars in reparations for the inconvenience visited upon the saboteurs.

6

Scofflaws in Striped Pants

LIKE THE GOMEZ ARABS from Cuba and the Swede Wenner-strom and Poland's Monat, foreign representatives who serve as spies or saboteurs wager only their own diplomatic careers on their excursions into espionage. Even if they are caught in the act by the FBI or some other American law enforcement agency, they are protected from prosecution in the United States by their diplomatic immunity. The worst fate they risk is being expelled by their host government. Wennerstrom, who was arrested by Swedish police on Swedish soil, undoubtedly would have faced the same prosecution had he been caught here and returned to his native land, but he most likely would have sought asylum in a Communist country or embassy. Monat, who did his spying for his own country, would have suffered no more than a rebuke for getting caught.

In short, a foreign diplomat accredited to the United States can commit any crime—from speeding to murder to espionage—and go free. He can scoff at parking tickets, refuse to pay his bills, burn down the Capitol or even, conceivably, assassinate the President, and no American court can touch him. Washington's only recourse is to declare him *persona non grata* and demand his recall by his government. Thus, when an American conspires with a Russian to steal defense secrets from the Pentagon, the American may be sentenced to death and the Russian only to some tedious bureaucratic assignment in Moscow.

The theory of diplomatic immunity, which goes back to antiquity, is that without it the diplomat would find it impossible to satisfactorily

77

perform his functions. Today, as in Biblical times, he must be protected against the arbitrary action of the government which is having a row with his own; he must have a license even to advise his bosses back home to declare war on the country in which he is a temporary guest. He also has the right to communicate freely with his own country, except when he is in a city which is under siege. Winston Churchill invoked this exception to deny the diplomatic colony in London the right to dispatch couriers or send messages in code during the several days immediately preceding the invasion of the continent in 1944.

This immunity is extended to the envoy's wife, family and official entourage and, in some cases, to his servants, on the ground that otherwise his freedom of action would be inhibited by consideration of their safety. It was invoked in the case of David Hearne, young son of the Irish Ambassador, whose car struck and killed a woman pedestrian in Washington. Police were ordered to free young Hearne, and the coroner's inquest was called off. Eventually, the young man was sent home to Ireland—not by the State Department, which was powerless to act, but by his father. In this case, as in many others, there were growls from the police, but no American cop is about to run the risk of violating Title 22 of the United States Code, which provides that a law officer is liable to three years imprisonment if he attempts "to imprison or offer violence to" any person with diplomatic status.

However, some diplomats fail to read the fine print of the international convention relating to diplomatic immunity and wind up in the same trouble visited upon plain citizens. One of these was the Guatemalan Ambassador to Belgium, Mauricio Claudio Rosal, who was engaged by a dope-smuggling ring to act as a courier for its shipments to various countries. Rosal stopped off in New York City en route "home" to Guatemala and aroused the interest of U.S. Bureau of Narcotics agents when he booked a flight back to Europe. They shadowed him as he paid several calls in the city, including one to a man suspected as an international go-between for narcotics smugglers, and finally arrested him.

While Rosal protested his immunity, the agents tore his luggage apart and came upon a large quantity of heroin and $27,000 in payoff money. To Rosal's screams that he had diplomatic status, the agents replied that his immunity applied only when he was en route to or from his post of duty. Rosal was disavowed by his government and sentenced in a Federal court to fifteen years in the penitentiary.

Rosal was both unlucky and careless. He was not the first nor the last diplomat to attempt to use his diplomatic status for personal profit by taking part-time employment with racketeers. The diplomat is a perfect cover for the smuggling boys, since ordinarily his luggage may not be opened in customs, and the Narcotics Bureau has in its files virtually airtight cases against scores of diplomats who have brought jewels, gold, diamonds and narcotics into the country in diplomatic pouches or their private baggage. Where the evidence is conclusive, the State Department steps in and quietly arranges with the foreign government involved to recall the culprit without, of course, offering any explanation for his departure.

Other diplomats have discovered that the cloak of immunity does not necessarily protect an employee of the United Nations or a member of a delegation to the UN. This fact was established several years ago when the Cuban Santiesteban was arrested for conspiracy to commit espionage and tried to invoke diplomatic immunity. Federal District Judge Edward Weinfeld looked up the agreement between UN headquarters and the United States and ruled that the defendant had status only with the United Nations. Judge Weinfeld noted that to accord UN staffs automatic diplomatic immunity without U.S. accreditation "would open the floodgates for the entry of saboteurs, *agents provocateur,* and others under a built-in guarantee that, no matter what the criminal conduct, the government would not prosecute them."

What the agreement between the UN and the U.S. said then—and still says—is that the chief of a UN delegation is automatically immune, but that other delegation members are accorded immunity status only if there is an agreement among his government, the United States and the UN.

Such an agreement was in force for members of the Czech delegation when one Karel Ziska, an attaché of the Czech UN mission, shot his wife to death and fled in his car. Ziska was a fool. While he was speeding south from New Jersey to Pennsylvania, New York police were announcing that no action was planned against him because of lack of jurisdiction. A few hours later, Ziska became a dead fool. His car overturned near Easton, Pennsylvania, and he apparently became so unnerved that he fatally shot himself in the head.

Only one Russian diplomat has ever been arrested, prosecuted in an American court and convicted of espionage. This was Valentin

Gubitchev, a member of the Soviet mission to the United Nations, who was nabbed for receiving information from the pert Judith Coplon in 1949. The Coplon conviction was thrown out on appeal, on the grounds the FBI used wiretap evidence in its case. Gubitchev got fifteen years but was released on condition that he return to Russia. Meanwhile, the U.S. has expelled a number of Soviet diplomats for spying, including the man-and-wife team of Ivan and Aleksandra Egorov, and Gennadi Sevastyanov, cultural attaché of the Soviet Embassy, who tried to persuade a Russian-born employee of the Central Intelligence Agency to turn double agent. By the fall of 1966, sixty-four members of Soviet or satellite diplomatic missions had been "removed" from the United States for various reasons, but the names of only thirty-one were made public. Such secrecy is a reciprocal thing; the United States is not eager to publicize the case of every American diplomat who is kicked out of an Iron Curtain country. Whenever a case is suddenly made public after several years, it is usually in retaliation against a similar action by the other party to this unwritten agreement.

Indeed, the successful practice of the theory of diplomatic immunity depends largely on what might be called an international gentlemen's agreement; its occasional lapses are due almost entirely to the paucity, in a given time, of gentlemen. From the days of the Medes and the Persians, the theory has worked when governments have wanted it to work and failed when there was bad faith between nations. Often there is ill grace on both sides, as in the case of an envoy from one of the Italian principalities of Emperor Otto I in 968 A.D., who was dispatched on a mission to the Byzantine court of Emperor Nicopherus. The envoy made some derogatory remarks about Byzantine culture, whereupon he was clapped into jail and kept prisoner for one hundred and twenty days, with five lions eyeing him hungrily from the next cell. Upon his release, the envoy was presented with several bolts of purple cloth to compensate for his ordeal, but these were dutifully confiscated at the border by customs officials who indignantly found him guilty of the crime of being a foreigner.

In this more-or-less enlightened era, most members of the diplomatic corps are conscientious about obeying the law of the land and generally invoke immunity only to avoid time-consuming court actions. Besides, it is damaging to a diplomat's career to be recalled for embarrassing his government. Sometimes, if the ambassador himself is involved, he is relegated for the rest of his professional life to exalted clerkships. In Washington and in New York, the worst offenders are those from Iron Curtain embassies who tend to be contemptuous of American laws, and diplomats from the so-called emerging African states, who appear to be more puzzled, or fascinated, by the ramifications of the immunity theory than inclined to mischief.

When the Mephistophelean Georgi Zaroubin was Soviet Ambassador to Washington, for example, he earned an unsavory reputation for refusing to pay his bills. Grocers and proprietors of liquor stores and men's clothing shops found him maddeningly casual about accounts that were twelve and fourteen months overdue. One local decorator pulled his crew off a painting job at the embassy because Zaroubin wouldn't pay him for some work he'd already completed.

William Vlahos, owner of the Cathedral Painting and Decorating Company, claims that his crew painted sixteen rooms and had six more to go when he walked out. "I just couldn't get anybody to pay me," he explained. "When I took the job I made up a detailed list of the work to be done and put the price opposite each item. Then I had this big shot initial each job. The next time I saw the list, three days later, the prices we'd agreed on had been crossed off and lower ones written in."

Merchants and other storekeepers find it exceedingly difficult if not impossible to sue successfully a diplomat for nonpayment of a bill. The plaintiff must depend on the good faith of the diplomat's government, which is a sometime thing. However, a French-born hairdresser had his revenge after spending six months trying to collect a $700 account from the wife of a European diplomat.

The coiffeur merely showed up furiously drunk at an Embassy party, staggered up to the hostess, handed her the bill and screamed: "I want my money!"

He got his money the next day—but henceforth he got no more business from anyone at the embassy.

There was also the case of the African diplomat who rented an apartment in a swank building in northwest Washington. The management succeeded, after several weeks of negotiation, in convincing the diplomat that it was not considered *de rigeur* to permit his children to urinate out of the windows. But ejection papers had to be served when the diplomat's wife persisted in cooking dinner over a campfire on the kitchen floor. The diplomat moved out, but he refused to pay damages and successfully pleaded diplomatic immunity when the landlord tried to sue.

In Eighteenth Century England, a more activist approach by several irate merchants was responsible for the convention by which diplomatic immunity attained the force of law in a sovereign nation. The shopkeepers seized and beat up the ambassador of Czarist Russia because he owed them money, then turned him over to the authorities, who forthwith clapped him in debtors' prison. Shortly thereafter, in 1708, the British Parliament passed Act 7 of Queen Anne, which banned interference by local law enforcement officers in the affairs of diplomats. But it was not until 1815 that the first Congress of Vienna established a set of internatonal regulations covering immunity; these were codified by 84 nations at the Second Congress of Vienna in 1961.

Although the regulations are all there, in black and white, Americans are still occasionally shocked by their meaning. When a diplomat's car injures a plain citizen or wrecks the citizen's own car, the American is always furious to learn that he cannot take the diplomat to court but must accept whatever compensation is offered him by the insurance company. In fact, he's lucky to get that much of a sop. To pay damages is an implicit admission of guilt, and many diplomats refuse to make that admission lest they get into trouble with their home office; therefore they instruct their insurance companies to refuse to pay any claim, however small.

This sort of thing several years ago prompted Virginia's Representative Joel T. Broyhill to introduce legislation to make the United States Government liable for claims against diplomats. Broyhill's bill made considerable sense in arguing that since it was the government that granted the immunity, it should shoulder the losses incurred by the citizen who is a victim of that immunity, but the bill died in committee. Meanwhile, a Virginia motorist was stuck with more than five thousand dollars in hospital and garage bills contracted after his car was demolished by a vehicle operated by a diplomat.

Any American with investments in foreign countries is subject to similar frustrations, for nations themselves are protected by sovereign immunity. That is to say, a nation may not be sued in another nation's courts lest such action cause damage to foreign relations. In 1952, the United States decided that in certain cases a foreign government could be sued in U.S. courts but specified that if the foreign government lost the case, its holdings in this country would still be free from attachment. American companies have filed more than 4000 claims against the Fidel Castro regime in Cuba, which has nationalized various U.S. interests, but they haven't a chance of collecting unless or until the Communists are overthrown.

Meanwhile, diplomats in Washington and New York for years have infuriated the citizenry by their almost utter disregard of traffic laws. In Washington during one twelve-month period, privileged foreigners with their DPL license tags accumulated more than eleven thousand traffic tickets without paying a dime in fines. In New York, police attached blue cards to illegally parked cars bearing DPL tags, begging their drivers not to park in front of fire plugs. The idea was to "shame" or "persuade" these scofflaws to obey the law; predictably, it didn't work. Some irate New Yorkers took unofficial action by letting the air out of illegally parked diplomatic cars. Curiously, the police were unable to track down a single one of these vandals.

Early in 1967, New York's Mayor John Lindsay outraged United Nations diplomats by ordering that their illegally parked cars be towed away. On the first day of the police action, seven cars bearing the DPL tags of diplomats or the FC tags of foreign consular personnel were towed off to Pier 74 and stashed with 105 other cars belonging to members of New York's common herd. Unlike ordinary American citizens, diplomats were not subject to fines or towing charges, but there was an immediate outcry from United Nations headquarters.

The outcry was followed by the dispatch of a special UN committee to City Hall, where Mayor Lindsay was petitioned for a moratorium. On their own, other diplomats threatened reprisals against American diplomats in foreign countries.

Two weeks later, Mayor Lindsay surrendered. He agreed that his policemen would try to find the owner before a diplomatic car was towed away and ordered that diplomatic cars be towed to UN headquarters to save their owners inconvenience. He also promised that the city would crack down on nondiplomatic cars parked in diplomatic parking places and would provide more diplomatic parking spaces near UN missions. Meanwhile, it was announced that the American mission to the UN would be staffed around the clock to help diplomats with their parking problems.

State Department men chuckled over Lindsay's surrender. "Lindsay will find," noted one State Department graybeard, "that you can't lick diplomatic immunity." State itself has tried everything, without success.

Prodded by citizens' protests and newspaper editorials, the State Department cracked down on Washington scofflaws in 1965 by ordering police to ticket every diplomatic car parked illegally more than two blocks from its embassy. (It was explained that the Department had to make allowance for the fact that the District of Columbia government had failed to provide sufficient parking spaces around the embassies). Between April 1 and December 31, the crackdown campaign resulted in the tagging of 6038 diplomatic cars. Twenty-six violators were ordered to pay fines, and six did so. Although the State Department had threatened to cancel the license tags of the most flagrant violators, no such action was taken—on the grounds the diplomatic colony needed time to get used to the new system.

On another occasion, Secretary of State Dean Rusk sent letters to all ambassadors notifying them that in the future diplomats would be expected to pay fines for traffic violations. In the first ten days after the letters were mailed, Washington police ticketed 205 cars with DPL tags and collected forty-six fines. But the diplomatic colony rose up in legalistic wrath and dispatched the dean of the corps, Nicaraguan Ambassador Guillermo Sevilla-Sacasa, to deliver a protest to Rusk. The campaign was abandoned.

It goes without saying, of course, that American diplomats abroad enjoy the same privileges of immunity, and it is largely in their interest that the State Department insists upon strict respect for the immunity of diplomats stationed in the United States. Any deviation from the code in the United States, spokesmen point out, would lead to reprisals against American diplomats in foreign countries. Since the U.S. has more than seventy-five hundred Americans serving abroad, it actually gets the best of the bargain in the number of personnel protected. Moreover, many of the more primitive countries have harsher laws, and a violation which would be punishable in America only by a fine might subject an American abroad to imprisonment or even corporal punishment, such as flogging.

As in so many other things, American diplomats are under strict orders to bend over backward to make certain they are not violating any local laws. They have learned from the experiences of others that even a small collection of tickets for speeding could lead to their recall. Indeed, one staffer at an American embassy in a Middle Eastern country was hauled back to Washington and sentenced to the State Department equivalent of counting paper clips when the authorities accused him of a series of violations of a jaywalking statute—all committed at or about seven o'clock in the morning in the course of his daily constitutional. Another was sent home by his ambassador for gambling on a Japanese train, a grave offense in that country but about which the defendant could, and did, plead that he was ignorant of its gravity.

In all the hullabaloo about diplomatic scofflaws in Washington, the outstanding example of propriety was the Swede Wennerstrom who was stealing the country blind of military secrets for his Moscow masters. Wennerstrom promptly paid his own traffic fines and insisted that his wife do the same. Given the normal behavior of members of the diplomatic set, this alone should have made him suspect.

7

Fun, As It Were,
and Games

HISTORIANS WITH a penchant for the off-beat footnote in the dusty archives of the civilized world were intrigued by a juicy item offered by a staffer at the Indonesian Embassy several days after the May, 1956, visit of the then Indonesian President Sukarno to Washington. It took diplomacy back to the lustier days of antiquity, when an ambassador's duties included periodic shopping tours to acquire fresh females for the palace or tent of his monarch or ruling lord.

As related by the Indonesian staffer, one of the chores assigned an unnamed but highly-placed member of the embassy was the rounding up of a dozen ladies of liberal moral outlook, and of various nationalities and colors, to entertain Sukarno during his stay. Although the State Department maintains a frosty silence on such matters, they are frequently a fact of diplomatic life when certain chiefs of state come to Washington to seek a bigger share of foreign aid, understanding of their latest tiff with a neighbor, or merely to live it up a little. Visitors from the Arab and African states are notable among those who express the desire for a little feminine companionship after a day in the salt mines of statesmanship, although there have been West European VIP's who have kicked up an erotic heel or two.

At any rate, some embassies maintain unofficial contacts with the more raffish elements of show business against the day when they may be called upon to provide such nighttime diversions for an exalted voyager. Whatever means were employed, a passel of comely damsels was engaged by the Indonesian Embassy's Mr. X and at the prescribed moment introduced to Sukarno and a couple of his top-ranking aides.

Presumably all went well, for Mr. X heard no complaints from on high about his taste in pulchritude. But the next afternoon he was unexpectedly confronted by a husky spokeswoman for the mobile harem.

"We want more dough," the lady informed Mr. X crisply. "Fifty bucks more apiece."

Mr. X, a properly frugal diplomat, naturally was appalled at this unethical assault on the embassy's purse. They had an understanding, he reminded the eye-filling wench. The price was agreed upon.

"Yeah," replied the lass, "but you didn't tell us that little guy—Sukey—had halitosis."

In an earlier, and possibly better, day, the lady and her friends would have lost their heads. "But what would you do?" the informant asked. "She had him where she wanted him. He had to pay up."

When Sukarno paid another visit to Washington in April, 1961, he complained to President Kennedy that this story was being passed around on Embassy Row and that it had been hinted at in some American newspapers and magazines. "Yes, yes, I love women," he told Kennedy. "I admit it. But I am not the kind of a playboy they make me out to be. I merely like to be in the presence of women. *Time* magazine says Sukarno can't see a skirt without getting sexy. That's inaccurate. I like only young women. A woman is like a rubber tree. She's not good after thirty years. I'm tired of being played up as though I were *Le Grand Seducteur*. But what crushes me most is that anyone should complain that I have bad breath."

As the nation's Number One diplomat, Jack Kennedy naturally tried to sympathize with Sukarno. But the Indonesian playboy's Washington representatives were giggling behind his back. Memos concerned with Sukarno's visit were inscribed with a heading which translated roughly into English as "Broads, Bribes and Booze."

However, such wild life once enjoyed by Sukarno and a few others is rarer on the diplomatic scene than most people might think. The last thing the average diplomat—or visiting head of state—desires is the kind of publicity that would get him in trouble back home. When an ambassador gets drunk or dallies with some feminine ball of fluff, he does so in private. In that part of his social life which is public, he behaves not unlike the citizen from Cedar Rapids at the annual fish fry of the Lions Club.

Indeed, some critics have complained that what passes for diplomatic high jinks in Washington is essentially joyless because of its transient quality. Any innovation is greeted as *le dernier cri* in entertaining, as was the case when Madame Charles Lucet invited a horse to be guest of honor at the cocktail party she threw in November, 1966, in connection with the annual Washington, D.C. international horse race at Laurel Race Course.

This may have seemed a little hard on the horse, because it was obliged to mingle with the other, human guests, and in any given season diplomatic cocktail parties are not overpopulated with Oscar Wildes or Noel Cowards. But the horse, a pretty black filly, arrived on schedule accompanied by a palomino brood mare, and was figuratively enthroned on the French Embassy's front lawn, where it was surrounded by admirers throughout the long chilly evening. In due course, the filly was raffled off and assigned to the holder of the winning $100 ticket, Robert Kleberg of Texas' spacious King Ranch, who needed another horse as badly as he needed another million dollars. Happily, however, fair play won the evening when the filly was auctioned off for $5200 to Frank Ewing, former Deputy Assistant Secretary of Defense, who confessed that the daughter of Nasrullah would become the first horse in his stable.

Betty Beale, the indefatigable and often acerbic society columnist for the Washington *Star,* took the party in her wonted stride the next day. "After all," she wrote, "people are used to unusual types at Washington parties." Miss Beale, perhaps, was thinking of the contretemps that ensued at another cocktail party a couple of nights earlier at the Sheraton-Park Hotel.

The cocktail party was given by John D. Schapiro, president of Laurel Race Course, and Mrs. Schapiro, as one of the social accessories to the annual International Ball. This latter event is attended by swarms of diplomats and their ladies, some of whom can afford the price of the tickets, and most of them showed up at the Schapiro blast. Ordinarily, the damage accruing from such a party is limited to the stains imposed on male shirt fronts and female spines by spilled drinks and flying blobs of cheese dip, but at the Schapiro party there was action.

It started when the tall, redheaded wife of a wealthy New Yorker showed up dressed in what appeared to be a simple black dress, with the skirt fashioned like a redingote. But when the skirt swung open, the lady was seen to be wearing a breathtakingly short miniskirt. A male guest promptly made a remark about her daring, whereupon the lady's husband flung a glass of whiskey in the man's face. The two men then duelled with glasses of assorted beverages, and the husband's pince-nez spectacles were knocked off, before they were separated. Meanwhile, the lady's diamond earrings fell and she was quoted by Dorothy McCardle in the Washington *Post* as saying blithely, "Oh, don't bother with the earrings. I've got all the jewelry in the world."

Had the rather tiresome man from Mars attended the Lucet and Schapiro parties he would have concluded that Washington diplomats do indeed play zestfully after hours. The fact is, however, that Mme. Lucet's horse and the drink-tossing duel were exceptions proving the rule that diplomatic social functions provide all the titillation of a Mississippi convention of Baptist bishops. Some society columnists and slick-paper magazines paint a picture of international intrigue conducted by dazzling *femmes fatales* and distinguished statesmen, and there are hints that the course of history is often altered by a few words whispered in the ear of the Cambodian Ambassador by the wife of some retired Des Moines chiropractor, newly elevated to the post of Third Assistant Secretary of State. The facts are considerably more pallid. At the average diplomatic party, the conversation is more likely to center around what Fishbait Miller, doorkeeper of the House of Representatives, said to a White House chauffeur in the House barbershop. A remark about the weather confided by a Commerce Department official to the Papal Nuncio is reported with all the awe ordinarily accorded to a Papal Bull. Deals occasionally are made at these parties, but for the most part the international problems discussed are more likely to concern the awful rumor that the chef at the Spanish Embassy has been given the sack, thus cutting off free-loaders from some of the best food in town.

But the myth of the Washington cocktail party as a sort of nightly international conference, with bad hooch, survives simply because the town is filled with influential men of all nationalities who are presumed to be thinking, if not uttering, important secrets. This is, for the most part, harmless twaddle, because by the time a Secretary of State or an ambassador from an important country arrives at one of these elegant routs he is either thinking about how sore his feet are or wondering how soon he can escape and go home for an honest drink. "Always find out where the rear exit is located," advised Hervé Alphand, former French Ambassador. Reality, of course, does not deter the fresh young attaché from the Peruvian Embassy or the *nouveau riche* hostess from trying to cure their secret fears of inadequacy by plunging into the Washington social swim. In any gathering of anonymous diplomatic faces they know that some of those faces belong to persons of importance who may be trapped into exchanging a few words with them. A line in the Washington *Post* reporting that Under Secretary of State Nicholas deB. Katzenbach was seen talking to the young attaché can be negotiable in Lima.

There are pitfalls to be avoided by diplomatic hosts, however. Gate-crashing is endemic in Washington, and the guest with the distinguished air who was so knowledgeable about the latest loan to Laos may turn out to be a passing tourist from Charley Horse, Arkansas, who found the door open and walked in. Indian Ambassador Braj Kumar Nehru once got a call from a friend at Georgetown University asking if the famed nuclear scientist, Edward Teller, might attend a party the Nehrus were giving. That night, the Nehrus welcomed a short man with fierce black eyebrows and a long nose and paid him the obeisance due a cardinal of the scientific world. When an individual of identical appearance arrived and announced he was Teller, the Nehrus discovered that the earlier arrival was a pianist they'd hired for the evening.

Intimate embassy dinner parties, of course, are often elegant affairs featuring both superb food and stimulating conversation. But most diplomats below the rank of ambassador or minister-counselor seldom gain admission to any but the mass gatherings, called receptions, which feature wall-to-wall people. These were once described by a beauteous Irishwoman as "Just a lot of people with French shoes and Irish feet." They are a device for paying off obligations to an assortment of diplomats, journalists, third-level types from the Executive departments, members of Congress, and lobbyists. After all, in the United States the diplomatic host must keep in mind that that jerk counting paper clips in some cul-de-sac at Agriculture could become a somebody someday.

There are certain characteristics common to all diplomatic receptions. The air would set a veteran of the Black Hole of Calcutta choking and reeling. The booze is cut-rate stuff, and the mixed drinks apparently are concocted by unfrocked morticians whose hands possess all the cunning of a blacksmith. The canapés are poisonous. Cigarets are jabbed into human eyes or used to ignite creations by Balenciaga, Dior, and Sears Roebuck. Drinks are spilled. Female shoes are ruined. Abrasions and contusions are sustained.

One is not obliged to speak to anyone at a diplomatic reception. Indeed, it is virtually impossible to manage more than a nod or a brief greeting because of the guests' compulsion for swift and sudden movement, especially in the direction of one or another of the three bars. Occasionally a guest finds himself trapped by the crush and forced to listen to a series of inchoate non sequiturs released by the aging widow of some World War I general. But if he keeps his eye peeled and his feet alert he can slide through a gap in the mob and find relative solace in the company of a Third Secretary of the Tunisian Embassy a few yards away. He had believed the man was dead, of course.

There is a kind of desperation to the consumption of alcohol, because a diplomatic reception calls upon reserves of vigor not manifested since the storming of the Bastille. As a result, a staid matron from Cleveland Park suddenly will find herself being pinched in the behind by a brilliantined dandy from some Latin-American embassy. A Budget Bureau type will be moved to arrange a tryst in some dimly-lit Howard Johnson's with a sultry secretary from the Italian Embassy. Most of the conversation consists of grunts and groans, dressed with tinkling female laughter. Lyndon Johnson's accession to the White House contributed to these affairs a hearty patois which might approximately be described as shirtsleeve Texan.

Embassy Row does its entertaining within the varied walls of a conglomeration of structures which seem to have sprung from some architectural Babel. There is the spectacularly contemporary embassy of oil-rich Kuwait, of modified Arabesque design and decor. There is Great Britain's red brick English country house, built in 1928. The Irish Ambassador presides over a residence, bought by the Irish government in 1964, which is officially described as Irish Georgian. The French Ambassador plays host in a Tudor castle, the Spanish Ambassador in a massive, brooding building in the now unfashionable environs of upper Sixteenth Street, which might have been transplanted from the Toledo of Goya.

Beginning in 1960, there was a surge in the construction of new embassies, as the old residences became too small and embassy budgets were fattened by world prosperity. New chanceries also were built, to accommodate the daytime burden of paper work—the German chancery on Reservoir Road is six stories of steel, tiered like steps on a hillside; the Iranian chancery, a copy of a fifteenth century mosque in Isfahan. The Dutch Embassy imported 350,000 bricks, rough stone and window frames for its new residence. The Danes installed teak floors from Denmark in their new glass-and-brick establishment. The Iranians imported both materials and some workmen to decorate their chancery; Communist-like, the Yugoslavs used all imported labor to build their new chancery, whose special Yugoslav locks were no defense against a terrorist bombing in January, 1967.

Probably the most interesting and undoubtedly the most beautiful of the newer embassies is the combination residence and chancery of the State of Kuwait, which brushes the fringes of Rock Creek Park on Tilden Street, just off upper Connecticut Avenue. It cost an estimated four million dollars, and its opulence predictably has been the target of Congressional critics, who have wondered aloud how many square meals the money would have bought for the more underprivileged among that Arab country's masses.

The structure is of antique beige brick trimmed with white marble; its exterior was designed by a Baltimore architect, its interior by an Egyptian of Italian heritage. Inside, the leather paneling on the walls and doors is tooled in 14-karat gold. The carved lattice screen enclosing the circular red-carpeted staircase leading to the private living quarters on the second floor and all the furniture were designed and carved by hand in Cairo and shipped to the United States in pieces. It took eighteen Egyptian laborers, working twelve to fifteen hours a day, three months to assemble the furniture and upholster the divans and chairs.

Hanging in the hall and dining room are large antique chandeliers of lace-like brass set with colored stones which are at least 250 years old. The sitting room is dominated by Islamic arches, and the walnut panelled walls are topped by an extensive collection of opaline glass made in Bohemia for the Persian kings of a thousand years ago. It took 27,000 pieces of carved wood to decorate the loggia, which is fifty by forty-four feet and two stories high. In the center is a pool with a low marble wall which is lighted at night, and three large glass doors at either end of the room open onto a small enclosed garden in front and a large tiled terrace in the rear. Outside, continuous colonnades expressing the Islamic arch face the building front and back, and beyond the rear terrace there is a swimming pool—a must in Washington.

In contrast to such ostentatious and exotic display, the other embassies around town seem almost drab, although both the British and Irish embassies have a warmth of style and grace that is charming. Unfortunately, the British were forced by the postwar expansion of their embassy personnel to erect a modernistic office building adjoining the residence. The structure cost $3.4 million and is the largest single building ever to have been built outside Britain by the British Ministry of Works. It surrounds a square central court; two of its sides are four stories, a third six stories and the fourth seven stories. There is also a rather monstrous conference hall in the shape of a rotunda with a copper-covered dome.

The French Embassy, bought in 1936 from the mining engineer, John Hays Hammond, for $450,000, has been altered somewhat to add Norman touches to the original Tudor architecture. It features Gobelin tapestries, Matisse still lifes, Sèvres nymphs—and a wine cellar whose temperature is always kept at 60 degrees Fahrenheit. Of the Alfred Norton '14 cognac, an embassy chef once remarked, "It is a sin to drink it. This was made for sniffing."

In such surroundings, most ambassadors live well but not lavishly. The notable exceptions are the Kuwaiti envoy, Thalat Al-Ghoussein; the Spanish Ambassador, the Marquis de Merry del Val; and French Ambassador Lucet. Periodically, there is criticism in print of the luxury enjoyed by some of these diplomats, especially those who represent countries on America's Foreign Aid list. But Mrs. Al-Ghoussein had a tart retort for a social pal, Mrs. Barbara Howar, when the latter mentioned the matter on a local radio show.

Mrs. Howar, wife of a wealthy Washington contractor, commented that she found if difficult to accept the lavish hospitality of embassies of countries receiving aid from the United States. "In the countries where there is complete poverty, you wonder if the money should be spent even for such a thing as a National Day party," said Mrs. Howar.

Mrs. Al-Ghoussein's voice had a sly smile in it. She replied simply that she didn't feel it right to criticize expensive parties given by Americans "in spite of the poverty of many of the people in the District of Columbia."

Mrs. Al-Ghoussein arrived in Washington at a time when there was maneuvering room for a new diplomatic hostess desirous of crashing the Embassy Row Establishment. The social attrition resulting from President Charles de Gaulle's anti-American policies were having a predictable effect on the diplomatic scene, and Mrs. Al-Ghoussein did manage to make quite a splash. Unfortunately, however, there was shortly another new arrival in town—the Marquesa de Merry del Val, wife of the Spanish Ambassador—and Mrs. Al-Ghoussein found the going a little slow after the first few months. Eventually, the Marquesa de Merry del Val out-distanced that lively Frenchwoman, Mme. Lucet, for the coronet as the town's leading Embassy Row hostess. The Marquesa made it mostly on her blue blood. Quite aside from the fact that De Gaulle was becoming a bore, the Merry del Vals represented a noble family distinguished over the centuries for its production of statesmen and high dignitaries of the Roman Catholic Church. Even with the best chef in town and a penchant for inviting horses to take pot luck—or feedbag—at her embassy, Mme. Lucet remained a democrat and thus fatally handicapped.

The Marquesa de Merry del Val is handsome and cultured. She is also wily. Before she arrived in Washington, the Spanish Embassy threw an annual bash on October 12 to honor the memory of Christopher Columbus. But then the Italian Embassy got into the act by inaugurating a wreath-laying ceremony at Columbus' statue outside Union Station, and when the marquesa arrived, she saw to it that the significance of October 12 should be pure Spanish. Invitations to her party read; "To commemorate the 474th Anniversary of the Discovery of America *by Spain*."

She also won the hearts of Washington's captive political population when she told a gathering of ultrachic New Yorkers, "Washington is the capital of the world. You are living in the provinces." Several Washington hostesses reportedly sacked their psychiatrists forthwith, with the explanation that they had licked their insecurity.

Meanwhile, the marquesa was getting in on all the little acts so important to Washington socialites and social-climbers. She was honorary chairman of the 1966 Junior League Christmas Shop. She gave a cocktail party for members of the Men's Committee of the United Performing Arts of Washington, which prompted former Postmaster General J. Edward Day, a kind of ex-officio wit, to take a crack at Mrs. Jacob Javits, wife of the senator from New York. "I am sorry Senator Javits couldn't come today so he could tell his wife how cultured we are all getting," said Day. He was referring, of course, to Mrs. Javits' disparaging remarks about the state of the capital's cultural life. The marquesa also sent some of Washington's "Beautiful People" into a tizzy by having a Spanish television crew on hand to record for the home audience a dinner party at the embassy. Presumably, any citizen of Franco's Spain who could afford a television set would be only casually envious of the lavish hospitality dispensed by the chatelaine of his embassy in Washington.

All these activities, however, were preliminary to what Spanish Embassy spokesmen modestly referred to as "the climax of the season." This was the visit to Washington in January, 1967, of Prince Juan Carlos, pretender to the throne of Spain. Juan Carlos and his wife, Princess Sophia of Greece, were the guests of honor at an elaborate and ceremonious dinner at the Spanish Embassy, attended by everybody who was anybody and the usual smattering of those who got in because they knew an anybody or two.

Later, the Marquesa de Merry del Val was said to have been annoyed at the directness shown by one Washington society writer who cornered the Prince and asked him point blank: "Are you going to be king?"

Juan Carlos's reply would have warmed the heart of that plain speaker, Harry Truman. "I hope so," he replied, while Spanish hearts slowly receded from Spanish mouths. The Prince also handled himself well when asked about his father, Don Juan, only son of the late King Alfonso. "I hope he becomes king, too," said Juan Carlos. "As his son, I think he should be king, but I also want what is best for Spain." Secretary of State Dean Rusk later remarked that he "could use a diplomat like that."

The Prince got in a question of his own, to Lynda Bird Johnson, who was wearing a new ring given her by the actor, George Hamilton. "Is it serious?" he asked. Dimpling, Lynda Bird would reply only "We're going steady." Naturally, this exchange was reported with all the breathlessness of a State Department spokesman announcing the rumor that Mao Tze-tung had run off with Brigitte Bardot.

Meanwhile, the Washington *Post*'s Maxine Cheshire was able to shed some light on how a member in good standing of the Beautiful People Club wangles an invitation to go yachting. In another corner of the drawing room of the Spanish Embassy, Mrs. Sargent Shriver, wife of the director of the anti-poverty program, learned that Mrs. Alexander Goulandris of the Greek shipping family had invited her

brother, Senator Ted Kennedy, to go along on a cruise of the Greek
Isles. Mrs. Shriver sought out Mr. Goulandris.

"Do you happen to know Mrs. Sargent Shriver?" she asked the shipping magnate. Goulandris confessed he did not.

"Well, I just wanted to tell you to be sure to invite her on your
cruise this summer," said Eunice Kennedy Shriver. "She is one of the
most fascinating women in Washington and would be a great addition
to your party."

Such repartee admittedly is not of the kind that topples chancelleries and causes dictators to toss restlessly on their silk sheets at night.
But it is the kind that dominates at diplomatic social affairs, largely
because important government figures are fearful lest they say something they shouldn't, and thus take refuge in the frivolous or even
inane. Besides, Washington is not overcrowded with stimulating con-
versationalists of the breed of the acid-tongued and scholarly Joseph
Alsop, the columnist, and the delightfully candid Princess Alice
Longworth, who once said of Tom Dewey that he looked like the little
man on a wedding cake. Moreover, most diplomats are as ordinary as
those the United States sends to Madrid or Nairobi. Usually, the only
difference is that the foreigners have interesting accents, reek of
cologne, and are more successful in putting off creditors.

As far as the social pecking order itself goes, there are those along
Embassy Row who insist that the diplomatic colony will not soon find
a worthy successor to Nicole Alphand, who preceded Mme. Lucet as
mistress of the massive yet graceful Tudor-style French Embassy at
2221 Kalorama Road, Northwest. It is true that during the latter part
of the Alphands' tenure they were replaced as the Number One diplomatic pals of the John Fitzgerald Kennedys by Jack Kennedy's old
friend, British Ambassador Sir David Ormsby-Gore and Lady Ormsby-
Gore, but until they were recalled to Paris, the Alphands retained first
ranking in the colony's social order. The Merry del Vals were em-
braced because of who they were; the Alphands because they had style
and gave parties, not infantry charges.

Long after the Alphands had left town, the colony continued to
exclaim over the dinner party Nicole Alphand gave for ninety persons
to celebrate the safe arrival of the *Mona Lisa*. The ranking guests,
predictably, were President and Mrs. Kennedy. Mme. Alphand once
invited fifteen women friends over for what she called a *pique-nique
au boudoir* and presented each of them with a new hairdo—on the

spot—by Alexandre de Paris. She sponsored a showing of 120 Dior designs and a hula-hoop contest. She gave a party for three hundred to display Pierre Cardin's new fall fashions, and had thirty women over to try on Jean Barthet's fall hats. When her husband gave her a second mink coat, she converted her old one into button-in linings for six cloth jobs.

The Lucets tried hard, but they were never quite accepted as worthy social successors to the Alphands. Besides, Mrs. Lucet's interests inclined more to little parties after opera performances, and there were not as many music lovers in the Johnson Administration as there were among Kennedy's New Frontiersmen. Moreover, there was the distinct reaction to De Gaulle's tactics of seeming to bait Washington.

This caused considerable concern in February, 1967, when the French Embassy sponsored a "very small" dinner dance for the benefit of the Alliance Française of Washington, the Gallic equivalent of the English Speaking Union. Members of the Alliance found it difficult to dispose of the tickets, and not alone because they cost a hundred dollars apiece. There was resistance from among those who proclaimed they loved the French—"but that goddam De Gaulle . . ." But Madame Gerard Gaussen, wife of the counselor of the embassy, put her considerable charm to work on Washington society, the ticket sellers redoubled their efforts, and the result was a sellout attendance of 210 socially presentable—and rich—guests.

"The French Embassy is back in style," proclaimed Nancy Ross in the Washington *Post*. And the *Star*'s Betty Beale, who had awarded the social throne to the Merry del Vals, reported that Washington society had "buried the hatchet that De Gaulle has been flinging our way lately . . ." In Washington salons, doubt was cast on the credentials of the freshman Congressman who had cracked that an invitation to the Spanish Embassy was worth one-half Kuwaiti, and a Kuwaiti invitation was worth five French.

Yet De Gaulle's continuing intransigence had set up a kind of battle royal among the more social-minded embassies to replace the French as Number Two. Only the British Embassy remained aloof from this scramble. Sir Patrick Dean, the new British Ambassador, and Lady Dean were aware that invitations bearing the lion-and-unicorn crest would always be coveted in Washington, and continued to give the sedate, infrequent dinner parties for which the embassy was always noted. The British, however, had the bankroll to splurge if they saw fit; as noted earlier Her Majesty's ambassador gets $95,000 a year in salary and for housekeeping and entertainment.

There is also plenty of money for the spending elsewhere along Embassy Row. Although West German Ambassador Heinrich Knappstein gets $78,500 a year in pay and for housekeeping and partying, German parties are dull and marked by an overdose of old-world politeness. "Everybody's afraid someone will drop a spoon," reported one dinner guest. The Peruvians entertain gaily at their palatial embassy tucked into twenty-five bucolic acres in Chevy Chase, and so do the Mexicans, who can frequently count on the Lyndon Johnsons as ranking guests. Chilean Ambassador Radomiro Tomic and Mrs. Tomic are favorites among the more serious types because of their emphasis on people-to-people projects. Most of the parties at the Russian Embassy are crowded affairs, because the Russians like to pay their obligations all at once. Arriving at one of these wholesale routs, Columnist Bob Considine squeezed his way to the bar and then turned to survey the milling mob. "Where," he asked, *"IS* everybody?"

Although very little diplomatic business is done at these after-dark affairs, the socializing does pay off occasionally. Thus, Merry del Val once cornered a couple of United States senators at a party at the Spanish Embassy and was able to persuade them to oppose an Administration proposal to reduce financial concessions concerned with the maintenance of American bases in Spain. A few weeks later, the senators led a successful fight to keep the concessions intact. American military aid to India to India during the 1962 Red Chinese border attacks was agreed upon at an impromptu session in the kitchen of the Indian Embassy in which the participants were Ambassador Nehru, the then Attorney General Bobby Kennedy and Defense Secretary Robert McNamara. The then Under Secretary of State George Ball dotted some i's and crossed some t's for Soviet Ambassador Anatoli Dobrynin during a discussion of the nuclear test ban treaty at a shindig at the French Embassy. In 1963, Mexican Ambassador Antonio Carrillo Flores huddled with Vice President Johnson and United States Ambassador to Mexico Thomas Mann in a drawing room during a reception at the Mexican Embassy and got an agreement on the settlement of Mexico's 52-year-old claim to 640 acres on the Texas border.

Mostly, however, diplomatic party-goers insist upon making the same kind of small talk which could be heard at any reception of the

National Association of Manufacturers. For example, during the period in the winter of 1967 when all varieties of "peace feelers" from North Vietnam were in the air, guests at a white-tie party given by Secretary of State and Mrs. Rusk were intrigued to discover Indian Ambassador Nehru and Soviet Ambassador Dobrynin in deep conversation. It was naturally assumed the two diplomats were talking about something significant.

But when the Marquesa de Merry del Val joined the two men, she was delighted to learn that they were discussing the best laundry in Washington to get a stiff shirt and wing collar done up. Ambassador Merry del Val then confessed that he sent his stiff shirts and collars all the way to Spain to be laundered, and it was recalled that former Australian Ambassador Sir Howard Beale used to send *his* formal armor to London.

At the same party, guests were recalling the practical joke played on the White House during the Kennedy Administration by the Prime Minister of Afghanistan, Mohammed Hashin Maiwandwall, then his country's ambassador to Washington. The incident concerned the horse, Sardar, given to Mrs. Jackie Kennedy by Pakistan's President Ayub Khan, during her visit to that country. In order to process the horse through United States Customs, Mrs. Kennedy's social secretary, Tish Baldridge, had to get an estimate of the animal's worth. She put in a call to the Pakistan Embassy, and the switchboard operator absent-mindedly dialed the Embassy of Afghanistan—an error made ironic by the fact that there was considerable ill-feeling between Pakistan and Afghanistan at the time.

Maiwandwall took the call, and Miss Baldridge dutifully asked him to put a value on Sardar.

"Well," Maiwandwall replied, "knowing where the horse came from, I'd say about twenty-five dollars."

Maiwandwall would have been appreciated by the newest diplomatic "in" group, which is not concerned so much with significant conversation as it is with what it calls "fun-action" and *avant-garde* fashions. This is the so-called Swing Set, comprising mostly the younger diplomats and their handsome wives, with a sprinkling of such vigorous party-goers as the ineffable Mrs. Barbara Howar. The Swingers announced rather arbitrarily that the hitherto prestigious British, French and Spanish establishments were too old-fashioned and that henceforth the people who mattered would be found dancing the frug and other spine-shattering adventures at the Moroccan, Kuwaiti and Algerian embassies—all Arabic and all heavily infiltrated by youth.

One of the more attractive among the Swing Set's arbiters is Mrs. Al-Ghoussein, the Kuwaiti chatelaine, who startled the more staid among the diplomatic colonists by wearing pants to go shopping and even suggested that britches of a somewhat more elegant and costly design might be suitable for evening receptions and dinner parties. Indisputably, Mrs. Al-Ghoussein possessed the aplomb to survive the glares directed at her by the comfortably stout among the diplomatic matrons. She once expressed herself as "charmed" when a Commerce Department wife from Iowa confronted her at a party at the Venezuelan Embassy and confided rather breathlessly, "I love the name Al. My husband's name is Al." Washington, of course, is the town where a wire-service photographer trying to arrange a picture bellowed at Morocco's King Hassan to "Shove over a little, King!"

At any rate, Mrs. Al-Ghoussein found supporters in such socially evident women as Mrs. Nicholas deB. Katzenbach, wife of the Under Secretary of State, Mrs. Sander Vanocur, wife of the NBC-TV correspondent, and the beauteous and unpredictable Barbara Howar. Mrs. Howar was the first to flout convention. She wore pajamas to a Moroccan Embassy black-tie party in the spring of 1966. It was social Washington's Magna Carta. Mrs. Vanocur shortly followed by donning a shocking pink silk number to a black-tie dinner at the Venezuelan Embassy. "No one asked me to leave," reported Mrs. Vanocur to *The New York Times.*

However, both Mrs. Katzenbach and Mrs. Edward Kennedy, wife of the *other* brother from Massachusetts, showed early signs of an awareness of the pitfalls awaiting a politician whose wife is too daring an innovator. Mrs. Kennedy wore her plum-colored velvet evening pants suit only in private. Mrs. Katzenbach told *The Times* she "very definitely" wore pants outside the house, but said she stopped short at diplomatic receptions.

Mrs. Katzenbach seemed exasperated by the dull routine in the capital. "There are very, very few chic people in Washington," she told *The Times* Reporter Myra MacPherson. "Washington just undermines you after a while, and I guess I'm tired of fighting the battle. For therapy, I have to get to New York or London or somewhere where individuality is part of your existence."

Nevertheless, the ranks of pants-wearing females at diplomatic functions continued to grow as the Swing Set asserted itself. This posed somewhat of a problem for the male party-goer who wore his hair long, as one willowy attaché from the Chilean Embassy discovered to his embarrassment at a shindig at the Algerian Embassy, when he was approached by a beribboned general and asked if he was free for the next dance. He rose early the next morning and was the first customer to enter the Mayflower Hotel's barbershop. Other males reported discovering just in time that pants-wearing figures they approached were not quite of the sex they had hoped to regale with the latest story out of Uncle Billy's Whiz Bang. There was even a report that a Spaniard challenged to a duel a guest attired in bullfighter's outfit who turned out to be the wife of a big spender from Chicago. And it was noted that the more ebullient Latin-American diplomats were more cautious; they refused to pinch the derrieres of any but those guests safely sheathed in a genuine dress. Presumably, this saved them many a punch in the snoot from former All-American tackles with shoulder-length locks.

Despite the determinedly chic antics of the Swing Set, it remained for the staid British Embassy to provide the most delightfully shocking *pièce de résistance* of the 1966 season. The occasion was an official dinner for Britain's unpredictable Foreign Minister George Brown, who had won a reputation on the Continent as a kind of professional *lourdon* by his barefoot-boy approach to high society.

The dinner was all that the British Embassy could offer, stately but warm, and with just a hint of the effortless pomp which is the hallmark of any representative of Her Majesty anywhere in the world. Brown seemed restless, but he behaved himself until the dessert, when he suddenly turned to his dinner partner, the wife of a member of the Johnson Cabinet, with what can only be called a practiced leer.

"You're an enchanting woman," he told her. "Shall we have an affair?"

Brown explained to a group of American reporters the next day that "the lady refused quite gracefully." He then added that he had made the same proposition to a diplomat's wife at a London dinner, and when he was chided later by an aide he had promised never to do it again "until after the soup."

As a matter of fact, the British Embassy has not been without its incidents. One of the most notable in the memory of Washington old-timers took place at the reception in honor of the King's birthday in

1938. This is a magnificent affair, held annually on the embassy lawn at tea time. And traditionally, the domestic staff of the embassy has its own little party at noon, when the maids, chauffeurs and butlers kick up a figurative heel in honor of the monarch.

But at the 1938 staff party, one of the butlers had a trifle more than his share of champagne and a few hours later almost got World War II started ahead of time. No one noticed his condition until it was too late—that is to say, until the horrified onlookers watched him unceremoniously dump a glass of iced coffee, complete with clotted cream, onto the lap of German Ambassador Hans Heinrich Dieckhoff.

There was also the evening, just after the 1965 inauguration of Lyndon Johnson for his first full term in the White House, when a fun-loving and bibulous British diplomat buttonholed Alexander Zinchuk, minister counselor of the Soviet Embassy, and confided a piece of startling intelligence.

"It's not Johnson at all, you know," he told Zinchuk. "He was assassinated during the campaign, but they kept it quiet and elected a double. It was quite easy, with Goldwater running on the Republican ticket." Zinchuk, one of the more urbane Soviet diplomats, tore himself away as soon as it seemed safe, convinced the Englishman was mad. But the British envoy later reported he had checked with "an intelligence bloke" and discovered that Moscow was making discreet inquiries about a reported "accident" to Johnson during the 1964 campaign.

8

The Suez Conspiracy

A FEW WEEKS AFTER the seizure of the Suez Canal on July 25, 1956, by Egypt's President Gamel Abdel Nasser, two bright young diplomats met at Washington's swank La Salle DuBois for one of their periodic martini-to-brandy luncheons. One was an underling in one of the elegant rabbit warrens of the State Department. The other was military attaché at a neutral embassy. Their meetings were only ostensibly social; they were businessmen who exchanged tidbits of information about their trade.

On this sultry August afternoon, the military attaché had some startling intelligence for State's young man. He said he had picked up a report from an unimpeachable source that the British, French and Israelis were planning an invasion of Egypt, designed to crush the Nasser regime, recover the Suez Canal and win more land for the fledgling Israeli nation.

This was more than a tidbit. It was a gift-wrapped package of dynamite that could blow up the alliance of the West's three major powers. And although the man from State considered the intelligence cautiously—its very outrageousness made it subject to suspicion—there was good reason to accept its authenticity. He had been getting information from the neutral military attaché for the past eighteen months and had never been given a bum steer. Moreover, he had independent knowledge that the military attaché had important contacts at the Israeli Embassy.

From what he had been able to learn, the attaché said, the invasion plan was still in its tentative stages and therefore subject to change without notice. But his information was that it was scheduled for "some time after" the American Presidential election in November— probably in January, 1957, and in any event not earlier than late December. America's allies, it seemed, had a nice concern for the domestic problems such an action might pose for the Eisenhower Administration.

So far as is known, the military attaché acted in good faith. However, only half of his information was accurate—plans had been launched for an invasion of Egypt, but D-Day had been set tentatively for sometime during the last two weeks of October. Moreover, the information had been planted with the attaché by a member of the staff of the French Embassy for the express purpose of having it leaked to the State Department.

The reason for this ploy on the part of the French was a simple one—they were attempting to cover their tracks. The French had been told a nosy operative for the Central Intelligence Agency had picked up some shreds of information about the invasion from an agent in French Intelligence in Paris, and the French Foreign Office wanted to spread a little confusion in Washington. Indeed, at that early stage of the planning, the three conspiring nations were quite resigned to abandoning the plot should Washington raise a substantial fuss. In the meantime there was always the chance they could brazen it through by a campaign of befuddlement, of which further exercises were planned for later.

It has never been revealed, even after more than a decade, whether a CIA man did in fact pick up a whisper about the invasion. If he did, there is no available record that it was passed on either to Washington CIA headquarters or to the State Department. Cold, after-the-fact research suggests that the State Department had received no hint of the invasion plan prior to that offered by the neutral diplomat because Secretary of State John Foster Dulles seems to have dismissed as unreliable gossip the intelligence passed over the luncheon table at La Salle DuBois.

In any event, Dulles did nothing about it. Monday morning quarterbacks among Washington experts have submitted that Dulles just couldn't believe our allies would dare to engage in such an adventure behind America's back. Others have suggested that since the report indicated the attack would not take place until after Election Day Dulles preferred to sit on the problem for a while rather than take any action which might stir up trouble during the campaign. Given Dulles' tendency to indulge in intricate and sometimes devious diplomatic maneuvers, the probability exists that he thought the invasion a grand idea—Nasser *had* to be got rid of—and at that early stage decided against any immediate attempt to interfere.

Whatever Dulles' thoughts, the French had succeeded far beyond their hopes with their planted information. To the conspirators, it didn't matter whether Dulles secretly approved their plot or hesitated to raise a fuss during a political campaign or disbelieved the whole story—they had avoided exposure and an early confrontation with their Atlantic partner. In the Gallic phraseology, events were marching satisfactorily, and there was reason to believe they would continue to do so if the conspirators could continue to feed false information to Washington via Embassy Row.

The Suez crisis, which very nearly plunged the world into nuclear war, was the fruit of high international finance, power politics between the Soviet Union and the West and the wounded pride of an Egyptian dictator. One development followed swiftly upon the other. When Nasser insisted upon accepting arms from Moscow, the while slipping in and out of the Soviet political bed, the United States withdrew its offer of a loan for construction of Egypt's huge Aswan Dam. Nasser retaliated by promptly nationalizing the Suez Canal. Subsequently, Secretary Dulles sought vainly to sell our allies on the Suez Canal Users' Association as a cooperative venture with Egypt, but even before he broached the project on September 12, France and Israel were laying the ground work for a war-making alliance—with a fully-informed Great Britain ready to join up at the right moment.

Israel wanted arms, to match those Nasser was getting from the Soviet Union, but Foreign Minister Moshe Sharett got the cold shoulder from both the Western Allies and Moscow—all except France. Prime Minister Guy Mollet and Foreign Minister Christian Pineau, under cruel pressure from Paris bankers and industrialists, had adopted a policy of getting the Suez Canal back by any means including, and perhaps inevitably, force. Early in September, therefore, Mollet and Pineau informed Simon Peres, chief of the Israeli Ministry of Defense, that France would supply Israel with aircraft and other armaments. Peres travelled secretly to Paris to receive the welcome news.

Dutifully, Monnet and Pineau informed Britain's Prime Minister

Anthony Eden and Foreign Secretary Selwyn Lloyd of their decision to become an ally of Israel. At the same time, steps were taken not only to keep the United States in the dark but to give Washington a false impression of the situation.

An Israeli attaché at the Washington Embassy was given the role of official pessimist. First through a member of the Belgian Embassy and later by direct contact with a State Department staffer, the Israeli diplomat revealed that Sharett had had "no luck at all" in trying to persuade France to provide arms to Israel. His manner was darkly gloomy. He feared an imminent invasion by Egypt and wondered aloud if Washington could be persuaded to come to the rescue of his fledgling nation.

At the State Department, serenity continued to reign. No one believed Egypt would attack Israel, and now there was assurance that France would not be a partner to any girding of the Israeli loins. Presumably, Secretary Dulles was stiffened in his belief that reports of an Israeli-French-British invasion of Egypt was mere cocktail talk. Top-level officials of the State Department continued to push the American advocacy of an eighteen-power proposal for settlement of the Suez dispute, which had evolved from an August 16-23 London conference of maritime powers.

Nasser rejected these proposals early in September. Washington pressed its allies to continue negotiations with the Egyptian dictator and was assured by both Eden and Mollet that they would do so. Dulles apparently placed considerable faith in the efforts of Dag Hammarskjöld, Secretary General of the United Nations, to wheedle a reasonable counterproposal from Nasser. Britain and France had no such illusions. While neutral diplomats in Washington were carefully leaking the comforting intelligence, provided by both the British and French, that our allies were encouraged by Hammarskjöld's mission, Eden and his Cabinet decided to throw in with the French-Israeli partnership and "insulate" the Canal from Nasser's control.

By this time, it was mid-October and Nasser had resumed his *fedayeen* raids into Israel. More seriously, he was trying to organize an Arab joint military command. The British-French point of view later was explained in Eden's memoirs: "Unless Israel was prepared just to sit it out and wait until it suited her enemies to strangle and finally destroy her, it was clear that before long she would have to take some counteraction, at least to put an end to the *fedayeen* raids." And during the postmortem period, Pineau would tell the National Assembly that because Israel's position was "precarious," France and Britain had made "joint plans of a military nature to deal with the Canal situation."

That was not the way French and British diplomats were talking to Washington through their neutral mouthpieces. At just about this time, State Department people were being told that there was considerable dissatisfaction among politicians in both Britain and France, because Eden and Mollet were refusing even to consider any plans of a "military nature" to deal with the Canal situation.

Certainly, President Eisenhower was fooled by these unctuous assurances. During a campaign television news conference on October 12, he made "the best announcement that I could possibly make." Egypt, Britain and France, Eisenhower reported, "have met through their Foreign Ministers [at the United Nations] and agreed to a set of principles on which to negotiate, and it looks like here is a very great crisis that is behind us . . . I talked to the Secretary of State just before I came over here tonight, and I will tell you that in both his heart and mine at least there is a very great prayer of thanksgiving."

In line with his policy of never troubling Eisenhower with knotty details, Dulles had clearly played down to the President the very real difficulties involved. And Eisenhower had no reason to doubt his optimism when, four days later, the British and French issued a communiqué in which they agreed to adhere to the so-called Six Principles for governing international cooperation in managing the Canal. The communiqué did note that Egypt seemed to be questioning these principles, but said the two nations would be willing to consider any Egyptian proposals.

But on that same October 16, the conspirators set the date for the invasion of Egypt. It was to be no later than two weeks from October 16. France would supply planes to Israel and provide air and naval cover and, probably, land forces. The British would take over military leadership of the enterprise and assume responsibility for the movement of attacking forces from Marseilles and Malta.

Having thus committed themselves to war, the plotters then went about the task of making certain the United States was taken completely off the scent. French and Israeli diplomats in Washington contacted their pals in two neutral embassies and with heavy casualness revealed intelligence of a spectacular nature: There was to be no invasion, ever.

They explained it was not clear whether the invasion had been cancelled or whether earlier rumors of an invasion had been false. In any
event, no such adventure was planned. The State Department got
this sensational news the same day—October 18.

Meanwhile, the French and Israelis covered their other tracks.
France's shipments of aircraft and arms to Israel had far exceeded the
limitation imposed by Eisenhower and Dulles in their sincere efforts to
avoid adding fuel to the Middle Eastern fires. French diplomats since
have said that Washington was aware of this, which gives credence to
the theory that Dulles, acting alone, was not completely opposed to
Israeli military action against Egypt if Tel Aviv could come up with a
credible *casus belli.* But Eisenhower certainly was still in the dark, and
Dulles also may have been. At any rate, France took no chances. The
sales contracts for the arms were expertly doctored to conform with the
limits agreed upon with Washington.

Although Mollet and Pineau were using staff members of the French
Embassy in Washington to spread false rumors, they had so far declined to let the Foreign Office operating personnel in on their prepa-
rations for the invasion lest someone be tempted to spring an honest
leak. When a direct radio connection was installed between the Paris
Ministry of Defense and Tel Aviv, total secrecy was insured by the
dispatch from Israel of an Israeli intelligence officer to act as interpreter
for the messages from Tel Aviv. Mollet and Pineau met secretly with
Israeli Prime Minister Ben-Gurion, driving themselves in their private
cars to the hush-hush sessions so no one would be tempted to make too
many deductions.

Then, on October 18 or 19, Paris heard again that the CIA had
picked up intelligence on the invasion plans. And once again Paris
acted to befuddle Washington by planting a series of conflicting stories
among neutral embassies in Washington. From various diplomats, the
State Department learned: 1) that the invasion was scheduled for the
day after the election; 2) that France had backed out of the invasion
plot; 3) that France and Britain were making solid progress in secret
negotiations with Nasser.

Finally, Dulles was getting a little jumpy. Normally, there was a
steady, daily flow of communications from both London and Paris into
the State Department. The three countries traded information around-
the-clock on military, intelligence and economic matters. But suddenly
there was a blackout. The regular reports from London and Paris were

missing from his desk. At long last, Dulles took official recognition that something might be afoot.

He charged over to the White House and, catching Eisenhower between campaign trips, told him of his suspicions. Eisenhower was both surprised and furious. He told Dulles to call in Israeli Ambassador Abba Eban and make it clear to him that the United States wouldn't stand for any warlike monkeyshines. "And don't soften my words, Foster," he told his Secretary of State.

Dulles transmitted Eisenhower's message to Eban virtually verbatim. It was that the President hoped Eban would not allow any misinterpretation of sentiment in America to sway him, particularly possible Jewish sympathy for what seemed to be an intention to build up mobilization in Israel. Eban should know that the Administration would do its very best to prevent any outbreak of hostilities, and that if he thought American action would be affected by the election he should disabuse his mind of it.

Eban accepted the lecture in silence and departed—to return to his office and report to Tel Aviv that Washington was suspicious, but nothing more. Yet Secretary Dulles' brother, Allen W. Dulles—at that time director of CIA—would tell the author several years later that "we had the Suez operation perfectly taped . . . we reported that there would be a three-nation attack on Suez." If this was so, it is strange to recall that on October 21 John Foster Dulles appeared on the CBS television program, "Face the Nation," and reported that the Suez situation was under control.

The brother of the man who later claimed to have had the Suez invasion "taped" told his viewers that the Allies "have developed a common policy, and I think it's amazing, the degree to which we have had a common policy . . . While we have sometimes started out with somewhat different points of view, we have ended up together, and the fact that there are certain *minor superficial* differences [italics the author's] as to details about just how you handle tolls or how much is going to get paid to Egypt and how much isn't, doesn't detract from the fact that basically we do have a common policy."

Ambassador Eban may have reinforced the curious, wishful euphoria which seemed to suffuse Washington in a speech at the United Nations on October 25 in which he inveighed against the UN for its inability or unwillingness, or both, to compel Nasser to implement its unanimous resolution of September 1, 1951, that the Canal must be kept open to Israeli ships. "If we are not attacked, we shall not strike," Eban told the Security Council. "If we are attacked, we fully reserve the inherent right of self-defense." However that statement was analyzed, it seemed to say plainly that there would be no invasion of Egypt.

An hour before Eban's speech, a French diplomat assured a member of the State Department that the Suez problem would be solved peacefully.

But as Eban was speaking, Prime Minister Ben-Gurion signed the order for the mobilization of Israeli's armed forces.

United States military intelligence in Israel dutifully reported the mobilization to the State Department. Frantically, American diplomats sought out their opposite numbers at the French and British Embassies—and were told their allies knew nothing about it. At the Israeli Embassy, an official told William M. Rountree, head of State's Near East Division, that the mobilization was only partial—it was total—and that it had been ordered as a defensive measure.

In Paris, London and Tel Aviv, the decision was made some time during that busy October 25 to attack Nasser's Egypt via the Sinai Peninsula on October 29. The British had argued for November 2 or 3 for reasons of military exigencies; the French and Israelis wanted to attack on October 27. D-Day thus was a compromise. In Washington, the State Department assigned one of its officials to maintain contact, on a twenty-four-hour-a-day basis, with Reuben Shiloah, political counselor at the Israeli Embassy. In diplomatic circles, the title political counselor is an euphemism for intelligence operative.

For the next two days, Eisenhower and Dulles busied themselves with dispatching appeals to Israel and our two Western Allies to reject the use of force—Eisenhower from Walter Reed Hospital, where he was undergoing a medical checkup, and Dulles from the State Department and later from Dallas, where he addressed the Council on World Affairs. Israel, meanwhile, completed its mobilization.

Dulles returned from Dallas just before cocktail time on October 28, to be told by Deputy Secretary of State Herbert Hoover Jr. that on the President's instructions the State Department was arranging for the evacuation of Americans from Israel and nearby Arab states. Dulles called in Ambassador Eban and asked him what was going on. Eban replied that so far as he knew the mobilization was a defensive action against Jordan. The newly-appointed British Ambassador, Sir Harry Caccia, had not yet arrived in Washington, and French

Ambassador Hervé Alphand was out of the city, so Dulles then summoned the British and French chargés d'affaires, J. E. Coulson and Charles Lucet (later to succeed to the ambassadorial post). Coulson and Lucet listened in silence to a Dulles lecture on international morality and his warning that the United States would appeal to the United Nations to stop any fighting that broke out. But the Frenchman and the Englishman offered Dulles no information. They told the Secretary that of course they would pass on to their foreign offices what he had told them.

Several weeks later, Dulles would remark to an aide: "Even then, even on that terrible afternoon, I could not believe that those men were laughing at me."

The Israeli armed forces attacked Egypt at about 9 A.M. Washington time on Monday, October 29. Even at that moment, the conspirators attempted to conceal their real plans in an Israeli communiqué which said the attack was aimed at a cluster of *fedayeen* bases. At two o'clock that afternoon, Ambassador Eban was conferring with Rountree and Fraser Wilkins, an Arab-Israeli specialist. Eban was telling them once again that the Israeli mobilization was defensive, when Rountree was handed a dispatch from the Associated Press ticker telling of the invasion of the Sinai Peninsula.

Eban expressed profound shock. He insisted he had known nothing about it and knew nothing about it now. His story, which Rountree naturally found suspect, was that his government apparently had purposefully kept him in the dark to avoid a leaking of its plans. To John Foster Dulles, the British and French chargés d'affaires told essentially the same story. Dulles said later he had scrutinized their faces and was sure they were hiding behind a "cover." Later in the day, Eisenhower gave Britisher Coulson a most undiplomatic tongue-lashing couched in vigorous barracks language.

Meanwhile the fighting went on, with the Israeli forces obviously far superior in both fighting skill and weapons to Nasser's hordes. It was the opinion of Admiral Arthur W. Radford, chairman of the Joint Chiefs of Staff, given at an emergency meeting that night at the White House, that "The Israeli boys can beat all the Arab armies combined with one arm tied behind their back." This, of course, would not be necessary, since the British and French served notice the next morning that they would join in the invasion, and did so twenty-four hours later.

It was the chore of French Ambassador Alphand, shortly after the

British-French ultimatum was announced, to explain his government's position. He was ushered into Dulles' office in mid-afternoon on October 30. The elegant Alphand was not at his accustomed ease, but he made a good argument. France, he said, could not accept Nasser's nationalization of the Canal because it was a prelude to an attack by Egypt on Israel and any fighting between the two countries would obstruct operation of the Canal.

But Dulles was in no mood for explanations. The invasion conspiracy, he said, had placed him in "an impossible position," because Washington had no idea that such action was planned "although during the last three weeks I suspected that something was brewing. This is the darkest day in the history of the Western alliance. It might even be the end of the alliance itself."

Alphand murmured courteously that surely this was overstating the case.

"It is no exaggeration," Dulles thundered. "The action and intervention of France and Britain is just the same as the behavior of the Soviet Union in Budapest."

This was something Alphand couldn't take. As France's representative, he was perhaps suffering from a guilty conscience, but he could not permit an action his nation considered honorable and necessary to be compared with the gangsterism practiced by Moscow in Hungary.

"Your accusation is not true," he shouted. "I am bound to protest."

Dulles calmed down immediately and begged Alphand's pardon. He explained that he was "speaking under the stress of a great emotion that such a terrible thing could have happened . . . I am laboring under the anxiety of how I can remedy the damage to the confidence between our governments."

Alphand saw Eisenhower a little more than a week later, after a cease-fire had been imposed, and the President was less emotional although constrained to take a moral tone. "Well, you've got the right to do as you want," he told Alphand. "I think you are wrong. History will tell." And then, "Mr. Ambassador, life is a grand staircase which rises to Heaven. I shall arrive at the top of that staircase, and I wish to present myself before the Creator with a pure conscience."

There is a suspicion that by that time Eisenhower's pique was directed not so much at his wayward allies as at his good friend and faithful adviser, John Foster Dulles. The Secretary of State kept protesting that "We had no advance information of *any* kind" on the Israeli attack and "the British-French participation also came as a complete surprise to us." And, to be sure, both Eisenhower and Dulles got their first information on the invasion from wire service tickers. Yet there has never been a denial by anyone of Spy-Boss Allen Dulles' assertion that the CIA "reported there would be no attack by Israel on Jordan but that there would be a three-nation attack on Suez. And on the day before the invasion, CIA reported it was *imminent.*"

Since there presumably were no secrets between Brother John Foster and Brother Allen, the conclusion seems incredible either that Allen's reports were considered worthless by John Foster or that somehow they slipped his mind. Obviously, when John Foster said the State Department had "no advance information" he could not have referred to being informed through diplomatic channels—which in the Suez case were employed not to conceal information but to doctor it.

9

Ormsby-Gore Lends a Hand

THOSE WHO KNEW him best found it characteristic of John Fitz-gerald Kennedy that he should remember the counsel of an old friend from London days, when congratulations were being offered him for his spectacular success in the Cuban missile crisis in the fall of 1962. After the Bay of Pigs fiasco the preceding year, Kennedy had insisted there was "blame enough to go around, but I'm the President and most of it belongs on my shoulders." Now, on a balmy November evening at the White House, he reminded those who would do him honor that "a lot of other people were involved in that one." He ticked off the names—his brother, Bobby, United Nations Ambassador Adlai Stevenson, Defense Secretary Robert McNamara, former Secretary of State Dean Acheson. Then he grinned, and nodded toward the Englishman. "And let's not forget the foreigner," he said.

Kennedy was referring to Sir David Ormsby-Gore, Her Britannic Majesty's Ambassador to the United States, whom he had known since the days when he was merely Ambassador Joe Kennedy's son. He had reason not to forget Ormsby-Gore's contributions. In the tense October days when the world teetered on the brink of nuclear war, Ormsby-Gore had performed with brilliant competence the duties of the *compleat* diplomat by rendering advice and assistance to a head of state which were at once in the interest of his own country, the country to which he was accredited, and the world.

Indeed, there will be future historians who will argue that among all those who had Kennedy's ear during the missile confrontation,

David Ormsby-Gore stood preeminent because of two suggestions he made at the height of the crisis. One was a major contribution to the credibility of the American position. The other gave Khrushchev the time he needed to make, with some grace, the hard decision to climb down from his own position.

Specifically, it was Ormsby-Gore who successfully urged Kennedy to release the aerial photographs taken of the Soviet missile sites in Cuba to counteract skepticism abroad—including speculation in Great Britain that the missiles might be a figment of the Central Intelligence Agency's imagination. And it was Ormsby-Gore who advised the young President to switch his signals and order the Navy to delay intercepting the Soviet ships, with their missile cargoes, until they reached Cuban waters. This second decision might well have been the difference between peace and war, because each additional hour made it easier for Khrushchev to back down.

Kennedy, of course—and the United States—were lucky to have a British ambassador in town who was the President's longtime and intimate friend. He and Ormsby-Gore had met in London in 1938, and young Kennedy's sister, Kathleen, had married the Marquis of Hartington, a cousin of Ormsby-Gore. Later, she was godmother of Ormsby-Gore's oldest child. Both the young American and the young Briton had climbed the political ladder in their countries. In 1959, when Kennedy was all but officially running for President, Ormsby-Gore was Minister of State for Foreign Affairs and an expert on disarmament. Kennedy's speeches during the 1960 campaign on the Eisenhower Administration's neglect of disarmament planning were partially a result of long talks between the candidate and his English friend.

But Kennedy also could lay claim to prescience. As Arthur Schlesinger Jr. relates in his book, *A Thousand Days,* the President-elect called Ormsby-Gore at the United Nations in New York after the election and told him that "he must come to Washington as ambassador." Ormsby-Gore, who was related to Britain's Prime Minister Harold Macmillan by marriage, got the job in October, 1961.

Indisputably, Kennedy's admiration for Ormsby-Gore was enormous. Although their relationship was enlivened by practical jokes, gamesmanship on the golf course and a constant exchange of dry wit, Kennedy had a profound appreciation of the Briton's swift and brilliant mind. McGeorge Bundy, Kennedy's ex officio Secretary of State, was said to have been mildly miffed when another Presidential aide quoted Kennedy as remarking that Bundy was the smartest man he knew—next to Ormsby-Gore.

Because of this high respect for the Briton's intellect, Kennedy frequently stood still for some unpleasant opinions from Sir David. After the Bay of Pigs, he told Kennedy that the invasion attempt had been "stupid" and that British intelligence estimates showed that the Cuban people were solidly behind Castro and highly unlikely to support any insurrection. "In Europe," Ormsby-Gore told Kennedy, "the politicians now see you as a blundering imperialist." And on one of his trips to Washington, as a member of Parliament, Ormsby-Gore read his friend a lecture criticizing the United States' policy of backing the right-wing General Phoumi Nosavan in Laos. "You've got to stop holding up corrupt dictators," he said.

This was the man who in October, 1962, presided over the stately British Embassy on Massachusetts Avenue. Almost upon their arrival, the Ormsby-Gores replaced French Ambassador Hervé Alphand and his determinedly chic wife, Nicole, as most favored guests at the White House. Alphand was a man of great wit and charm and a surpassingly talented mimic of public men, and both he and his wife were close to the Francophile First Lady, but Kennedy demanded more red meat with his conversational fodder. He seemed unaware that his preference for the Ormsby-Gores caused hard feelings at the French Embassy and even some growls from Le Grand Charles in Paris, who once demanded of Alphand an explanation of Kennedy's intimacy "with this young Englishman." Alphand, it is said, cabled back that Ormsby-Gore and John Kennedy had "gone to school together."

At any rate, it appears that Kennedy couldn't quite take the elegant Alphand seriously. He was amused, but hardly impressed, at the French Ambassador's habit of using the French-speaking and ultra fashionable Jacqueline Kennedy as a messenger for some of his most urgent official representations. And he was contemptuous of Alphand's suggestion in 1963 that if De Gaulle agreed to visit America in March of the following year, Kennedy should entertain him at Palm Beach.

"I'll be damned if I'll show De Gaulle the worst side of American life," Kennedy told Alphand. "Cape Cod is where I'm really from, and it can't be any more gloomy in March than Colombey-les-deux-Eglises," De Gaulle's home base.

With Ormsby-Gore, on the other hand, Kennedy could both relax and lay his serious conversations on the line. He once told his aide, Ted Sorensen, "I trust David as I would my own Cabinet." The President and the young Englishman enjoyed their private jokes, and were forever devising excuses to quote Prime Minister Macmillan's observation that President Eisenhower "wouldn't let Nixon on the property," and Anthony Eden's crack that John Foster Dulles was "a card-carrying Christian." While he was still in the Senate, Kennedy told Ormsby-Gore he was not sure he was cut out to be a politician because he saw the other side too well. Both had a pragmatic belief in the advantages to be gained by doing diplomatic business with the Soviet Union, and Kennedy was much influenced by Ormsby-Gore's argument that it should be easier to do business with the new generation of Soviet politicians. When they played golf, Kennedy would bewilder Sir David with a complicated system of bets which he outlined on the first hole; the bets would then be doubled on the tenth tee.

David Ormsby-Gore had been British Ambassador to the United States for only nine months when, in late July, 1962, Soviet shipments of medium-range nuclear missiles began to arrive in Cuba. This was Nikita Khrushchev's supreme ploy in the Kennedy era of the Cold War; he wanted to apply a test to American intentions. If it succeeded, he could go on to reopen the Berlin question before a world audience which no longer trusted America's willingness or capacity to protect it from Communist imperialism. With nuclear missiles successfully installed only ninety miles from Florida, the United States would fall into disgrace among those weaker nations which depended on Washington's resolution for their safety.

The CIA in mid-August submitted a report to the President which told of considerable activity in Cuba—new military construction, more Soviet ships unloading equipment and materiel, an increase to about 5000 of the number of Soviet "specialists" in Castro's unhappy little principality.

At this point, it was generally agreed that Moscow was merely adding muscle to Cuba's defenses, probably by installing a network of surface-to-air (SAM) sites. After the Bay of Pigs, of course, the world would not be likely to deplore Castro's attempt to insure his regime against external attack, and the Soviet Union had a clear advantage in shoring up its bridgehead in the Western Hemisphere. Only CIA Director John McCone suggested that someone might consider the possibility that Khrushchev was planning to install offensive missiles.

From Kennedy down, everyone else argued that Moscow wouldn't dare take an action which would bring an immediate—probably military— American response. McCone bowed to the majority and whipped off for a three week's honeymoon in Europe. (In Washington, before Lyndon Johnson, the government understood that a certain priority should be given to such things.)

Accordingly, Kennedy was merely touching all the bases when on September 4 he dispatched a warning to Krushchev that the United States would not tolerate the installation of offensive weapons in Cuba. At almost the same moment, Khrushchev was assuring the President, through Soviet Ambassador Anatoly Dobrynin, that he would stir up no fuss before the November Congressional elections, and shortly thereafter replied to Kennedy's warning with a blustering statement that the Soviet Union had no need to shift its weapons anywhere outside its own territory, and described the installations in Cuba as "exclusively for defensive purposes."

At this point, Ormsby-Gore observed to Kennedy at a White House luncheon that "the Soviets seem to be making a great thing of secrecy, if all they are doing is setting up some SAM sites." The Ambassador added that he would be suspicious that Moscow was protesting too much, if it were not for the fact that "the Russian makes it a state secret every time he goes to the loo [toilet]."

Kennedy did what had to be done. He stepped up U-2 flights over Cuba. These showed a continuing and expanded military buildup but no signs that it was anything but defensive in character. But reports from refugee circles—which had not always been reliable—continued to tell of nuclear installations on the island. From the same sources, Senator Kenneth Keating, the New York Republican, built several speeches on these reports and demanded that the government "do something." Under pressure, the CIA got permission from the White House on October 10 to send a U-2 over western Cuba. Bad weather delayed the flight until the fourteenth when a reconnaissance plane flying in cloudless skies recorded photographic evidence which showed a launching pad, buildings for ballistic missiles and a missile on the ground in San Cristobal.

(Later, it would be learned that the Soviets had under construction twenty-four launching pads for medium-range and sixteen for intermediate-range missiles. Forty-two medium-range missiles were landed in Cuba, and another six were on the way when Kennedy confronted Khrushchev with evidence of his perfidy.)

From then, almost continuously until the President went on national TV to tell the nation, the Soviet Union and the world of the American response, Kennedy and his closest advisers debated what that response should be. At the outset, they estimated they had about ten days before the missiles would be in firing positions. There was, therefore, no time to submit the problem to the United Nations, where the Soviet Union and its ideological pals could delay matters until the missiles were in place. The responsibility was solely the President's, or, as Kennedy put it, "This is the week when I had better earn my salary."

Military men, supported by Dean Acheson, argued for a massive, surprise air strike. It was that, they declared, or "acquiescence"—as Acheson said. Kennedy ruled out acquiescence but sought alternatives to the air strike. Attorney General Bobby Kennedy was appalled at the thought that the United States would even consider "another Pearl Harbor."

Meanwhile, Major General Sir Kenneth William Dobson Strong, director of the Joint Intelligence Bureau in the British Defense Ministry, who was attending an intelligence conference at the Pentagon, began to smell something. Although the secrecy was total, General Strong was intrigued by the sudden disappearance, in mid-session, of a number of the American participants in the conference. He noticed beds being carried into the offices of certain top officials. The man who had been Dwight Eisenhower's intelligence chief during World War II telephoned Ormsby-Gore with a carefully-worded recital of his suspicions, and the next day the Ambassador received Strong and Sir Hugh Stephenson, Deputy Under Secretary of State at the Foreign Office.

"Something funny is going on," Strong told Ormsby-Gore. "The Americans are up to something they don't want to tell us about."

They decided it had to be an international crisis of major seriousness. "I suspect Cuba is acting up," remarked Ormsby-Gore. "Let's see what we can find out and meet again tomorrow."

Next day, the Ambassador decided the time had come to go out on a limb. With the concurrence of Strong and Stephenson, he concluded that Kennedy's repeated warnings against any Russian move to install offensive weapons in Cuba meant that missiles probably had been discovered there. Ormsby-Gore had not seen Kennedy and did not now attempt to do so. He wrapped up his conclusion in Foreign Office vernacular and sent it off by cable to London. Thus the British government became the first of our allies to know of the crisis. Kennedy had neither informed nor consulted anyone outside American official circles in Washington.

By now, Kennedy had made his decision—the United States would impose a blockade on Soviet ships seeking to land at Cuban ports. The idea had originated with Secretary McNamara, who plumped for it as a device that not only would bar the further entry of missiles into Cuba, but would also probably force the Soviets to remove the missiles already there. It was the middle course, which gave Khrushchev time to reconsider his actions. It was a serious step, but not necessarily a step that would lead to war, since it permitted subsequent moves toward peace while Khrushchev was pondering the seriousness of the situation.

This was on Saturday, October 20. That night, Kennedy phoned Ormsby-Gore and invited him to Sunday lunch. At the lunch table, the President told the Ambassador what was happening in Cuba and, without disclosing what actions had been decided upon, outlined the various alternatives—an air strike, a blockade or submission to the United Nations.

"What do you think we should do, David?" Kennedy asked.

Ormsby-Gore spoke out at once against the air strike. World opinion, he said, would hardly condone an attack without warning, and the United States would lose its standing as a responsible, rational power committed to decency in its international relations. He agreed that the United Nations couldn't work fast enough to do any good. The blockade, he said, seemed the sensible alternative, because it preserved flexibility, gave the United States control over the future, and avoided war.

Kennedy grinned. "You'll be happy to know that's what we are going to do."

The President addressed the world on television at seven o'clock Monday evening, October 22. His voice was calm and emotionless, although his face was grave, as he declared that the purpose of the missile bases "can be none other than to provide a nuclear strike capability against the Western Hemisphere," and called the Soviet action "a deliberately provocative and unjustified change in the status quo . . ." Beyond his words could be heard the unmistakable rattle of the saber when he described the blockade as the "initial step," and then warned that any missile launched from Cuba would be regarded as an attack by the Soviet Union on the United States.

World reaction was generally favorable, although the British greeted the speech with unexpected cynicism. There was talk that the CIA had dreamed up the missiles as a pretext to justify an American invasion. The *Economist* counseled against forcing a showdown with the Soviets over the shipment of "Russian arms" to Cuba. The *Manchester Guardian* declared that "In the end, the United States may find that it has done its cause, its friends, and its own true interests little good." England's Bertrand Russell dispatched an insulting cable to Kennedy and an obsequious one to Khrushchev.

It was against this background that the President dined at the White House on Tuesday, October 23, with Ormsby-Gore and some other English friends. As soon as they could, the President and the Ambassador broke away from the other guests for a talk about the crisis.

Sir David was disturbed by the pockets of unfavorable reaction in his own country and in France, Italy and West Germany. He pointed out that even Kennedy's old friend from the London School of Economics, Hugh Gaitskell, leader of the Opposition, had referred sarcastically to the "so-called missiles in Cuba." It was imperative, said Ormsby-Gore, to provide evidence that would persuade even the ordinary layman that the missiles were indeed being installed.

"Why don't you release the photographs taken by your U-2 plane?" Sir David suggested.

It seems incredible, but at that point no one else seems to have thought of such an obvious move to bolster American credibility. Kennedy sent for the file of the photographs and together the grandson of a lace-curtain Boston-Irish politician and the English aristocrat re-examined them, picking out those which would have the greatest impact on Main Streets all over the world. The pictures were published the next day, and later they would be thrown in the face of Moscow's ambassador to the United Nations, V. A. Zorin, during Adlai Stevenson's memorable indictment of the Soviet Union before the "the courtroom of world opinion."

On that same evening, Bobby Kennedy was spending a fruitless hour with another diplomat, Soviet Ambassador Dobrynin. Bobby had gone to the Soviet Embassy in an attempt to find out whether Moscow had ordered the Soviet ships to turn back if challenged by American naval forces following imposition of the blockade.

But Dobrynin appeared to be a shaken man, who was not even sure what day it was. He told Bobby he was unaware of any instructions. "I am out of the picture," he added.

When Bobby reminded Dobrynin of his own past assurances that there were no offensive missiles in Cuba, Dobrynin replied that he had meant that the missiles were "not capable of reaching the United States."

"I trust you realize that on the strength of your false and hypocritical assurances, the President told the American people earlier that there was no danger from Cuba," Bobby told Dobrynin.

"I am guiltless," Dobrynin replied. "So far as I know there are no Soviet missiles in Cuba with sufficient range to reach the United States."

"We're in for a difficult time," Bobby reminded him, "thanks to Soviet deception."

"I don't understand," said Dobrynin. "If the President knew about the missiles, why didn't he mention it to Mr. Gromyko [the Soviet Foreign Minister] when Mr. Gromyko was at the White House the other day."

"What was the use?" asked Bobby. "Gromyko certainly knew the truth and the President was so shocked by his lying that any attempt at intelligent conversation was impossible."

The Attorney General reported his conversation with Dobrynin to his brother at the White House while Ormsby-Gore was still there. The Briton suggested that the Russians had been stunned, all the way down the line, by the firmness of the American response.

"Everyone, especially Khrushchev, is now faced with the job of making some hard decisions," he said.

"I hope they realize how important it is that they make the right ones," the President said.

"I'm sure they do," Ormsby-Gore said. "But couldn't you give them a little help? That is, give them a little more time?"

"Show me how, and I'll do it," said Kennedy.

Sir David then recalled that the Pentagon had insisted on the importance of stopping Soviet ships as far out of reach of Cuban jet planes as possible in order to avoid a clash. He argued that this policy might not give Khrushchev enough time to ponder the gravity of his action.

"Why not give him as much time as possible to squirm out of the situation?" he suggested. "Why not make the interceptions as close as possible to Cuba?"

It was then that John Fitzgerald Kennedy made what could have been the most important decision of that critical autumnal interlude. He telephoned Secretary McNamara, told him to brush off anticipated protests from the Navy, and pass the order to delay interceptions until the last possible moment.

Arthur Schlesinger would write later that "This decision was of vital importance in postponing the moment of irreversible action." He based his statement on plenty of evidence. For many long hours after the imposition of the blockade, Soviet officials from Khrushchev down assumed a posture that was a mixture of truculence and injured feelings. Khrushchev threatened nuclear war and warned the "young American President" not to stand too long on the brink. Work continued on the missile sites, Soviet ships continued their Cuban course, and an American force of one hundred thousand men in Florida prepared for invasion.

Secretary General U Thant of the United Nations did nothing to relieve the tension when he proposed that the Soviet Union suspend its arms shipments and the United States in turn call off the blockade to pave the way for negotiations. Predictably, Khrushchev eagerly accepted this proposal, but the President would have none of it. He pointed out that it suggested the American response was as evil as the Soviet aggression, and that a pause would permit work to go forward on the missile sites. Kennedy could safely reject the U Thant formula; the time awarded Khrushchev to think things over was working in the interest of peace.

When his truculent statements failed to swerve Kennedy from his announced path, Khrushchev realized that his gamble had failed. He had suggested to the poet Robert Frost, during the latter's visit to Moscow, that democracies were too liberal to fight, and had now discovered that he was wrong. He was, as the veteran American trouble-shooter, Averell Harriman, suggested, looking for an out, and the United States had to give him one.

What John Kennedy later described as "the great Ormsby-Gore delay" was already buying at least some indecision in the Kremlin. A little less than two days after the blockade was set up, half the Soviet ships had put about and were heading home. Others appeared to be dawdling about, waiting for orders. When a Russian tanker entered the quarantine zone, Kennedy gave Khrushchev a little more time. He ordered that the tanker, which obviously was not carrying nuclear weapons, be permitted to proceed once it had identified itself to the blockade forces.

"It looks as if David is going to be proved very right," said Kennedy.

That was, indeed, the beginning of the end. But before that end another diplomat, this time a Russian, would play a starring role along with an American television newscaster. The diplomat was Aleksander Fomin, a counselor at the Soviet Embassy; the newsman was John Scali, State Department correspondent for the American Broadcasting Company.

Scali had had previous social contacts with Fomin, and he was not surprised when the Russian asked him to meet him at the Occidental Restaurant. There Fomin put to Scali the proposition which would be the basis of a peaceful settlement of the crisis. He asked Scali to inform the State Department that the Soviet Union would promise to remove its missiles from Cuba under United Nations inspection and promise never again to introduce such weapons onto the island, in return for the President's public promise not to invade Cuba. Scali was naturally skeptical, but he carried the proposal to the State Department, and was told by Secretary Rusk to inform Fomin that the United States saw "real possibilities for a negotiaton." Scali forthwith passed the word to Fomin, this time in the coffee shop of the Statler Hilton Hotel, and two hours later on the evening of Friday, October 26, the White House began to receive by cable a long letter from Khrushchev verifying the Fomin proposition.

That, of course, was the ball game. There was a scare on Saturday morning, October 27, when Kennedy received another letter from Khrushchev demanding that the United States remove its missiles from Turkey in return for the Soviet withdrawal from Cuba, but Kennedy decided to act as if he'd never received the second letter. He dispatched a reply to the first letter, in effect accepting the proposition made therein. At that time, no one knew which Khrushchev letter contained the true terms, but the chance had to be taken that Khrushchev had been prompted by the apparent eagerness of the State Department to do business, to try to sweeten his end of the agreement.

The gamble paid off. On Sunday, October 28, Kennedy received Khrushchev's acceptance of the peace terms—terms which, through the adoption of "the great Ormsby-Gore delay," could now bear the stamp "Made in Moscow." Khrushchev had had time to find a graceful out, and a young Englishman could take one of the triumphant bows.

Mao, Chiang and Sugar

10

The Red China Lobby

PLAIN CITIZENS across the United States were outraged in late 1963 when it was disclosed that a propaganda motion picture on the Viet Cong which had been shown on a number of college campuses had been smuggled into the country in a diplomatic pouch by the Cuban mission to the United Nations. The film was produced by the Communist-oriented Australian journalist, Wilfred Burchett, and it predictably presented the Viet Cong as a flower-loving, mother-worshipping conglomeration of brave heroes.

But no one in that part of official Washington concerned with foreign affairs was surprised by Burchett's ruse. The Australian had merely, and logically, employed the good services of Communist China's unofficial diplomatic representative to the United States—the Cuban delegation to the UN. And Washington was not about to raise any serious fuss with Carlos Lechuga, Cuba's Ambassador to the world peace organization.

For one of the facts of international life, unknown to most Americans, is that the United States and Peking *do* maintain diplomatic relations. State Department staffers have regular informal contacts with the Cuban UN delegation, from which they siphon off the official, if frequently unpublicized, Communist Chinese line on a variety of issues. Similarly, the American viewpoint is passed on to Red China through an assortment of neutral embassies in Peking. Only infrequently does either side get anything very important from these sub rosa exchanges, but the contacts are maintained simply because they

are the only contacts possible under the circumstances, and a diplomat
never can tell when an unspoken word, a nuance or an emphasis will
tell him something he isn't supposed to know.

Thus, by piecing together morsels of gossip from a variety of diplomatic sources, the United States had advance knowledge of the timing
of three of the first nuclear explosions set off by Red China. During
the Cuban missile crisis of 1962, the State Department received assurances from one of these sources that Peking positively would not become "militarily involved."

In January, 1967, there were denials by both the State Department
and the French Foreign Office that Communist China transmitted
through French diplomats its terms for staying out of the Vietnam
war—and that the United States observed them. But such denials are
standard operating procedure in the diplomatic set and not necessarily
credible. Even as the denials were still hot on Page One, State Department people were admitting privately that the deal revealed by
Rene Dabernat, foreign editor of *Paris-Match,* in an interview with
U.S. News and World Report, was the sort of arrangement that could
logically have resulted from informal, unofficial diplomatic relations
between Peking and Washington.

At any rate, the Dabernat interview agreed with the State Department view that Peking had a selfish interest in the concept of a limited
war by the United States. According to Dabernat, Red China informed Washington, through Paris, that it would stay out of the war if
the U.S. would not: (a) invade China; (b) invade North Vietnam;
and (c) bomb North Vietnam's Red River dikes. At the same time,
Washington was getting reports from Chiang Kai-shek's intelligence
agents on the mainland that Mao Tze-tung was toying with the idea of
intervening in the war to give his subjects a "foreign enemy" upon
which to vent their wrath and thus unite his squabbling country.

Another go-between in the "diplomatic relations" between the
United States and Red China is the Polish Embassy. The State Department has done some significant business with the Poles in this
field, especially during the months immediately following the schism
between Moscow and Peking, when the Mao Tze-tung regime was
trying to split off the satellites from the Russian motherland. Although
Warsaw remained true to Moscow, it managed for a long time to
maintain cordial relations with Peking. At the same time, the Poles

were extremely active in trying to arrange negotiations between North Vietnam and the United States aimed at ending the Vietnam war. Most of the so-called "peace feelers" of 1966 and 1967 were of Polish origin.

Unfortunately, one of these feelers was doomed to go down in the history books as a cruel fiasco, wreaked by the unpredictability of North Vietnam's President Ho Chi Minh. It had its beginning in a conference at the State Department between Secretary of State Dean Rusk and Zdzislaw Szewczyk, charge d'affaires of the Polish Embassy. Szewczyk had sought an appointment to discuss the possibility of persuading Ho Chi Minh to agree to conditions for peace talks. Szewczyk said he had been authorized by his government to seek American approval of the attempt. Rusk told him to go ahead, that it couldn't do any harm. That same day Szewczyk cabled the Polish Embassy in Hanoi to arrange an audience with Ho. The result was like something out of an Oriental *Alice in Wonderland*.

Armed with Szewczyk's assurances that the Americans had expressed no objections, two Polish diplomats met with Ho Chi Minh early in January, 1967. They suggested various terms as a basis for initiating talks, but Ho rejected them all. Finally, in desperation, the Poles asked Ho if he could offer any alternative to his Four Points.

At first, Ho said he saw no reason to amend the Four Points, which included an end to the United States bombing of North Vietnam and withdrawal of U.S. troops from South Vietnam; enforcement of the 1954 Geneva agreement barring any military alliances by the Vietnamese with foreign countries; settlement of Saigon's internal affairs by the South Vietnamese on the terms of the communist puppet National Liberation Front, and reunification of Vietnam by the Vietnamese without foreign interference. Finally, after another hour of conversation, Ho said the prime objective of any talks should be the immediate establishment of a caretaker government which would guard the rights of the NLF. Then, he said, there could be elections to establish a permanent government not dominated by General Nguyen Cao Ky and his military clique.

The conferees discussed these suggestions for another hour and came up with this proposal: The Americans would halt their bombing of North Vietnam and a cease-fire would be declared on existing lines. A caretaker government would be set up composed equally of representatives of the Ky regime, the Buddhists and other religious groups, and the NLF. There would then be elections, supervised by an international commission.

Naturally, the Poles believed they had accomplished something big. That night, the new terms were dispatched by coded cable to Warsaw, and within a few days selected diplomats from a number of Soviet bloc and neutral countries were carefully leaking them to the rest of the world. It was the consensus among Washington diplomats that Ho finally had switched from his Four Points and was sincerely signalling a willingness to talk peace.

But on February 3, the same two Polish diplomats in Hanoi were summoned to Ho's presence on another matter. When that business was concluded, they mentioned that Ho's "overture" had been well received in the outside world. Ho seemed puzzled. There was nothing new about the "overture," he said, and added that he had not intended it as a substitute for his Four Points. He said he had merely been talking about some of the things which would have to be done once the United States agreed to his Four Points. Besides, Ho told the Poles, it was well known that the United States had no intention of withdrawing its troops from Vietnam after an armistice. He said he could not enter into any discussions not based on the immediate withdrawal of American forces.

No one pretended to know for a certainty why Ho had changed his mind. One explanation was that Communist China learned of the "overture" and persuaded Ho to back away from it. Much more likely, the NFL wouldn't buy it because it dropped the provision in the Four Points calling for settlement of Saigon's internal affairs on the NFL's terms. Szewczyk called on Secretary Rusk to report the Poles' failure. Rusk thanked him and told him to keep trying. Meanwhile, presumably, the Secretary of State turned back to the chore of sifting the voluminous reports from America's other unofficial "ambassadors" to the Communist Far East.

For the State Department also picks up tidbits of intelligence about Hanoi's and Peking's views and problems from Indian, Pakistani, Ceylonese and Burmese diplomats. A particularly good source has been Pakistan's Ambassador Ghulam Ahmed, obviously because of the recent romance between Pakistan and Red China. Until recent years, the Department had little success in its attempts to trade information about Red China with the Soviet Embassy and other Iron Curtain diplomats, but the feud between Moscow and Peking made the Russians and their satellites much more talkative.

But in a lobbying sense, Peking is represented much more successfully by those individuals and organizations plugging for better relations between the United States and Communist China. With some exceptions, there is nothing disreputable or "un-American" about these people or their views. For example, no rational observer would consider the American Friends Service Committee or the National Council of Churches of Christ subversive. Yet both have been in the forefront of those urging recognition of the Peking regime, the inauguration of trade relations, and the admission of Red China to the United Nations. For the most part, it is the view of what might be called the Peking Lobby that since Communist China is a fact of life, it must be lived with and, hopefully, done business with. In the Red Chinese view, of course, such people and organizations constitute a sort of propaganda free ride. For any foreign country, it is always much more effective to have American citizens plugging its cause than to depend on the efforts of an embassy whose official status makes it suspect.

There are also those, however, who are paid or unpaid agents of the Peking government. Every practicing Communist in America qualifies for this category, as well as some others who embrace the Communist ideology without carrying party cards.

Felix Greene is a British citizen with permanent residence status in the United States, a journalist, author and sometime producer of documentary films, who has been described in a report of the private, right-leaning American Security Council, introduced into the Congressional Record, as a "paid agent" of the Chinese Communist government. Others, including Senator Milward Simpson (Rep., Wyoming), have called Greene Peking's "unofficial ambassador to the United States."

Although Greene could neither speak nor write Chinese, he has visited Red China several times during the past decade and has become a most articulate advocate of the Peking regime. On the lecture circuit, he usually sums up his viewpoint in these words: "I know something, too, of the suffering and bloodshed that has accompanied the birth of this new China. But all this seemed trivial in the light of the accomplishments I could see around me wherever I went." Greene has never explained how he managed to dismiss as "trivial" a genocide movement which has caused the death of an estimated twenty million persons.

In his travels to China, Greene has produced both motion pictures and books, all, according to the American Security Council report, made possible by the cooperation of the Mao government. His most spectacular effort was a sixty-five-minute color film entitled "China," which was shown in theaters across the United States in 1965. In the film's prologue, Greene pleaded with viewers to try to see the Chinese people "as fellow human beings," and not exclusively "in terms of their politics." Greene's film was described by the American Security Council as "a stunning piece of Communist propaganda, the most effective yet to reach the West."

The film gives credit to the Official China Film Corp. for its "cooperation" in the making of "China." As the American Security Council pointed out, this meant that "nothing Felix Greene photographed nor one step of the fifteen thousand miles he tells he traveled was accomplished without the express permission and control of the Peking government. Nothing in Red China moves without such permission." ASC also refutes Greene's statement that he went to China for British television—"Greene made the film independently with Peking's OK."

Variety seemed suspicious of Greene in its review of "China." The show-biz newspaper pointed out that "Although he says he traveled over most of China, most of the film deals with two cities—Shanghai and Peking—both with heavy political overtones. The few rural or village shots could have been immediately outside either city."

Greene admits in the prologue that others might leave Red China with a different set of impressions. *Variety* agreed, and offered the reminder that the noted French author, Jules Roy, summed up his impressions following a long tour of mainland China with the words: "Having come to China in an ecstacy of love and admiration, I left bitter and frightened." *Variety* then summed up the film itself: "Greene has tried to minimize political aspects of the film without losing the evident dramatic impact of the industrial growth of China. . . . He has been unsuccessful in both attempts."

In 1961, Greene also published a book, *Awakened China—The Country America Doesn't Know* (Doubleday). The book received a rave review from the Communist newspaper, the *Worker,* as "a rare combination of excellent reporting—objective, yet human—a fine appreciation of the human miracle being wrought in the building of socialism in China . . ." But the Los Angeles *Herald-Examiner* called it "a blatant piece of propaganda . . . an apology for Communist China."

Meanwhile, Greene remained in the news as a participant in rallies staged by various organizations plumping for the withdrawal of American troops from Vietnam, as a lecturer and radio and TV personality. He was one of the speakers at a "China Forum" program in New York's Town Hall on May 17, 1966, sponsored by an ad hoc group set up by the American Friends Service Committee, the Committee of the Professions Against the War in Vietnam, SANE, the ADA, and Women's Strike for Peace. Greene attacked U.S. policy in Vietnam, the American economy, the Pentagon and the Central Intelligence Agency, and urged that Americans support "wars of national liberation" throughout the world.

For the other side, Greene's role has perhaps been best summed up by Senator Milward Simpson, Republican of Wyoming, in a Senate speech on July 21, 1966. Greene, said Simpson, "represents a new kind of China Lobby, quite unlike the lobby of the 1940's which endeavored to tell Americans that Mao Tze-tung and company were not agrarian reformers. This new China Lobby of the left works on Mao's side of the ideological fence. Mr. Greene, as an articulate, sincere-sounding and persuasive advocate of the People's Republic of China, is the new China Lobby's blue chip asset."

However, the blue-chip value of Felix Greene has fallen considerably since he came under attack on Capitol Hill for his various activities. It is a safe bet that Peking has come to a keener appreciation of an accidental asset—the support given by various organizations of American citizens to the drive for Red China's recognition. From the United Auto Workers to the Republican Ripon Society have come resolutions and declarations, for the most part filled with sincerity and good intentions, which must warm the cockles of whatever passes for Peking's heart.

In May, 1966, the UAW called for diplomatic recognition of Red China in a resolution which said Peking "must be brought into the family of nations, where their government will find it necessary to rely increasingly upon the force of politics, rather than upon the politics of force." The Unitarian Universalist Association, at about the same time, urged recognition of Red China, admission of the Peking regime to the United Nations, "relaxation of cultural and economic relations with the Communist countries, and immediate inclusion of Red China in world disarmament talks." The liberal Republican Ripon Society, based in Cambridge, Massachusetts, asked for "a full normalization of relations, including an exchange of ambassadors and admission to the United Nations" for Red China.

Remarked Secretary of State Dean Rusk, playfully: "With capitalist enemies like that, Mao needs no Communist friends."

Best financed among all the independent agencies in the Peking Lobby is the comparatively new National Committee on United States-China Relations, formed in June, 1966, by a group including such articulate spokesmen for "normalization" of relations with Red China as Columbia University's Doak Barnett, Harvard's John K. Fairbank, and Columbia's O. Edmund Clubb. Also named as founders were Bayard Rustin, the civil rights leader, and A. Philip Randolph, a civil rights moderate and vice president of the AFL-CIO. The committee raised $250,000 for its first-year's expenses.

Nevertheless, by 1967 the most effective outfit probably was the Americans for Reappraisal of Far Eastern Policy. Organized at Yale, ARFEP describes itself as "an entirely new kind of interest group organized by students who found that while they disagreed on many political issues, they were united in their frustration over U.S. Far Eastern policy." Its strength was sufficient to finance a full-page advertisement in *The New York Times* on December 10, 1965, signed by eighteen hundred Yale students and three hundred faculty members. But although purportedly a student organization, ARFEP was controlled by a national committee sprinkled with the old familiar names of Peking's advocates—Harvard's John Fairbank, Socialist Norman Thomas, Roger Baldwin and Michael Harrington. The committee has seen to it that the outfit has "area coordinators" working at Beloit College, Brown University, Dartmouth, Georgetown, Duke, Oberlin, Smith, Princeton, University of Chicago, Stanford, University of Oregon, University of Texas, University of Utah, Yale and Wellesley.

Then there is the Association of Asian Studies, a collection of 2700 reputable, expert students of the Far East, whose support is constantly sought but not always obtained by the more blatant pro-Peking groups. *The New York Times* discovered this in March, 1966, when it devoted a full column on Page One, and most of an inner page, to a pro-Peking document signed by 198 persons. Editorially, *The Times*—which could never be accused of being pro-Formosa—deposed that "this shows where the weight of informed American opinion lies."

There was wide disagreement with this. Both *The Reporter* and *Time* revealed that the document was not distributed by the Association of Asian Studies, but seemed to have descended on *The Times* from thin air. The document purportedly was sent to all 2700 members of the AAS, but only 7.3 percent of the total membership endorsed or signed it. In an official statement, the AAS said it had "nothing to do with the document on United States-China policy that was published in *The New York Times* on March 21, 1966 . . . Some of those listed in *The Times* as signers of the statement are not members of the Association." Remarked *The Reporter,* "*The Times* built the release into major significance by giving it inordinate prominence and a largely spurious authority . . . This is irresponsible journalism."

One of the unfortunate results of the liberal organizations' rush to the side of those advocating a soft policy with Red China has been the involvement of the American Friends Service Committee, which has a brilliant history of relief work throughout the world.

For example, the AFSC in 1965 distributed under its imprimatur a curious piece of Communist literature. This was a booklet, "Chinese Aggression—Myth or Menace," by Charles Burchill, a professor of history and economics at Royal Roads University in Vancouver, British Columbia. To the detached observer, it appears that Burchill did his research in some strange Alice's wonderland of history, for he purports to "prove" that the Chinese Reds have never been aggressors anywhere—in Korea, Tibet, China or Vietnam. Even the Washington *Post,* which takes a mature, tolerant view of some of the more outrageous ideological kooks, expressed its disgust at this handout and chided the AFSC sharply for pinning its name to its distribution.

The AFSC put out in the same year a pamphlet entitled *A New China Policy—Some Quaker Proposals* which was replete with the tiresome appeasement clichés of another time. Most Americans identified the Friends movement with this twaddle, although the fact is the AFSC is an independent corporation with no organizational relationship to the Friends movement. The Friends Yearly Meeting no longer names representatives to the AFSC.

The Quaker publication, *California Friend,* explained the Friends' dilemma: "A careful study of the report [*A New China Policy*] brings out the fact that the paper was prepared by the American Friends Service Committee. However, not one in a thousand reading the article would know that the position taken by the report would be the position of only a *very small minority* of Friends . . . The so-called 'New China Policy' is not a proposal of the Society of Friends, but who will believe our report?"

But if the AFSC only implies that its proclamations represent the thinking of all Quakers, the National Council of Churches of Christ presents its activities as The Word from 38 million Protestants, a presumption of which Peking regularly makes hay. For example, when the Council issued a declaration in Cleveland in 1958 advocating recognition and UN membership for Red China, the Communist *Worker* gleefully headlined:

38 MILLION PROTESTANTS TELL IKE: RECOGNIZE CHINA!

That was not quite the case. A poll of the clergy of the Council's communions was taken by The Committee of One Million under the direction of a committee of dissenting churchmen. The poll showed that 7437 ministers were opposed to the resolution and only 963 approved of it. A poll by *Christianity Today,* a periodical circulating among two hundred thousand Protestant clergymen in the United States, Canada, Australia and the British Isles, revealed eight to one opposed.

All resolutions issued by the Council of Churches, including a particularly effusive document passed by a ninety to three vote of the General Board in 1966, stem from the Council's so-called "Message of Cleveland." In that curious collection of wishful thoughts and euphemisms, the Council leaned heavily on the sentiments of Columbia's Doak Barnett, whose arguments were laced with pessimism concerning the dynamics of Western political thought.

Said Barnett: "We must realistically face, therefore, not only the question of what we can or cannot do in respect to Communist China itself, but also the question of whether or not we are capable of *competing effectively* with Communist China and with the ideas, the values, and the institutions which it represents, in the whole non-Western, Asian-African world." (Italics the author's).

This was pretty rough stuff even for the ears of political clergymen, but the "Message of Cleveland" subsequently embodied Barnett's despairing cynicism in its text.

Another draft speaker was the Rev. Dr. M. Searle Bates, professor of missions at Union Seminary, who blamed the United States for what he called "the barriers of separation" between the U.S. and Red

China. The barriers, said Dr. Bates, were "attributable to wrongful acts on our own part or on the part of our government." As a sort of *mea culpa* proxy for the villains, Dr. Bates confessed that the then Secretary of State John Foster Dulles, other politicians and some churchmen were "accounted spokesmen of Christianity in statements and policies utterly intolerable to the tide of Chinese feeling in these years."

It did not seem to occur to Dr. Bates that "the tide of Chinese feeling" on the mainland is imposed by the Communist dictatorship.

Then there was the peripatetic Bishop G. Bromley Oxnam. Bishop Oxnam asked querulously if there was not "something fundamentally wrong with a policy that seems to keep us isolated from six hundred million people, or a quarter of the human race." Admittedly, United States China policy over the past twenty-five years had been enough to send Talleyrand spinning in his grave, but it seemed curious that Bishop Oxnam had no apprehensions about the "permanent belligerence" of the new imperialism of Communism.

The Rev. Dr. Daniel A. Poling, editor of *The Christian Herald,* was quick to point out that the Cleveland resolution "represents only the men who endorsed it and not the Protestant community of the United States." Dr. Poling, who not always had seemed to possess the tolerance desired in a man of the cloth, this time put his finger on the principal reason why some churchmen might find the resolution distasteful. Said Dr. Poling: "It is a brutal betrayal of our Protestant brothers in China who have remained steadfast . . ."

Later, the International Society of Christian Endeavor, a youth organization active in many Protestant churches, took the same stand. "We deplore the recommendations of the Cleveland Study Conference . . . for recognition and admission," it said in a resolution of its own. "We take our stand against a betrayal of our Christian missionaries and the Chinese Christians on the mainland of China."

Nevertheless, the Council of Churches shortly went beyond its defense of the study conference's findings as an exercise of free speech. Its General Board inaugurated a year-long study course in all the churches under its direction, and the Council's Department of International Affairs prepared and distributed twelve pamphlets to all member-churches in the United States. The *Message of Cleveland* and the souped-up 1966 *Policy Statement on China* were promoted across

the land as a commitment by 38 million Protestants in favor of recognizing Communist China and admitting it to the United Nations.
Aside from those communions which opposed the resolution, this was a
hard line for those denominations which did not belong to the Council, including the Southern Baptists, the Missouri Synod Lutherans and
the Lutheran Communion, representing more than six million com-
municants.

Such volunteer trumpeters of the Peking line also make it difficult
for the State Department to achieve even a casual meeting of minds in
its only official diplomatic contacts with the Chinese Communist
regime. These are the periodic sessions between the American and
Red Chinese ambassadors in Warsaw, initiated in 1954 to discuss the
question of American prisoners-of-war captured during the Korean
conflict. In June, 1966, U.S. Ambassador John Gronouski was forced to
admit under questioning by reporters for the magazine, *U.S. News and
World Report,* that after 130 meetings the State Department saw
"relatively little progress toward any thaw." State Department officials
state bluntly that they are handicapped because the Chinese Reds
believe they can get all the concessions they want through pressure put
on Washington by the Red China sympathizers.

"They don't have to deal with John Gronouski," said one Assistant
Secretary. "They say Gronouski should deal with what Wang Kuo-
chuan, Peking's ambassador to Warsaw, calls 'the majority among your
religious community.' "

Yet during the early years the sessions were relatively fruitful in that
the American representatives succeeded in securing the release of most
of the prisoners. That, as some State Department people point out, was
before the Peking Lobby really got rolling. Moreover, as Gronouski
pointed out, there have been many occasions when it has been "useful" for both the United States and Communist China to get their
points of view and positions across. In Gronouski's view, the periodic
talks are important if only because there are some seven hundred
million people in mainland China whom the United States cannot
completely ignore.

Gronouski described the talks as "a forum for discussing a whole
series of issues that confront both nations, in Southeast Asia particularly, but also throughout the world. The very seriousness of the situation in Southeast Asia makes these meetings even more important. We

are in a position to express our point of view very clearly, so that neither side makes any mistake with respect to what the attitudes and positions are on the other side."

For example, the United States launched its bombings of North Vietnam in the late winter of 1965 after there were some indications from the Chinese ambassador in Warsaw that Red China would not necessarily take a hand in the war unless its own territory was violated. The impression Washington got at the time was that the Peking regime was not interested in committing its own troops to protect the territory of another state, because it feared massive retaliation by the United States.

In order to get this kind of valuable information, the American ambassador must sit through an endless series of meetings with his Chinese counterpart in Warsaw. The meetings are held in a room in the Mysliwiecki Palace provided by the Polish government. Each ambassador has an adviser, an interpreter and a secretary—in the American case all Foreign Service personnel. The adviser flies over from Washington a few days before the meeting for mutual briefing sessions with the ambassador. Meetings have been held on an average of about once every two months, and there is no agenda. The ambassador whose turn it is to open the discussion establishes the agenda in his opening re-marks. The one rule of procedure is that the ambassadors take turns speaking first. Since a great deal of time is spent in a give-and-take discussion of the issues, both sides are able, in Gronouski's words, "to explore the nuances of the argument." In such a way, Washington learns, in effect, how Peking is feeling at a given time.

Both sides put forth suggestions for easing tensions between the two countries, but usually they make little progress in this area. Again, however, the suggestions reveal the thinking of the two governments.

The meetings have usually lasted about two hours, but one session went three hours and fifteen minutes when Wang became excited about what he called the "conspiracy" between Moscow and Washing-ton to encircle Red China. There is no socializing, no after-meeting drinks, but the two ambassadors always have a little chat about such things as the weather, a concert they've both attended or an art gallery show they've seen or—incredibly enough—women's fashions. Wang, something of a Puritan, was playfully caustic about the short-ness of Western women's skirts.

As Gronouski put it, "Wang is quite formal, perhaps in keeping with Chinese traditions or custom. In any event, we haven't developed a buddy system."

The time may come, of course, when a buddy system will suit Peking's purpose. But it is not in the Communist textbook to be chummy when no strategic reason for chumminess exists. Besides, like the Formosa regime, Communist China has an American lobby to handle the hail-fellow bit. The State Department, which is willing to take its chances in handling both Peking and Taipei across the baize-covered table of diplomacy, cannot be blamed if it sometimes is constrained to call down a plague on both these houses of American meddlers.

11

The Formosa Lobby

T H O S E W H O P R O C L A I M Winston Churchill the most successful
diplomatic lobbyist of modern times acknowledge that over the long
haul his personal efforts on behalf of a besieged Britain have been out-
distanced by the China Lobby. Churchill, in the words of the late
Secretary of State Cordell Hull, may have "owned Frank Roosevelt,"
but the Chiang Kai-shek regime sold itself to FDR and maintained its
influence over Congress and a reluctant Executive Department for
more than twenty years. During that period, Chiang cost the American
taxpayers more than fifteen billion dollars, including over five billion
dollars in postwar economic and military aid, and received an estimated half billion dollars more in private contributions channeled
through a variety of fund-raising organizations.

By the close of 1966, the old China Lobby of the late forties and Joe
McCarthy fifties no longer existed as such. That is to say, there were no
more strident demands for new billions for Chiang or for support of a
Chiang invasion of the Chinese mainland. The old gang had been
replaced by a new lobby with a new aim—The Committee of One
Million, whose objective was to prevent recognition of Red China and
its admission to the United Nations. The Committee was part of the
modern system whereby a foreign country, through its diplomatic
representatives, arranges pressures through organizations of public-
spirited citizens.

For those whose lives are titillated by nostalgia, however, a glamorous
member of the original China Lobby cast was still making her "final"

appearances. Madame Chiang Kai-shek spent most of 1966 in Washington and New York, mending both health and fences. Never modest in her concern for her creature comforts, Madame Chiang paid two thousand dollars a month for a house in Washington and another twelve hundred dollars a month for a New York apartment; her landlord said she spent a total of forty-nine days in her capital pad during her ten-month stay in the United States.

Perhaps one of the reasons Madame Chiang spent so little time in Washington was that official Washington had so little time for her. She saw President Johnson only twice, each time briefly, during her stay in the United States, although the Chinese Embassy regularly peppered both the White House and the State Department with demands for appointments with the President.

"Your President doesn't want to see me," Madame Chiang told a Washington reporter, "because he doesn't want to hear the truth about how he is being betrayed by some of his diplomats in the Far East."

A White House aide concerned with foreign policy begged anonymity before he would offer any comment. "It's no use the President seeing her," he said. "She always wants something he can't give her." With Vietnam, Charles de Gaulle, Mao Tze-tung and the Republicans on his mind, Lyndon Johnson clearly found the once-glamorous Madame Chiang a trifle tiresome.

Two months after Madame Chiang returned to Formosa, after apparently having given The Committee of One Million an exotic shot in the arm, The Committee suffered its most important defection. Senator Jacob K. Javits, Republican of New York, announced he had withdrawn from membership in the group on the grounds that he regarded its inflexible position on Communist China as "foreclosing even the hope of negotiation" with Peking. In a letter to The Committee, copies of which he sent to forty-nine other senators and two hundred and forty-eight representatives who were members of the group, Javits said he was withdrawing "in the interest of my duty as a United States senator to retain freedom of action regarding Communist China."

Meanwhile, The Committee seemed to be beating a retreat of a sort. On the day Javits withdrew, The Committee's secretary, Marvin Liebman, sent a memorandum to all Congressional members which said that the group would discontinue the use of the names of Congressional members on letterheads and committee publications. Liebman said the declaration opposing United Nations membership for

Communist China and United States recognition of the Peking regime had "served its purpose" because the UN General Assembly had just rejected a proposal to expel Nationalist China and give the Security Council seat to Red China.

The Committee, of course, remained very much in business as part of a new Nationalist China front whose other advocates worked much more subtly than the old China Lobby. In the fashion of the times, these included the New York law firm of Nordlinger, Riegelman, Benetar and Charney, and Formosa's registered legislative representative, Robert L. Farrington of Washington. Farrington, chief counsel of the Agriculture Department in the Eisenhower Administration, concerned himself mostly with the sugar interests of the Chiang regime.

In the field of international politics, The Committee of One Million has been Chiang's principal instrument of pressure on Congress. The group has always admitted that it depended on agitation at the grassroots level to work its will on Capitol Hill. Its 1964 general program, for example, stated:

"The key to the entire program . . . will be local community action. Because of increased pressures this year, we will have to mobilize and enlist greater grassroots action than ever before. We can count on the active cooperation of a number of national veteran, youth, fraternal, and civil organizations toward this end."

It goes without saying that the mere threat of pressure from the grassroots sends the average member of Congress into the cold shakes. And in an era which found Americans fighting Communists on the battlefields of both Korea and Vietnam, there was little doubt in most Congressional minds that the general public took a tough line toward Communism. Indeed, The Committee found little difficulty in enlisting the endorsement of such outstanding liberals as Hubert Humphrey—who later withdrew his name—former Senator Paul Douglas of Illinois, and Senator William Proxmire of Wisconsin. Douglas, whose liberal credentials will be recorded by history as impeccable, even affixed his name to an article prepared by Formosa's American public relations representative, the Hamilton Wright Organization, citing arguments against United States recognition of Communist China.

Douglas, always refreshingly candid, wrote a Senate committee that he had found himself in general agreement with the sentiments and arguments contained in the article and, after making some changes, authorized its distribution over his signature. Unlike some liberals,

Douglas has never seen any difference between Fascist and Communist aggression.

The Committee of One Million, founded in 1953 as the Committee *for* One Million only two months after the truce in Korea, could not be more respectable for the purposes of the Chinese Embassy. It operates on a modest budget from unpretentious offices in Manhattan, and takes no money from either the Formosa regime or from millionaire Far Right fanatics. Admittedly, its relations with the Embassy are both intimate and cordial to the point of affectionate, and it has used material prepared by the Hamilton Wright Organization, which at one time received from the Chiang regime $300,000 a year in fees. But it seeks no millions for the Formosa government, nor even any important political privileges for it. Clearly, its purpose is anti-Peking rather than pro-Taipei. That, of course, is all right with Taipei.

The group was the brainchild of Nicholas de Rochefort, a Russian-born university lecturer. Dr. Walter H. Judd, then a House member, helped get it started. During its first ten months of existence, The Committee obtained more than one million signatures on petitions to the President opposing Communist China's admission to the United Nations, whereupon it suspended its activities. But it was revived in 1955 as The Committee *of* One Million, to launch a new, continuing drive aimed at persuading a majority in Congress to pledge itself to a hard line on Red China. It works through petitions and declarations. Each fall, just before the General Assembly voted on the question of admitting Peking, The Committee has bought space in a handful of leading newspapers to mobilize public sentiment behind its opposition.

In 1961, The Committee strengthened its declaration by coming out against diplomatic recognition of Peking and got the signatures of 345 members of Congress on the declaration. In 1965, it also opposed trade relations between the United States and Communist China and "any policy of accommodation which might be interpreted as U.S. acquiescence in, or approval of, Communist China's aggression, direct or indirect, against her neighbors." This was a pretty all-inclusive statement, but it was endorsed in print by 312 Senators and Representatives, evenly divided between the two parties.

In pursuing its single-minded purpose, The Committee is fortunate to employ as its secretary and vigorous day-to-day executive, Marvin Liebman, a former member of the American Communist Party. Leibman has illustrated the point that there is no more energetic convert than the former Communist, and he has also brought to the group the discipline and organization he learned as a Communist. Liebman always has been quick to put out Committee rebuttals of any public utterances by government officials which seem to suggest a compromise with Peking. He leaped with both feet upon Roger Hilsman, former Assistant Secretary of State, when in a speech in December, 1963, Hilsman failed to find anything wrong in the Two-China policy. From time to time, Liebman also has issued circular letters reminding his "Fellow Americans" that even while "young Americans" were being slaughtered by Communists in Vietnam, "all too many American individuals, organizations and publications . . . continue to urge concessions to these same Communists . . ."

Over the years, it has been the contention of such literary observers of the international scene as James A. Wechsler, an editor of the *New York Post,* that The Committee of One Million is a paper tiger. Anybody, said Wechsler, could form a Committee of One Million to push any issue. "The John Birchers," Wechsler noted, "could probably produce a Committee of One Million for the impeachment of Earl Warren," and the White Citizens Council a similar group to endorse the appointment of Mississippi's Senator James Eastland as Attorney General. With more than 190,000,000 million Americans in the country, asked Wechsler, "why should 1,000,000 . . . loom as so powerful an array, worthy of such continuous newspaper attention and so much Congressional apprehension?"

Wechsler, of course, could have found an answer to his question in the activities of some of the more radical civil rights groups which regularly cause members of Congress to quake in their insecure boots, although they represent only a minority of a minority of ten percent of the population. But The Committee of One Million found it unnecessary to quibble with Wechsler. The fact is it has influenced public opinion while, in Liebman's words, serving as a "watchdog for the public on China policy." No diplomatic lobbyist in the Chinese Embassy, spending hundreds of thousands of dollars a year, could have equalled the results achieved by The Committee on an annual budget of sixty thousand dollars.

It is for this simple, compelling reason that a succession of recent Chinese Nationalist ambassadors in Washington have found it not only unnecessary but distasteful to spend huge sums from the Taipei treasury to hire high-pressure press agents. "The American people can make up their own minds," said Ambassador Chow Shu-kai in 1966.

"We are confident the plain citizen will continue to support a free China. The Committee of One Million represents American fair play and American common sense."

Yet in the past, the Chiang regime had not hesitated to spend, and squander, millions in pulling political strings in Washington. The story of the old China Lobby is an unsavory one in which Madame Chiang Kai-shek and her wealthy brother, T. V. Soong, lobbied successfully with high officials of the American government to rescue and then rehabilitate a corrupt and demoralized regime which was detested by the common people and which had been driven off the mainland by the Communists. They not only got all the money they wanted, but their agents in the fifties fed information to Senator McCarthy for his wild charges against "Communists" in government. Soong was fond of boasting, "There is practically nothing that goes on in the American government of which I do not learn within three days."

Soong was a rich and influential man when he came to Washington in 1940 to get more help for the government of Chiang Kai-shek, and he added to his wealth during his stay in the United States. In 1944 his American holdings alone were estimated by a friend at forty-seven million dollars. And during the days of World War II, he had the expert assistance of a charming Pole named Ludwig (Lulu) Rajchman, now in exile in Paris. Between them, and with the glamorous assistance of Madame Chiang, Soong and Rajchman funnelled more than two billion dollars into their wartime China Defense Supplies, Inc., patterned loosely on the British Purchasing Commission, to represent China on lend-lease matters. Soong himself soon made friends of such White House intimates as Harry Hopkins, Henry Morgenthau Jr. and Lauchlin Currie. Soong had come to Washington without a title, and when an American official once questioned his authority to sign a document, Soong brushed him off with the remark, "I am China."

Even though Soong, Rajchman and Co. were able to dispatch a river of dollars to the Chiang regime during the war, the coming of peace found a change of atmosphere in Washington. For one thing, Harry Truman had moved into the White House and the New Dealers had moved out. For another, official Washington had become disenchanted with Chiang. Had it not been for the outbreak of the Korean war, the Truman Administration would have disengaged the United States from its involvement with the defeated Chiang government. It was during the Korean conflict that orders came to the Chinese Embassy from Taipei to launch an all-out propaganda campaign on behalf of the Formosa regime. The objective was to prevent the cutting off of American economic assistance and to forestall United States recognition of the Communist government.

Fortunately for Chiang, he found allies among influential Republican politicians such as Senators William Knowland of California and Styles Bridges of New Hampshire, who saw a powerful political issue in the China question. And indeed, for all their bumbling ways, the Knowlands and Bridgeses and their Capitol Hill and journalistic allies undoubtedly prevented both the Truman and Eisenhower administrations from making an expedient, seemingly logical, but in retrospect dangerously premature deal with the Communist regime. Throughout their fight, however, the Knowland-Bridges forces were handicapped by the average American's disillusionment with and distrust of the China Lobby. Too many American dollars had disappeared into the jungle which was Chiang's political headquarters in Taipei. There was too much evidence of venality in the little clique of Chiang's cronies, there were too many instant millionaires among those who had served Chiang's cause.

Senate hearings, however, revealed there was still life in the Chiang propaganda machine. Although the China Lobby was exposed in 1952 when *The Reporter* magazine devoted the better part of two issues to its untidy activities, the Chiang regime was not convinced that it was taking a risk by continuing its obvious attempts to influence American public opinion with American dollars. Senate hearings disclosed that directly and through its Washington embassy, Taipei entered into a four-year contract with the Hamilton Wright Organization through which the New York public relations firm undertook to "create a sympathetic understanding of Free China that would have dramatic impact on members of the United Nations and prevent the seating of Red China in the United Nations and the lifting of trade sanctions against Red China." Hamilton Wright promised that its campaign would "bring vociferous support from the American people when the day comes for a return to the mainland."

Taipei agreed to pay Hamilton Wright $300,000 a year for its services. In turn, Hamilton Wright "guaranteed" that Nationalist China would receive at least $2,500,000 worth of publicity in newspapers, magazines, television, newsreels and other media. Since $300,000 is a lot of money, Hamilton Wright Sr. wrote Dr. Sampson Shen, director of the Government Information Office, in Taipei: "This campaign is extremely difficult and expensive . . . Money is the 'oil' that will make it work smoothly."

Eventually, in March 1963, the Senate Foreign Relations Committee took an interest in the contract and later made public some of the testimony and documents offered during a hearing. The transcript provides fascinating material for the student of the twentieth century's Madison Avenue approach to diplomacy.

At the outset, Chairman J. William Fulbright put into the record a letter containing the Hamilton Wright proposal to Dr. T. F. Tsiang, Nationalist China's Ambassador to the United Nations. In the letter, Hamilton Wright Sr. promised Tsiang his organization would "research, create and manufacture feature news," that it would release such features free to the press and other media, and that it would make the American people "Free China conscious."

Both Hamilton Wright Sr. and Hamilton Wright Jr. appeared as witnesses, and after some effort Senator Fulbright got Wright Jr. to admit that the objective of the campaign was "political." The father insisted it depended on one's point of view. Fulbright then referred to a second letter, from Shen to Wright Sr., in which Shen said he wanted the Wrights to correct the fallacy that "we have given up the goal of recovering the mainland." Shen also complained that the Two-Chinas theory "has never been fully discredited," and that there had been talk of admitting the Chinese Communists to the United Nations and relaxing the embargo of strategic material to the Chinese mainland. He wanted the Wrights to get at the job of overcoming "'sales resistance" on the part of the American public toward Nationalist China.

Questioned by Fulbright, Wright Sr. said he wanted it "particularly understood that the services taken by our organization shall not be construed as political propaganda . . . but rather to enlighten and inform the American public opinion . . . in an effort to uphold the processes of a democratic way of life."

Fulbright had no comment.

At any rate, the Wright firm also proposed to give the Nationalist China story considerable exposure in Latin America and arrange with the United States Information Service "to push HWO movies, newsreels and shorts wherever possible in South America."

Asked Fulbright, "What did you have in mind about arranging with USIS to push movies?"

Replied Wright Sr., "The U.S. Information Service has been using

Hamilton Wright short subjects in film for almost fifteen years. Every time we go into a country there is somebody from their office who is coming to our office and saying, 'Can we borrow a picture you made on Puerto Rico, Venezuela, Colombia?' and we say 'Yes, use it any way you want.' "

According to the Wrights, on at least one occasion they also paid a three-thousand-dollar subsidy to get an article favorable to Nationalist China published in the ultra liberal magazine, the *New Leader*. In fact, a guarantee that the article would be published was part of a sales pitch contained in a contract agreement with the Chiang government dated January 6, 1959: "Assist in arrangements to publish an article entitled 'China, the United States and the Continuing Struggle' in the *New Leader* magazine and to publish and distribute copies of said article to representative citizens, writers and leaders in the United States."

Asked Fulbright, "How did you fulfill this part of your agreement?"

Wright Jr. replied that he had been "bamboozled on this one. The *New Leader* came to me and hit me up for a little money that this would be a great thing to have, and I fell for it. They did the work, not me." He explained that the *New Leader* "had a professor 'someone' write an article which was, I think, a special issue of the *New Leader,* and they came to us and said: 'Now, this would be a fine story to have out. We don't have enough money to completely publish this. Will you contribute to its effort?' I thought at the time this might be a good thing and did contribute."

FULBRIGHT: What did you pay them?

WRIGHT JR.: A sum. I would have to check back and see.

FULBRIGHT: It was three thousand dollars.

WRIGHT JR.: It was?

FULBRIGHT: I think so.

WRIGHT JR.: All right, fine.

Sen. George Aiken, Republican, of Vermont, wanted to know why the *New Leader* warranted payment for publishing an article favorable to Nationalist China. "Did they circulate among a particular class of people?" he asked.

Wright Jr. could only report what he had been told by some anonymous "they" at the *New Leader*. "As I recall, they approached me and said, 'Look, you are representing the Republic of China. We have this wonderful article that has been written, and we are going to put this out as a special supplement. Now, it is going to go—you know our circulation is to the intellectual group, and gee, we just don't have enough money to get this into print all the way. We can certainly use a contribution.' "

"Who publishes the *New Leader,* anyway?" asked Aiken.

"I can't remember the gentlemen's name," replied Wright Jr. He added, in the manner of a man remarking upon the mysteries of some Middle Eastern sheikdom, "It is in New York City."

Fulbright asked if the Wrights had ever paid *Life* magazine to publish pictures on Nationalist China.

Wright Sr. jumped in. "Tut, tut," he said, "I should say not." Later, he remarked that *"Life* magazine, thank God, and there are probably several hundred publications here—you can't touch with a twenty-foot pole."

Fulbright also showed considerable interest in a letter written by Hamilton Wright Jr. to Sampson Shen which was dated October 19, 1960. In the letter, Wright Jr. told Shen that "In view of the critical United Nations developments and statements by Senator Kennedy that he would abandon Quemoy if elected President—it is our considered opinion that the time has come for Taiwan to fight back with a full-scale counterattack in the form of stepped-up high-powered publicity. Clarification and understanding on Quemoy and Taiwan, and what they stand for, must be brought into sharp focus to American people and people throughout the world, particularly during the U.S. presidential election campaign and after the new U.S. President takes office. Public opinion everywhere must be one hundred percent in favor of Free China continuously and on a nonstop basis. The public forgets quickly."

"Would you say that is a political objective you are stating there?" asked Fulbright.

WRIGHT SR.: I think that is trying to save the face of the United States.

WRIGHT JR.: It was political, yes.

FULBRIGHT: It was political.

WRIGHT JR.: Excuse me; may I also say it was a sales letter.

FULBRIGHT (drily): I was just going to say this is also a sales letter intended to inspire a continuation of the contract.

The hearings later revealed that the Taipei government had cut the Wright contract by one-third and then by one-half, and that the

Wrights had urged that "immediate steps" be taken "to treble" their effort. "This publicity," Wright Jr. told Shen, "must be clever—smooth—penetrating. We must show the public more short subjects—more newsreels—more still pictures—more feature articles; more of everything, everywhere." But as the time for renewal of the contract neared, the Wrights ran into more trouble.

Incredible as it may seem, Taipei demanded that the Wrights round up editorial support for an invasion of the mainland by Chiang's troops. Shortly thereafter, the contract was cancelled because the State Department informed the Wright firm that such an invasion was not in the best interests of the United States.

Here, the student of diplomacy by hired flack will discover some of the perils of beating the drums for foreign governments. Taipei was not only disappointed in the Wrights' unwillingness to seek editorial support for a mainland invasion, but was annoyed at their choice of other clients. In a letter to Wright Jr. from the Wrights' Taipei representative, David Roads, Roads reported that the Chiang government "are hurt about South Africa." Roads said he had had lunch with one Jimmy Shen, who had replaced Sampson Shen as director of the Government Information office, and that Shen told him, "Hamilton Wright Organization does not care who it takes as a client." Shen complained that the South African government had "brought grave insults to the Chinese people and government." Shen also asked if Wright Sr. was still in Africa—"I understand that he is not only taking pictures of wild life in the park but trying to show how good the Africans treat their Negroes."

"What does he mean, they are hurt about South Africa," asked Fulbright.

"They were a little upset because we were doing work for South Africa," Wright Jr. replied.

"Why?" asked Fulbright.

"Well, because I would say among other things, the report that I got was that the Chinese consul in South Africa was treated as the blacks were because of their apartheid policies."

Even for a regime afflicted for more than twenty years with a bad case of paranoia, Taipei was being oversensitive about the Hamilton Wright Organization's perfectly proper policy of offering its services in the public marketplace. American press agents merely work for foreign governments, they do not take oaths of allegiance to them, and the ethics of the business do not require that Madison Avenue embrace the political idiosyncracies of its clients. Jimmy Shen probably was both inaccurate and unjust in complaining that "Hamilton Wright Organization does not care who it takes as a client," but even if he spoke a rough sort of truth about flacks generally, Taipei's record in the lobbying business does not qualify any of its representatives to look down their noses at other practitioners of the elegant dodge.

Indeed, David Roads' report on Jimmy Shen's grumbling remarks about the quality of the Hamilton Wright product reveals the attitude of most governments toward the problem of burnishing their tarnished images abroad. "Jimmy said he was considered a hardheaded business-man and wanted something for his money," Roads wrote Wright Jr. "They are going to shop around and are willing to listen to any and everybody who can do a public relations job." Talleyrand and Winston Churchill would have gone along with that.

12

From Citizen Genet to Julius Klein

EVEN CAPITOL HILL reporters, who daily commit *lèse majesté* against members of Congress, thought Julius Klein's letter to Senator Thomas J. Dodd, Democrat of Connecticut, went a trifle too far in insulting a senator's dignity. After all, even if a lobbyist for a foreign government assumes that he owns and operates a member of Congress, he is not supposed to say so in print.

But there the letter was, spread in the 1966 record of the Senate's Select Committee on Standards and Conduct investigating Senator Dodd's dealings with Julius Klein, and it seemed obvious that in Klein's view Dodd had been a very naughty boy.

"What are you afraid of?" asked Klein. "Do you consider friendship a one-way street? All I can say is I am ashamed of you."

Klein was not quite accurate. He *could* say other things, and he did. As a registered foreign agent for various West German interests, Klein was furious at Dodd for failing to appear at a Senate Foreign Relations Committee meeting on May 7, 1963, to defend Klein's reputation. Instead, Dodd had written to Senator J. W. Fulbright, chairman of the committee, noting that Klein's testimony at the session included "a letter and draft resolution presumably sent to me by General Klein." Dodd wrote that he had never answered Klein's letter and had never introduced the resolution, which called for a plebiscite in the Soviet zone of Germany.

In his letter to Dodd, Klein seemed especially incensed that Dodd had overlooked an opportunity to say a few nice words about Klein in Senator Dodd's letter to Senator Fulbright.

"Now there is one thing I object to in your letter to Senator Fulbright," Klein wrote Dodd, "and that is your last line:

'I think it appropriate that my reply to you be made a part of the official record, and I hereby request that this be done.'

"You did not even add a few remarks about our personal friendship so that there should be no reflection on me. Please read on the same page [of the committee's hearing report] what Mayor Robert F. Wagner [of New York City], whom I hardly know, had to say about me.

"This would have been the proper attitude for you to take. No one knows more about the foreign agent registration than you. No one knows better than you my activities in Washington. I asked you to be present at the executive session. You promised me the night before that you would attend—but you were not there. I wired you to be present at the public hearings—you were not there either."

Klein appeared to have a point in asserting that Dodd was well-acquainted with his activities. For several years he and Dodd had been close political and personal friends, and the Senate record showed Klein had even written speeches for Dodd and briefed the Connecticut senator on how to talk to various officials of the West German government. Even after Klein had rebuked him, Senate hearings revealed Dodd dispatched letters of praise for him to key West German officials and put in a good word for Klein at a meeting with former West German Chancellor Konrad Adenauer in 1964. As a result, the Senate, prodded by an exposé launched by Columnist Drew Pearson, had become interested in whether Dodd had abused his office by acting as Klein's errand boy.

The evidence was that Klein required the services of an errand boy of some distinction. He had been tarred with some bad publicity during a 1963 Senate investigation of activities in the United States of agents for foreign powers at which Senator Fulbright had pointed to Klein as one of the agents who played up their influence with Washington figures to impress foreign governments. Fulbright's remarks, plus erroneous reports in some German newspapers that Klein was on trial for wrongdoing, led to Klein's loss of several lucrative West German public-relations accounts, including the prestigious Daimler-Benz auto company.

Julius Klein's troubles were a reminder that, since World War II, lobbying by foreign governments in the United States had become too big a business to entrust entirely to diplomats out of some Sussex village or Saxony mill town. International politics involves profits in the billions, and the peddling of foreign influence requires the services of hard-nosed American businessmen and public relations consultants with contacts in the right places. Julius Klein was one of these foreign agents, a latter-day successor to the impulsive Citizen Edmond Genêt, the French Minister in Washington in 1793 who dispatched French privateers from American ports to take British prizes in disregard of American neutrality, and who threatened to appeal to the "sovereign masses" President Thomas Jefferson's demand for his recall.

On any given day, more than four hundred public relations companies, law firms and individuals will be found registered with the Department of Justice as agents of foreign governments, or of companies or other interests abroad. They get business for their clients in steel, aluminum, sugar and toys. They promote tourism. They seek to influence both Capitol Hill and the Executive Department to pass certain laws and take certain actions which is in the interest of their foreign employers.

Senator Dodd himself once was a registered agent for the Guatemalan government between service in the House and Senate. Former Secretary of State Dean Acheson once represented the government of Venezuela, and former Governor Thomas E. Dewey of New York worked for the Republic of Turkey. Joe Louis, the ex-heavyweight champion, represented the National Tourist Commission of Castro's Cuba. Two sons of Franklin D. Roosevelt have found the business lucrative—Franklin D. Jr. as an agent for Dictator Rafael Trujillo's Dominican Republic in 1956 and 1957, and John as a press agent for Haiti in 1958. Franklin Junior shared a sixty-thousand-dollar fee with one of Washington's most eminent lobbyists, Charles Patrick Clark, for his services to Trujillo's little serfdom; John Roosevelt's firm collected $150,000 from Haiti.

Although Capitol Hill and assorted journalistic busybodies occasionally have asked some pointed questions about Charles Patrick Clark and a few other exalted flacks, no in-depth inspection of the foreign agent trade had been made until the Senate was forced to inquire about the relationship between Julius Klein and Tom Dodd. The Fulbright committee's investigation was a fascinating journey through the wonderland of name-dropping and influence-peddling. At one time or another, the record was littered with a variety of famous political names—from Vice President Hubert Humphrey through Senator Everett McKinley Dirksen, Republican of Illinois, and House Speaker John W. McCormack. All, according to the printed exhibits of the hearings, seemed to be devoted friends of Julius Klein, and all seemed determined to render him aid and comfort.

Klein himself was one of the more fascinating figures to step into the Capitol Hill spotlight in this century, a man of monumental ego who boasted that he brought the late Secretary of State John Foster Dulles and Konrad Adenauer "together." He covered the walls of his Chicago office with inscribed portraits of notables—Presidents Dwight D. Eisenhower, Lyndon B. Johnson and Herbert Hoover; Vice Presidents Richard Nixon and Hubert Humphrey; Dirksen, Senator Jacob Javits of New York; Generals Omar Bradley and Douglas MacArthur; Admirals Chester Nimitz and William Halsey. And always, Klein managed to give the impression that he was on the most intimate terms with these notables. It was the sort of ploy calculated to impress German politicians, who suffer from an awe of power.

Klein demanded—and got—bouquets from some of these men of power. If necessary, he would demand his due on the spot, as he did one night when Senator Dodd was addresssing an Italian-American dinner. Halfway through the speech, Klein tugged at Dodd's coat and ordered in a stage whisper:

"Say something nice about me, Tom."

Dodd did, and so did many others. In 1962, the then Senator Humphrey deposed that "Julius Klein has more friends in the Senate and the House of Representatives than any man I know." When Senator Javits visited Germany in 1961, Klein wrote Senator Dodd that "he brought greetings to our German friends from his Republican colleague, Senator Dirksen." The Senate investigation revealed that both Humphrey and Javits undertook to help Klein land the public-relations account of ADELA, an investment company to which 130 corporations in thirteen countries had pledged to contribute forty million dollars. Klein didn't get the account, he later explained, because the organizing corporations failed to meet the quota for contributions.

Klein had set up his own public relations firm in 1947, the same year he was elected national commander of the Jewish War Veterans. An ex-newspaperman, he commanded a truck regiment in the Pacific Theater during World War II, rose to the rank of brigadier general, and got the Soldier's Medal for heroism in directing rescue work following a dock explosion in New Caledonia. He preferred to be addressed as "general," but had to settle for "mister" from the Senate investigators.

The Senate record showed Klein was the target of considerable criticism in the Jewish community for his friendship with German industrialists and politicians, and particularly for his alleged relationship with Herman J. Abs, head of the Deutsche Bank, who had been a financial adviser to Adolf Hitler. Abs led a campaign to persuade the Eisenhower Administration to return 600 million dollars in German assets seized by the United States during the war, and Klein testified in favor of returning the assets and later served as American agent for the Society for the Protection of Foreign Investments. Klein, the record showed, also secured a contract with the Society for German-American Cooperation, allegedly through his close ties with Chancellor Adenauer and an Adenauer aide, Dr. Hans Globke, who was an official in the Interior Ministry in the Hitler regime and later an interpreter of the Nuremberg racial laws.

There were also various letters and documents spread on the Senate record:

When his appearance before the Senate committee in 1963 caused unrest among his German clients, Klein appealed to Dodd for help. He wrote Dodd that because of distortions carried in the German press, the Mannesmann Aktiengesellschaft had cancelled a contract that had two years to run, at a loss to Klein of a hundred thousand dollars. "Now other contracts are up and I suppose I will face a similar situation," wrote Klein. "I hope something can be done to remedy this."

In a second letter to Dodd, written on the same day—December 17, 1963—Klein expressed appreciation "for the action you have taken . . . Your letter to Fulbright demonstrated not only integrity but also courage . . . Incidentally, when next I see you, I will show you the file of letters that I received from your colleagues . . . every letter was similar in tone to the one that you wrote . . . I am attaching only Jack Javits' letter to Fulbright . . ." Klein said Fulbright had singled him out for personal attack, "trying to insinuate that I imposed on Senators and Congressmen. I was proud that not a single Congressman or Senator confirmed that statement. Dirksen and Barry [Goldwater] are fully posted, but what pleased me very much was that such liberals like Hubert Humphrey, [Senator Wayne] Morse and [Senator Stuart] Symington spoke out publicly in my behalf."

At just about this time, Senator Dodd was planning a trip to Germany to talk to various German officials on Klein's behalf. But by February 14, 1964, he was having trouble getting away from Washington because of a tax and civil rights bill. He wrote Klein that he would be unable to depart for Germany until sometime in March. Klein was in Germany himself at the time, and Dodd wrote him that "I certainly do not want you to wait around for me, especially since my schedule is so uncertain. Anyway, I have been thinking about this, and I believe that I might be more successful with the people in Germany if I talk to them alone. I don't think it is at all necessary for you to accompany me, and there is a chance that it might be misunderstood. You know how anxious I am to help you . . ."

Klein's reply was moody. He wrote Dodd that he had lost the Daimler-Benz contract and that the Flick syndicate had not yet renewed its agreement. He added that "the most important contract is the Committee for German-American Cooperation. This is my number one client and their contract is still in doubt. They fell into the trap opened up by the distortions in the German press as a result of the Fulbright hearings." Klein said news stories on the Fulbright hearings were "slanted in regard to my activities . . . as an attack on my industrial clients and the Federal Republic of Germany . . . What, if anything, can be done when you come to Germany is hard to say . . ." At one point, Klein would deny that the Committee for German-American Cooperation was subsidized by the Bonn regime, but later Dodd would discover that it was.

At any rate, Klein was petulant. He wrote: "Had I known that your schedule would have kept you in Washington, I would have asked either Senator Humphrey or Senator Symington to make a quick trip here on a weekend to speak on behalf of their Democratic colleagues, just as Javits did for Dirksen and others of his Republican colleagues . . ."

Among other things, this passage was pure Klein. One of his ploys was to go from one office to another in the Pentagon, chatting a bit, and then announcing that if he had any telephone calls he could be reached in the office of Secretary of Defense Robert McNamara.

Eventually, Dodd did get to Germany in April, 1964, and dutifully ran some errands for Klein, but before he did so he was soundly briefed—or brain-washed—by the public relations expert. In a "briefing memorandum" to Dodd, Klein told him to "Please ask for the following appointments when you are in Germany: (1) Chancellor

Ludwig Erhard. (2) Dr. Konrad Adenauer. (3) Dr. Hans Globke. (4) Dr. Heinrich von Brentano—former Foreign Minister. (5) State Secretary Karl Carstens—a Yale graduate. You met him in Washington. (6) Minister Gerhard Schroeder." Then Klein furnished a series of set speeches for Dodd to deliver to these Germans.

"I suggest, Tom, that you see each person alone," wrote Klein. "The Embassy would prefer this anyhow. This way you don't have to have a member of the German Foreign Office present, which would not be practical in view of the differences of opinion at the moment between the Chancellery and the Foreign Office . . . Also let Jack Javits brief you again; also Dirksen, Humphrey, Morse and Symington."

The speech Klein wrote for delivery by Dodd to Chancellor Erhard was a masterpiece of self-serving press agentry. It read, in part:

"We are very much disturbed to hear that due to the distortions in the German press and inaccurate reports that the role General Klein played in the political public relations field has been misunderstood . . . There has been no criticism of General Klein in connection with the Senate hearings. On the contrary, he received the praise and tribute from members of the Congress on both sides of the aisle . . . We in Congress who are working day and night have to rely on the assistance and help of General Klein in giving us proper briefings, research material and other vital information of interest to the United States in regard to the German Federal Republic . . . He has handled skillfully political public relations. He deserves not only our gratitude but yours and your continued support . . . we hope that this splendid relationship will continue . . . Your predecessor, Chancellor Adenauer, with whom we all worked, and former Foreign Minister von Brentano were pleased with the support and cooperation General Klein gave us at that time. We Democrats hope that will continue under your regime."

In his memo, Klein revealed that "Carstens [the German State Secretary whom Klein had mentioned to Dodd], was the man who gave support to the German group—the Society to Promote German-American Cooperation—that engaged me to handle political public relations . . . For your information, Carsten's office subsidized or contributed heavily to the Wiesbaden group [the SPGAC] which engaged me at the recommendation of Dr. Adenauer originally."

This was not the first time Klein served as a hopeful, self-appointed speech writer for Senator Dodd. In September, 1959, Klein had a member of his staff, Harry Blake, prepare an address which he told

Dodd to deliver on the occasion of Adenauer's tenth anniversary as German Chancellor. He instructed Dodd by letter: "As soon as you have edited the copy, please deliver it and have Jack Fleischer release it, not only to the American press, but also to the German correspondents accredited to the National Press Corps, and send a copy over to the German Embassy so that this will get widest circulation in Europe." Predictably, the speech mentioned Klein in a most kindly way. It noted that "The distinguished senior senator from New Hampshire . . . introduced into the Record a commentary by General Julius Klein on the mutual respect and confidence that had marked the relationship between our late Secretary of State, John Foster Dulles, Dr. Adenauer, and Foreign Minister von Brentano. General Klein's article was based on his personal acquaintance with Germany's government leaders and his knowledge of their high regard for Mr. Dulles."

Dodd did not deliver the speech. He explained in a letter to Klein that he did not have an occasion to do so "during the last crowded days of the session," but that he did make use of the "suggested draft" in a congratulatory message he sent Adenauer.

Over a period of years, the record showed, Klein managed to get endorsements from a number of members of Congress, including Dodd, House Speaker McCormack, Hubert Humphrey and Senators Dirksen, Javits and Morse, for a post on the American Battle Monuments Commission. He also rounded them up to support him for appointment to the U.S. Advisory Commission on Information. Klein didn't get either job, and he wrote Dodd petulantly, "You know, Tom, friendship is a two-way street."

When Dodd replied, "I am sure you will understand that I cannot guarantee any performance," Klein wrote back that he had never expected a guarantee. But he added, "As you can see, Speaker McCormack took the time to write me a letter in longhand."

Elsewhere, there were indications that Klein's pals on Capitol Hill were getting fed up with his importunities. Replying to a plea from Klein, Humphrey declined to write what the *Wall Street Journal* called "still another testament to the general's probity." He told Klein, "You have that in writing many times and you have demonstrations of respect by many personal acts on my part." But the Vice President did agree to attend a meeting in Dirksen's office with German Ambassador Heinrich Knappstein on January 10, 1964. A White House appointment prevented Humphrey from keeping the date, and Klein renewed his entreaties for a gesture of support.

Humphrey went along. "I would be more than pleased to sit down with you and the German ambassador so that we can have a good friendly discussion," he wrote Klein. "When you are speaking to some of your clients, I wish you would show them this letter. There is not a single thing in the reports of the Fulbright committee that indicates that you have done anything improper. To the contrary, those reports reveal that you have done a very good job of representing your clients . . ."

It is, of course, manifestly difficult for members of Congress to avoid the Julius Kleins who prowl the VIP corridors of Washington. After all, lobbyists for most foreign governments can present themselves as agents of friendly powers, and it is a legislator's duty to maintain contacts with persons who can offer them information unobtainable elsewhere. As Senator Javits once remarked, "I'm not afraid of foreign lobbyists. They're often quite useful to me. I couldn't afford to do the research necessary to obtain the information they hand out on a silver platter." Moreover, the State Department is not happy when it receives complaints that a Congressman has been rude to the lobbying representative of, say, South Africa, or refused to give him a hearing. Besides, America is still a nation of immigrants. When Italian Ambassador Sergio Fenoaltea was lobbying against Senator Dodd's firearms control bill, which among other things would have barred the importation of Italian guns, he had a lot of support from various Italian-American organizations.

In his monumental work, *The Lobbyists,* James Deakin put it simply: "All these men and women [the foreign agents] were exercising their Constitutional right to petition the government. The fact that they were doing it on behalf of others makes no difference . . . The right to petition government, guaranteed in the First Amendment, is a broad right. It includes the right to seek to influence legislation."

Thus it follows that a great deal of legislation passed by Congress is drafted or influenced by agents for foreign governments. They are professional witnesses before Congressional committees and they ghost-write a lot of the speeches heard on the floors of the Senate and House. The public relations firm of Selvage and Lee, Inc., which represented the Overseas Companies of Portugal, admitted writing speeches on Portuguese policy in Angola for fourteen legislators, including Rep. Joseph W. Martin Jr., Democrat of Massachusetts, former Speaker of the House. Selvage and Lee, said Deakin, boasted that Martin "used our stuff without change, apart from abbreviation."

Winston Churchill's popularity made it easy for a succession of British ambassadors to get what they wanted from the United States Treasury during and after World War II. West Germany's Embassy had a somewhat tougher time when Kurt-Georg Kiesinger, a former Nazi, ran for chancellor as the candidate of the Christian Democratic Party. Minister Georg von Lilienfeld, an old pal of Kiesinger's, broke the precedent which says embassies usually avoid involvement in politics by putting out a glowing biography of Hitler's former hired hand. Although Kiesinger never quit the Nazi Party, Lilienfeld effusively declared that Kiesinger was "deeply shocked and horrified by Hitler's sanctioning of the series of political assassinations committed by the Nazis in 1934, soon found himself more and more in opposition to the Nazi Party." Lilienfeld did not mention that Kiesinger continued to take Hitler's paychecks until the end of the war.

"The Germans tried to save money," commented one particularly astute practitioner of the foreign agent's art. "With a Churchill, you don't need any help. With a Kiesinger, you should hire someone like Charles Patrick Clark."

The point was well made. Charles Patrick Clark is the man who made Franco's Spain respectable, a feat which in the world of the upper-level press agent belittles the paltry endeavors of those who have sold ice boxes to Eskimos or the complete works of James Joyce to Billy Graham. Under Clark's skillful direction, the Congress between 1950 and 1962 approved loans to Spain totalling $1,711,300,000. It is no wonder that Franco's picture, hung with those of other dignitaries in Clark's office, is inscribed: "To Mr. Charles Patrick Clark, lawyer and advisor to the Embassy of Spain in Washington. With my recognition of a great work in the service of Spain. Francisco Franco."

Clark, whose lobbying business brings him two hundred thousand dollars a year, has earned as much as a hundred thousand dollars annually as agent for the Spanish government. He has been cheap at the price. It was Clark's subtle propaganda and influence with VIP's of all nationalities which got Spain admitted to both the United Nations and the Inter-Parliamentary Union, an association of international legislators. Although the Franco regime did everything short of firing shots in anger to help the Rome-Berlin Axis during World War II, Charles Patrick Clark managed to launch a massive aid campaign for Franco only five years after V-J Day.

Two of Clark's closest Congressional pals, Senators Owen Brewster,

Republican of Maine, and Pat McCarran, Democrat of Nevada, introduced a resolution in 1949 to lend Spain $100,000,000. With Clark working behind the scenes with Spanish Ambassador José Felix de Lequerica, the resolution only just failed to pass. However, a year later, the House and Senate agreed to give Franco $62,500,000.

Clark was an old friend of Harry Truman. He served the old Truman Committee, which investigated the national defense program during World War II, as associate chief counsel and acting chief counsel before resigning in 1942 to enter the Army as a private. Of Clark, Truman once said, "I am happy to say that as a public servant he has no equal." But Truman was opposed to aid for Spain, and so Clark concentrated on Congress, making hay with key committee chairmen. As a result, he not only got the loan for Spain but arranged matters so that for more than ten years Spain was one of the few nations for which American money was specifically earmarked in foreign aid bills. That is to say, the State Department and the foreign aid agency had no flexibility; the money had to go to Spain.

Like most foreign agents, Charles Patrick Clark admits that his contacts in Congress are most valuable. That, after all, is where the votes are. But he insists that he spends almost half his time in his office, doing research and preparing his presentations. "I may spend two or three weeks on research for a fifteen-minute appointment," he says. "I don't want to take up a man's time unless I'm prepared to offer him some information." Meanwhile, Clark restricts his grassroots propagandizing to occasional public speaking engagements, always armed with letters from a dozen or so members of Congress in which they vigorously support whatever views he expounds.

Like Julius Klein, Clark is an art collector whose tastes run to portraits of important people. Besides Franco's, the pictures on the walls of his office include those of Presidents Johnson, Kennedy and Truman, House Speaker McCormack, Senate Majority Leader Mike Mansfield, Senator John Sherman Cooper, Republican of Kentucky, King Ibn Saud of Saudi Arabia and Senator Stuart Symington. For years, Clark was host at an anniversary dinner for Harry Truman at Washington's posh Mayflower Hotel. At the 1961 dinner, Clark was flanked at the head table by President Kennedy, Mr. Truman and Vice President Lyndon Johnson. In 1963, Clark announced the establishment of a "Harry S Truman Chair of American History" at Westminster College in Fulton, Missouri, with a fund of $20,000 to endow the chair. In 1952, he punched Columnist Drew Pearson in the eye and was fined $25. He lives in a top-floor apartment in one of Washington's fashionable apartment houses, and keeps his coats on hangers made of red velvet with gold monograms.

If Clark throws in personality with his chores, most of the other agents of foreign governments concentrate on flooding the market with the propaganda of their principles. Selvage and Lee, for example, is an advocate of the printed word, multiplied millions of times. In 1963, the firm distributed 160,000 pamphlets, press releases, speeches and reprints of newspaper and magazine articles in behalf of the Overseas Companies of Portugal. All dealt with the sordid situation in Angola, where both Portuguese and natives indulged in an orgy of bloodletting. Among the material mailed out were reprints of a column by Robert Ruark and pamphlets with such titles as *The Communists and Angola* (Communist is *always* a good word), *Behind the Terror in Angola, Portugal and Her Overseas Provinces,* and *Angola: A Challenge and Opportunity.*

The agents, of course, are mouthpieces for the policies of their employers. Thus the Hamilton Wright Organization of New York was philosophical about the apartheid laws of South Africa when it was negotiating for a contract with that nation for a campaign estimated to cost between $150,000 and $350,000.

"Only a minority of people in the Western World itself probably appreciate South Africa's accomplishments in building a modern nation on the tip of Africa," Hamilton Wright Senior wrote Piet Meiring, director of the South African Information Service. "A smaller minority, certainly, understands Apartheid and how it is applied. . . . We believe that by concentrating on the actual progress of South Africa in its various endeavors—economy and investment, natural resources, culture and folklore, touristic attractions and social accomplishments—the best type of *positive* propaganda can be evinced . . . The scope of the audience we shall endeavor to obtain is worldwide . . . The tide of public opinion is flexible, but it needs material to bend with . . ."

Wright did not explain how he would reconcile apartheid with the South Africa regime's record of "social accomplishments." As a matter of fact, the Wright Organization's flirtation with South Africa got it into trouble with some of its other clients. During the 1963 Fulbright committee hearings, Wright admitted that officials of Nationalist China objected to the Wright Organization representing South Africa and that this was one of the reasons why the Formosa regime cancelled its contract with Hamilton Wright.

The Wright Organization also took pains to conceal from the South African government the fact it had a contract with the Ivory Coast government. In a cable to the Wright representative in Rome, Hamilton Wright Senior warned him to "Keep contract with Ivory Coast confidential, otherwise South Africa may quit."

"Was this contract kept confidential from South Africa?" asked Fulbright.

"No, they knew about it," replied Wright Senior. "I didn't care. It was such a small contract, it was a very small contract."

"If you didn't care, why did you send the cable?" asked Fulbright.

"Well, just for the nuisance value of it, just to avoid a lot of discussing and a lot of quoting," Wright Senior said.

There are, as Hamilton Wright Senior noted, "very small" contracts involved in this business of lobbying for foreign interests. But most of them are big ones. Charles Patrick Clark, for example, seldom touches a job for less than a $50,000 retainer fee. Selvage and Lee collected $500,000 for its campaign on behalf of the Portugal regime. But the biggest money changes hands during the periodic maneuverings for the allotment of sugar quotas to foreign nations. Under the present system, the United States buys guaranteed amounts of sugar from foreign producers at a price higher than that paid in the world market in an attempt to stabilize the market.

In any given year, the fees paid to registered lobbying agents by foreign sugar-producing nations will total just over one million dollars. The fees vary, depending upon whether Congress passes a two-year or three-year sugar law. For example, the Indian Sugar Mills Association agreed to pay the law firm of Dawson, Griffin, Pickens and Riddell $99,000, plus a maximum of $15,000 in expenses, if Congress passed a three-year law in 1962. Congress did just that. Mexico's sugar producers paid another law firm $50,000 a year for four years. During a fifteen-month period, the Colonial Sugar Refining Company of Australia paid a third firm $23,150.

Investigating the influence exerted by foreign agents on American foreign policy, the Senate Foreign Relations Committee turned its attention to the sugar lobby. It found that much of the big money paid American agents by foreign governments came from the American taxpayer's pocket. Many nations dip into foreign aid grants from Washington to hire lobbyists to argue their cases before Congress and the public.

Senator Fulbright found the Indian Sugar Mills Association's lobbying a case in point. He wondered how India, in view of its economic condition, could afford to pay that fat $99,000-plus to Dawson, Griffin, Pickens and Riddell. "In effect," said Fulbright, "we find ourselves in the strange position of paying to India large sums of United States dollars and then having large sums of those dollars paid to American citizens to influence the action of Congress . . ." He asked Under Secretary of State George Ball, "Doesn't this strike you as rather unusual?" Ball admitted he didn't think it was a "very attractive picture."

Then there was the case of Chairman Harold D. Cooley of the House Agriculture Committee, who for years was called the "Secretary of State for Sugar." Cooley, who was defeated for reelection in 1966, formerly doled out sugar quotas to foreign nations with all the authority of an absolute monarch. Lobbyists paid him constant court, especially assorted diplomats from the Dominican Republic, and Cooley was on cordial social terms with them. At any rate, in 1962— when Dictator Trujillo was still in power—the Dominican government offered Cooley an all-expenses-paid trip to the Dominican Republic. Cooley didn't go, but his sister, daughter and son-in-law did, as guests of Dominican sugar interests.

Although Trujillo's tame politicians had the cunning of sneak thieves, they seem to have been lost in the jungles of the legal lobbyists. They hired the Washington law firm of Surrey, Karasik, Gould and Efron to help increase their exports of sugar and paid the firm a fee of $95,000. The Senate Foreign Relations Committee gave the public a glimpse of one of the ways foreign agents work, when it put into the record a memorandum from Monroe Karasik, a partner in the law firm, to Jesus Maria Troncoso, then president of the Dominican Sugar Commission. It read:

"Through channels of personal obligation, we have made contact with a powerful law firm in the Senator's home state. The senior member of the firm is the executive officer of the Senator's political machine. The second partner is the son of the Senator's first campaign manager; there are very close family connections between this man and the Senator. The third partner is the private confidential attorney of the Senator; he handles important confidential matters for the Senator's machine.

"All three propose to call upon the Senator on Monday, January 30, to engage his sympathy for the position of the Dominican Republic with respect to sugar legislation. They will represent themselves as being interested purely because of their very close ties of friendship and business with my firm. Each of the three will adopt a different approach to arouse the Senator's sympathy.

"They ask for a retainer of $2500. In addition to this, they ask for a fee of $5000 if the Dominican allocation under the legislation, as finally enacted, is no less than that under the present House version . . . We believe that these lawyers can be effective in advancing the interests of the Dominican Republic and we accordingly recommend that the retainer fee be paid, and the contingent fee be agreed, all as outlined."

But when questioned by members of the Foreign Relations Committee, both Walter Surrey and Monroe Karasik said they didn't know who the senator was. "We were relying on you to know," commented Fulbright sadly. And Senator Bourke B. Hickenlooper, Republican of Iowa, growled "My disgust is complete."

Finally, the senator was identified by Samuel Efron, a former member of the law firm. He said the memorandum referred to Senator Harry F. Byrd of Virginia, since deceased. But all agreed that Byrd knew nothing about the little plan. The "powerful law firm in the Senator's home state" turned out to be Bendheim, Fagelson, Bragg and Giammittorio of Alexandria, but a spokesman for the firm said it was decided not to approach Byrd.

Efron explained: "I suppose Mr. Fagelson had told me certain things [about the Virginia law firm] and, perhaps, as is normal with lawyers, he may have puffed a bit. I may have puffed a bit to Mr. Karasik, he may have puffed a bit to Troncoso, and Troncoso may have puffed a bit to his government."

At the time, Senator Fulbright didn't seem to know what Efron meant by "Puffing a bit." Julius Klein could have explained it to the senator, and so could any other registered agent for a foreign government. It is one of the stocks in trade of the peculiar profession, and its principal ingredient is the casual dropping of names and places. Indeed, Fulbright later was offered a perfect example of the art during the committee's investigation of Michael Deane, another agent for the Dominican Sugar Commission.

Deane, it developed, had written his client, "I received an invitation from the President to attend a reception . . . at the White House." The invitation actually had been dispatched, routinely, by the Democratic National Committee. Deane explained, "Well Mr. Chairman, in your relationship with a client . . . you don't underplay your part . . . you tend to exaggerate a little."

In the world of Michael Deane and Julius Klein, it seems irrelevant that, by "puffing" the effects of their activities in behalf of their foreign clients, they might do more than boost the size of their fees. As Fulbright later put it, "The exaggeration by a lobbyist of his ability to control the processes of government in this country, when conveyed to a foreign client, can lead . . . to contempt on the part of the foreign client for United States institutions." Unfortunately, Fulbright neglected to add that too many representatives of United States institutions—not all of them named Tom Dodd—are pleased to stand still for this "puffing."

Growing Pains

13

Capital Without a Past

THE UNITED STATES has come far since January 10, 1781, when the Continental Congress created a Department of Foreign Affairs to deal, as Rhode Island's acidulous Elbridge Gerry put it, "with those foreigners." Indeed, the Department had no Secretary of State until 1790; no Cabinet post is mentioned in the Constitution and Cabinet members are merely Presidential agents serving at his pleasure. The first Secretary was Thomas Jefferson, who presided over an establishment renamed in September, 1789, the Department of State, consisting of five clerks, a part-time translator of French, and two messengers; the Foreign Service comprised legations at Paris and London, an agency at The Hague, six consulates and four vice-consulates. (There had been an American consul in Canton, China, before there was a United States.)

Like Elbridge Gerry, the Congress was inclined to belittle the importance of foreign relations. When the Department's name was changed its functions also were expanded to include various domestic duties, among them custody of the Great Seal of the United States, symbol of the nation's sovereignty. Besides handling foreigners, Secretary of State Jefferson was responsible for publishing the acts of Congress; making out and recording Presidential commissions to civil officers; filing all applications for Federal office; preserving the archives; operating the mint; issuing patents for inventions; receiving copies of all copyrighted material; publishing the census returns; corresponding with Federal judges, marshals and attorneys; and supervising terri-

torial affairs. In the years that followed, the Department was relieved
of almost all those early duties not related to foreign affairs.

Jefferson and the other early Secretaries of State lived and worked
among surroundings that were authentically backwoods compared with
European capitals. The State Department's first home was a twelve-by-
thirty-foot three-story brick building at 13 South Sixth Street, Philadelphia, which was the nation's capital until it was removed to the
newly-created city of Washington in 1800. In Washington, a desolate
wasteland of mud and wooden shacks, the Department first had quarters in the new two-story brick Treasury Building directly east of what
was then called the "President's Palace." By then its staff had been
expanded to eight clerks. During the next decade, the Department
moved twice—first to one of the so-called "Six Buildings," a row of
dwellings on the north side of rutty Pennsylvania Avenue between
21st and 22nd Streets, and then to the then newly-completed building
west of the "President's Palace," where it remained until British troops
burned the structure in August, 1814. State moved back when the
building was restored, and stayed there until 1947 when it moved to
"New State" in the old gashouse or Foggy Bottom district of Washington close to the Potomac River. An eight-story extension was occupied
in January, 1961, superseding the original structure as the Department's
"main building."

In the spring of 1967, there were 114 nations represented in Washington by ambassadors, ministers or chargés d'affaires, plus the acting
Consul General of Communist Estonia stationed in New York City. In
1800, the only countries represented were Great Britain, France, the
Netherlands and Spain. Denmark established its mission in 1801, Portugal in 1805, and Russia in 1809; there was no Netherlands mission to
the United States from 1802 to 1814. The rest of the civilized world
ignored the weanling Republic; indeed the so-called War of 1812 with
Great Britain seldom got little more than a short paragraph in English
newspapers and virtually no attention on the Continent except for the
self-seeking tirades in French journals. Even after the Battle of New
Orleans, Andrew Jackson remained unknown to the English public
until he was elected President fifteen years later.

Diplomats assigned to Washington regarded it as punishment. The
capital was officially listed as a hardship post in most European countries until well into the twentieth century because of its tropical summer heat and, earlier, its lack of such common conveniences as run-

ning water in its hotels. Predictably, those foreign envoys exiled there during its infant years found the city most disagreeable.

Edward Thornton, chargé d'affaires of the British Legation from November 28, 1800, to November 29, 1803, described Washington as "dismal—a wretched collection of hovels." In the dining room of Mrs. Suter's boardinghouse, where he lived, Thornton delivered himself one night of an impassioned and slightly drunken indictment of the capital as resembling "those Russian towns traced in the deserts of Tartary, in whose inclosures we behold nothing but naked fields and a few glimpses of houses." By coincidence or otherwise, the same description would appear in a book written by the Frenchman, Félix de Beaujour.

In those early days, all the diplomats lived in boardinghouses, along with high officials of the United States government, including the latest Secretary of State, James Madison; Secretary of the Treasury Albert Gallatin; Secretary of War Henry Dearborn; and John Marshall, fourth Chief Justice of the United States. Indeed, when Marshall arrived in Washington in 1801 he discovered that no provision had been made by the Congress to house the Supreme Court, and he convened the Court in a boardinghouse also occupied by Louis André Pichon, chargé d'affaires and "Commissioner General of Commercial Relations" of France.

This posed a peculiar problem for the Court, for Pichon was in the habit of beating his wife at all hours of the day and night, and her screams frequently distracted the justices in those early deliberations which would make indisputable the right of the Supreme Court to review federal and state laws and pronounce final judgment on their constitutionality. Informed that he was disturbing the Court, Pichon solved the problem by ordering his valet to play his flute whenever Madame Pichon was getting her comeuppances.

Pichon found Washington "hateful," filled with people "without a past . . . who are always boasting of what they will do because they can say nothing of what they have done." Although his language was sprinkled with the bedroom chatter of Versailles, Pichon affected to be shocked by Americans' profanity, which he accurately noted was "prevalent to a shocking extent." He also inveighed against the American habit of spitting, drunkenness in public, and "the remarkable virtue of the women." But he liked the Southerners with their quick tempers, their duels and their gambling. He also enjoyed horse racing and cock fighting and found attractive the "general dissipation of the landed gentry," mostly Southern.

Madame Pichon was a good-natured party-goer who loved her children but never let her pregnancies interfere with her social life. She told her American friend, Mrs. Margaret Bayard Smith, that she often went out "with the ague—sometimes with the fever on me" in order not to miss a soirée. Once both ladies were expecting at the same time. They agreed that "nothing will keep off the fit" and that they "may as well have it in one place as another." Mrs. Smith wrote a relative that she and Madame Pichon "seldom now go to bed" after a party, "but sit up or lie down on the sopha, have a bowl of tea and a basin by us, and then give no one further trouble, but take the fit with the greatest *sang froid.*"

The Britisher, Thornton, took notice of what he called the "peculiar use of many words or expressions" in America—"clever" for worthy or obliging; "smart" for clever; "I guess" for I suppose; "elegant" for excellent, "I reckon" for I think or I guess. But he admitted that even the "masses" spoke better English than many people in his native land. He said he heard nothing as bad as the Suffolk whine or the guttural of Newcastle. His chief complaint continued to be the physical state of the Federal City. In his letters home he spoke of it always as "this wilderness."

It was not quite that. At that time, the District of Columbia was a V-shaped green plain between the Potomac and East Branch rivers which merged into the blue, wooded hills of Maryland, and on the Potomac ended in high bluffs. Below these bluffs, Scottish immigrants in 1695 had established a trading port known as Georgetown, which by 1800 was doing a lucrative business with London, Liverpool and the West Indies. Besides Georgetown, there were in the area two other thriving port towns—Alexandria, or Bellhaven, on the Virginia bank, and Bladensburg, six miles up the East Branch. Most of the rest of the District was covered with large tobacco plantations, where the owners lived like English country gentlemen without England's manicured parks. But Washington city was a dreadful mess.

The city's population in the first decade of the nineteenth century probably never exceeded four thousand persons, and they lived with all the discomforts of a frontier town. They lived in small cottages, most of which were little better than log cabins, and Minister Thornton and the other diplomats and government officials performed their morning ablutions at the pumps stationed in every backyard. The streets were not really streets, but lanes. Even Pennsylvania Avenue, which the French engineer, Major Pierre Charles L'Enfant, visualized as a rival to the Champs-Elysées, was sprinkled with tree stumps and pockmarked with pot holes. There were no police and only a few broken stretches of sidewalk along Pennsylvania Avenue. There were still only three street lights—also on Pennsylvania Avenue—installed in 1801 at a cost of one hundred dollars.

Usually once a month, the diplomats made their way to an establishment which offered "Warm, Temperate and Cold Baths for the Use of the Citizenry—100 Cents." Both Thornton and Pichon thought the price too high, and also complained that they were being gouged for their meals. They found it scandalous that Suter's Tavern should charge thirty-five cents for a dinner that included roast beef, roast turkey and fried rabbit. Peder Blicher Olsen, the Danish Minister and Consul General, had a Puritanical comment on the city's vice. He suggested in a letter home that "although there are many prostitutes, the average person fortunately is unable to avail himself of their services, since they charge seventy-five cents for an evening's companionship." Carlos Martinez de Yrujo, Marquis de Case Yrujo, Envoy Extraordinary and Minister Plenipotentiary from Spain, seemed satisfied with his own romantic arrangements. As a regular guest of neighboring plantation owners, the Marquis availed himself of the pleasures afforded by some of the compliant slaves. He noted in his diary, however, that he insisted they be given "a good scrubbing" before he "approached them."

None of the diplomats seemed to be impressed with the "President's Palace" or the fare it offered. Both Thornton and Pichon complained about the lack of good wines. Thornton said it appeared that Americans had never heard of port, and Pichon made do with the new American whiskey, which he said "gave me terrible malaise in the mornings." The Dutchman, R. G. van Polanen, was appalled to find the Presidential laundry hanging in the great unfinished audience room, a chamber later to become famous as the East Room. He returned to The Netherlands in July, 1802, and it may have been his tales of the hardships encountered in Washington that prompted his government to delay dispatching a successor until 1814.

The mansion, which would not become the White House until it was painted after necessary repairs caused by its gutting by British arsonists in 1814, was impressive only on the outside. It was a modified Georgian residence of four stories designed by the Irish architect, James Hoban, after an Irish country home, and like the unfinished Capitol a mile up "The Avenue" it was built of Virginia sandstone from quarries recently opened at Acquia Creek by some friends of George Washington. Under the political circumstances, those who agitated to have the Capitol and mansion built of brick, in the Philadelphia fashion, didn't have a chance.

Thornton, Pichon and the rest of the tiny diplomatic colony were shocked to discover that not a single room in the mansion had been finished, and that there were no bells to summon servants. "In such a country, with its obsession with democracy, the servants probably would not come if summoned," Thornton noted. He also was dismayed to discover that the outdoor privies "lacked even the crude improvements of that offered by the lowliest tavern." The Marquis de Case Yrujo jokingly suggested that the mansion could be converted into a jail, "since its walls are quite thick," when the American colonies returned to the fold of the British Empire.

But by the time the fledgling nation decided to oppose militarily such a notion by grappling with Great Britain in the War of 1812, the "President's Palace" was in much better shape. James and Dolley Madison had moved into the mansion, and twenty-three of its rooms had been furnished in varied styles by Jefferson during his occupancy— Sheraton, Hepplewhite, Adams, the French Louis Quinze and Seize and Directoire—and much of it was gilded. Jefferson also had introduced cotton for draperies in the state rooms, and the floors were covered with painted canvas. Dolley Madison bought new sofas and high-backed chairs for the Oval Drawing Room, later renamed the Blue Room, and yellow damask draperies. She also installed the servants' bells that Abigail Adams had lacked, and bought a new rug for the main drawing room. When it arrived she thriftily sent the old one to the House of Representatives.

When food costs rose as a result of the unpopular war with England —the price of a turkey had soared to seventy-five cents, a whole pig was three dollars—ordinary folk criticized Dolley for her lavish spending on the mansion. But Dolley found a defender in the new French Ambassador Serurier, who lamented the penny-pinching of a Congress which prevented the First Lady from transforming the mansion "into an American Versailles."

Indisputably, Dolley Madison charmed Serurier. He approved of her house, her food and her dress, and praised her to the diplomatic colony as "worthy of belonging to a royal house." Serurier was especially delighted with Dolley's habit of offering male guests helpings of snuff from her lava snuffbox. He told one of his own dinner parties about the night Dolley shared her snuff with him and Kentucky's Congressman Henry Clay. When all three had had a dip, reported Serurier, Dolley fished out from a deep pocket in her dress a huge bandanna and after blowing her nose vigorously tucked it out of sight and flourished a dainty white lace handkerchief. She explained prettily that the bandanna was "for heavy work only," while the lacy square was her "polisher."

It was Serurier, together with the architect Benjamin Henry Latrobe, who had worked with Jefferson on improving the mansion and who persuaded Dolley to buy a state carriage of reddish brown trimmed inside with yellow lace. Dolley had wanted a black coach with red interior, but Serurier and Latrobe pointed out that black was too common and much too sombre for a lady of her cheerful disposition.

Serurier also tried to persuade Dolley to do more reading. He was unusual in that early day as a man who preferred intelligent women. But Dolley was charmingly candid. "Oh, I always read a lot at Montpelier," she told Serurier, "but I don't read a word here." He gave her a fine copy of *Don Quixote* to hold in her hand at parties so she would "have something not ungraceful to say and, if need be, to supply a word of talk."

In an age of gluttony, Serurier naturally was delighted with the dinners Dolley served at her soirées. They were meals calculated to separate the men from the boys—fried eggs, fried beef, roast turkey, roast beef, roast ducks, the new foreign dish "macaroni," trout, and several kinds of ices, cakes and tarts. And, "I am able to drink nothing but the finest French wines at the President's Palace," Serurier noted. President Madison tended to be abstemious, but it pleased Serurier to press French brandy on little Jemmy; "he is too sad, that one, "Serurier told his secretary. Meanwhile, in typical French fashion, he plied Madison with the latest gossip. When the British landed in Benedict, Maryland, and seemed about to march on Washington, Serurier told Madison he had heard that a British spy had visited Dolley disguised as a woman. Called over by her husband, Dolley found the report ludicrous. "I know personally all the females who have been in this house in the past six months," she said. "I shall not suggest which would pass as males, since that is not the point." Serurier was delighted; still, he asked, had not one heard of the spy who was "covered with leprosy, which was probably why he had turned traitor?"

Serurier lived almost as elegantly at home as he did at the "president's Palace." Not for him the boardinghouses of his predecessors; he was installed in Octagon House, just west of the Executive Mansion, which had been designed by William Thornton, one of the late-coming architects of the Capitol, for the capitalist Benjamin Tayloe. The house was not so much octagonal as it was partly triangular and partly circular, and it had a good deal of distinction. It was built of brick instead of the sandstone so politically popular in the government, and it had curving doors, window sashes and even curving window glass. An innovation was two small stoves in the wall of the vestibule which warmed winter guests on arrival.

At Octagon House, Serurier entertained lavishly, as often as not with tongue in Gallic cheek. Although he was Dolley Madison's complete slave, he found most others in American official life a trifle ridiculous and he enjoyed observing the antics of Cabinet officers, military men and Congressmen. Of Secretary of War John Armstrong, a man with a proven reputation for unreliability and undercover scheming, Serurier once remarked in an unwitting augury of the language of a later era that Armstrong "couldn't fight his way out of a burlap sack with a hatchet and a knife."

But Serurier was a gracious host, and guests always could be sure of a good time at Octagon House—a good time and a look at the latest feminine fashions, for the ladies of the capital were determined to impress the Frenchman. Occasionally, the guests were delightfully shocked by some of these fashions, as was the case on the appearance of the wife of a diplomat whom a more reticent—or more perfunctory—era seems to have left nameless.

This early-day jet-setter was described by Margaret Bayard Smith in one of her numerous letters to family and friends as "a scandal upon our fair city." She wrote that she saw no harm in speaking the truth: Madame———"has made a great noise here, and mobs of boys have crowded round her splendid equipage to see what I hope will not often be seen in this country, an almost naked woman." The lady's appearance at the Serurier party "was such that it threw all the company into confusion, and no one dar'd to look at her but by stealth;

the window shutters being left open, a crowd assembled round the windows to get a look at this beautiful little creature, for every one allows she is extremely beautiful. Her dress was the thinnest sarcenet and white crepe without the least stiffening in it, made without a single plait in the skirt, the width at the bottom being made of gores; there was scarcely any waist to it and no sleeves; her back, her bosom, part of her waist and her arms were uncovered and the rest of her form visible."

Next day the diplomat's wife had been invited to a tea by the wife of an American Congressman who "sent her word, if she wished to meet them there, she must promise to have more clothes on." Serurier was saddened by the reaction of his American friends. He had hoped, he said, to see the lady "even more unclothed at some future time."

Besides setting himself up as an arbiter of fashion and good taste, for which he had certain indisputable qualifications, Serurier also fancied himself as an expert on military affairs, for which status he had none. When the British were marching on Washington and nearing Bladensburg, he rode out to the bivouac of the capital's defender, Brigadier General William Henry Winder, to instruct that pusil-lanimous tin soldier to retreat to the center of Washington and there set up barricades. But President Madison was at the camp and told Winder to stay put, that if a battle was to be fought it must be fought at Bladensburg. Madison was right, of course. Almost any commander but Winder could have staved off the redcoats on that field. But when the British sent Winder's troops flying and poured into Washington, Serurier chided Madison with a collection of I-told-you-so's.

Madison may have been a trifle fed up with Serurier by then, for the Frenchman had spent most of his time before the battle lecturing the American military leaders on tactics. He even showed up at a council of war at the Navy Yard, presided over by Madison and attended by Secretary of War Armstrong, Secretary of the Navy William Jones, Secretary of the Treasury George Washington Campbell, Attorney General Richard Rush and General Winder.

The council probably was unprecedented in military history. News of its convening had spread through the city, and from time to time prominent citizens barged in on the session and stated their views on how the city could best be defended. Among them was the young lawyer, Francis Scott Key, who had been a violent opponent of the war but who had been converted into a fire-eating zealot by the British march on Washington. Key's metamorphosis eventually would lead him to write an unsingable national anthem to the music of a British drinking song.

Key tried to get the floor, but was gavelled down by the choleric General Armstrong, and Serurier thereupon launched into one of his lectures. Armstrong seemed uncertain of the protocol involved in squelching a diplomat and glanced over at Madison, who sought to interrupt Serurier's verbal flow. Serurier turned to Madison with an injured look on his face. "I pray you, sir," he begged, "Do not break in on my statement." Madison and the rest heard him out.

But Serurier was a good and loyal friend to the Madisons and America. When the Madisons had fled their "palace" and the British were about to put the torch to it, Serurier dispatched a note to the British commanders, General Robert Ross and Admiral Sir George Cockburn, pleading with them to spare the President's house. At the same time, so it should not be a total loss, Serurier asked that a guard be posted at Octagon House, saying that he feared mob rule.

When General Ross handed the note to the salty, brave and swaggering Cockburn, the admiral chortled. "That Serurier," he said. "He landed on both feet, the cat. Y'know, he represented Bonaparte too. Let us start a little blaze under his own feet."

Ross rejected this suggestion. He sat down at Madison's own desk in the mansion and wrote Serurier that unfortunately he could not accede to the Frenchman's request to spare the mansion because the British demanded revenge for the American burning of the Parliament buildings in Canada. But he gave Serurier assurance that the "King's Hotel" would be respected as though His Majesty were there in person, and to see to this a twenty-four-hour-a-day guard would be posted there. Serurier persisted with another note asking that the British leave the mansion undamaged as a sign of their "high civilization," but his messenger found the building already in flames and Ross and Cockburn departed. Next day, Ross called on the ambassador and shared a bottle of Serurier's Madeira while they chatted about the Peninsula campaign against Napoleon in which Ross had been one of the major heroes. Predictably, Serurier complained that the French had ignored his sound military advice during the Spanish adventure.

It was indicative of Serurier's intimacy with the First Family that when Dolley Madison returned to Washington from her hideout in the countryside after the British marched off to return to Benedict, she stopped first at Octagon House. Since dawn was just breaking, the servants had to rout Serurier from his bed. Sleepy-eyed and wearing a silk dressing gown, the Frenchman kissed Dolley's hand several times, sat her down to a *petit déjeuner* of coffee and croissants, and produced some official papers he had salvaged from the ruins of the mansion. Dolley had returned to the city in a farm wagon. Serurier helped her into his own ambassadorial coach so she could arrive at the F Street home of her sister, Mrs. Anna Cutts, in style. He also loaned her his own bedpan when a footman, come to escort Dolley to the Cutts home, confided to her that Mrs. Cutts was suffering from diarrhea and had misplaced "that utensil so needed at this moment."

America, as an independent country, was then only thirty-eight years old and had few friends in the chancelleries of the world. As an ally, the France which had recently restored a Bourbon to the throne was casually contemptuous of the upstart Republic, and indeed had sided with Washington solely to add to the bedevilment of John Bull. But it might be said that Ambassador Serurier, comfort-loving and hedonistic, made the supreme sacrifice for his *bons amis*. His sense of propriety could not tolerate the thought of Jemmy and Dolley Madison living like poor relatives with the Cutts, and so he turned over Octagon House to the First Family to occupy until their "palace" had been restored. It was there that Madison heard of Jackson's victory at New Orleans on January 8, 1815, and it was there, a month later, that the peace treaty signed at Ghent was delivered to him by Henry Carroll, one of the secretaries of the American peace delegation.

Serurier was one of the first to hear the news of the peace. He was content, for reasons perhaps peculiarly intelligible to a Frenchman. "Perhaps," he said, striking just a slight pose, "I contributed to Mr. Madison's comfort while he waited for victory to rise from the ashes of defeat." And with that touch of Gallic gallantry that so often begins with the gullet and proceeds to the stomach, he sent his coachman to Octagon House with some bottles of champagne and a new pâté a friend had discovered in Provence.

14

The Civil War
and Lord Lyons

RICHARD BICKERTON PEMELL, Lord Lyons, Minister to Washington from the Court of St. James, found his British imperturbability shaken by the proposal of his colleague, French Minister Henri Mercier. After a champagne lunch in a private room at the Willard Hotel, Mercier had shown Lyons a dispatch he was sending to his government urging that the major European powers act together to recognize the Southern Confederacy.

Lyons was not unreceptive to such a move, but he viewed it rather as a possibly desirable eventuality. In March, 1861, Queen Victoria's man felt the hour was yet too early for jumping. Moreover, he was startled by Mercier's proposal to Paris that if recognition was not forthwith granted, France and Great Britain should authorize their Washington representatives to do so should such action suddenly be deemed necessary. To forty-four-year-old Lyons, this smacked of the kind of free-lance diplomacy chilling to his proper, Whitehall-nourished soul.

At that juncture, Lyons took the action that quite possibly established the British policy of watchful waiting which was to preserve peace between Britain and the United States throughout the long years of the Civil War. He wrote to Lord Russell, Queen Victoria's Secretary for Foreign Affairs, and suggested that the Commissioners from the Confederacy, then en route to London, be greeted with polite and noncommittal restraint. Russell, grandfather of the Bertrand Russell whose penchant for radical causes would cause such a stir a hundred years later, adopted Lyons' policy and followed it thereafter in his dealings with the Confederacy.

It would not be unpardonable hyperbole to suggest that Lord Lyons was one of the unsung heroes of the Civil War. This red-faced British aristocrat with a love of fine wines and good living was the epitome of the traditional diplomat who saw his mission as that of keeping his country out of any trouble which might not serve its long-range interests. Unlike Ormsby-Gore, who had so much influence on the young Kennedy a century later, Lyons had no intimate relationship with either President Lincoln or Secretary of State William H. Seward. Indeed, he suspected almost from the start that Seward sought to use the threat of war with England to cover up internal dissensions. But he had the quality of common sense for which diplomats are not always noted, and he spent the war years making compromise as easy as possible for both Lincoln and Seward—always leaving a line of retreat open, always providing the opportunity for face-saving. His diplomatic skills, his judgment and his almost incandescent honesty made it possible for him to save the peace on many critical occasions when blood on both sides was boiling over incidents at sea or the threat of armed collision over Canada.

This is not to say that young Lyons was utterly charmed by America. He found Washington a dreary place with its muddy streets and wildly careening carriages, and he inveighed against the city's "atmosphere of heat, noise, dust, smoke and expectoration." He wrote that Washington was a poor place for young men, having no clubs, no good restaurants, no permanent theater or opera. However, he noted, there were "filthy saloons in profusion and a dreary collection of brothels." He hated the Willard Hotel because the only way a man could dine in comparative privacy was to engage a private room, and he found it strange that the only built-up section of the city was in the area between the Capitol and the White House. He found it small consolation that he received hardship pay for working in a tropical city. The extra money, he said, made breathing no easier in the humidity and dust storms of Washington's summers.

Yet Lord Lyons had been wrong, or perhaps merely very British, when he told his London friends he was being "exiled to a frontier nation." He found an America in which the Industrial Revolution was a fact of life and whose sinew had burgeoned to the point where Old Europe feared its effect on the balance of power. Indeed, Lord Russell was warning his conservative colleagues almost daily that the United States had become a growing threat to Britain's worldwide influence. It was not only sentiment which caused many Britons to side with the South but the hope that a divided America would be less trouble to the world's status quo.

America was beginning to fill up with people. In 1861 the country had a population of 31,513,000, and although Washington's streets were alternately muddy and dusty, the still-unfinished capital bulged with 75,000 inhabitants. Diplomatically, the world acknowledged the new importance of the Republic. Besides the British Legation, there were twenty-six other foreign missions in Washington, and newly-independent Liberia would send the twenty-eighth in 1864. The names on the doors of these legations testified as to how the world had changed in a quarter of a century. They included those of the new nations of Latin America, which had driven out their European masters—Brazil, Chile, Colombia, Costa Rica, Ecuador, El Salvador, Guatemala, Haiti, Honduras, Mexico, Nicaragua, Peru and Venezuela. All these countries represented the new influence of the United States, which had been the first to break away from the Old World. In a sense, too, they represented the revolt against slavery which lay behind the great issue of the American Civil War.

Consequently, Lyons' distaste for his American surroundings did not influence his cold-eyed detachment, his dedication to Lord Palmerston's thesis that England had no allies, only interests. He was well aware of England's stake in the war and of the obviousness of the arguments of those Englishmen who growled that Britain's industrial establishment needed Dixie's cotton. But he found these arguments a trifle too obvious. He insisted on hedging his country's bet against the possibility of a Union victory. Lyons was honest, but never altruistic; he wanted to make certain he got the best possible deal for England.

The South needed England as a warehouse from which to obtain the manufactured goods, ships and armaments necessary to the conduct of the war. For its part, England did not *need* the South, but found its business both useful and profitable. The South was a major source of income for rich English businessmen with interests in shipping and cotton, and its welfare was of importance to the old landed aristocracy because its secession challenged the vigorous, upstart republic which threatened England's position as a world power. Most of these titled folk had never forgiven the American colonies for their secession from the Mother Country; they distrusted the spread of democracy and wanted to put a stopper on its fountainhead across the Atlantic.

And yet there was a bone in England's throat—slavery. By then, Great Britain was almost completely anti-slavery. It had abolished the "peculiar institution" in 1833 at great cost, and twenty years later Harriet Beecher Stowe's *Uncle Tom's Cabin* had had a tremendous effect on Englishmen of all classes. While sympathetic to the South and repelled by the "Philistinism" of the North, scores of intellectuals refused to support a system based on slavery—Robert Browning, John Morley, T. H. Huxley and John Stuart Mill among them. Matthew Arnold was outspokenly pro-Southern, and so was Sir Edward Bulwer-Lytton, inheritor of a great family fortune. Dickens called down a plague on both houses—the South for its slavery and the North for its vulgarity.

All this intellectual ferment was merely window dressing, however. As in so many other international circumstances, the English politician and diplomat put their nation's welfare above glandular or cerebral considerations. Lord Palmerston, the Prime Minister, was a mixture of liberalism and old-school conservatism. He opposed slavery, but he was loyal to his own class, and that class was pre-eminent in Dixie. As a member of a Coalition Government, Palmerston could not afford to take chances, but he hoped the South could make secession stick and he listened sympathetically to the commissioners dispatched to London by the Confederacy. Happily for the Union, Lord Russell, the Foreign Minister, not only opposed slavery but suffered from a guilt complex. He blamed England for having forced slavery upon America when it was still a colony. Russell's sensitivity thus was a counterbalance to Palmerston's resentment of the North. Furthermore, Russell had the cool, suave and clear-thinking Lord Lyons to advise him.

Like the true diplomat he was, Lyons set a high priority on keeping his government informed. By the time he arrived in Washington in 1859, the transatlantic cable, which had been put into operation in August, 1858, already was a costly joke. It had failed a few days after its commissioning and would not be restored to service until 1866. Lyons therefore sent his dispatches via the *Great Eastern* steamship, which crossed the Atlantic in nine days, or by telegraph to St. John's, Newfoundland, where they were picked up by other ships which would deliver them to the telegraph station in Galway, Ireland, in six days.

Lyons supervised a corps of highly competent British consuls. Perhaps the most outstanding was Robert Bunch, who was stationed in Charleston, South Carolina and about whose intelligence reports Lord Russell remarked that "Bunch keeps me better informed than Lincoln is about what's going on over there." Shortly, however, Russell would be in need of services more vital than those of a perceptive reporter. Events were building up to the *Trent* Affair.

Aware of the importance of selling the Confederacy to England, President Jefferson Davis in March, 1861, dispatched three commissioners to London—William Lowndes Yancey, Ambrose Dudley Mann and Pierre A. Rost. Writing from Charleston, Bunch gave Yancey and Mann the rough side of his pen. He described Yancey as "impulsive, erratic and hot-headed . . . [who favors] a revival of the Slave Trade," and Mann as "the son of a bankrupt grocer . . . a mere trading politician possessing no originality of mind." Rost, said Bunch, was " a respectable sugar planter," but otherwise lacking distinction.

Bunch's appraisal of the three men was on the button. They spent six months in London and Paris without accomplishing much more than being seen frequently in the right clubs. So in August the Confederate government appointed James M. Mason Minister to the Court of St. James, and John Slidell envoy to France. Mason, a former chairman of the Senate's Foreign Relations Committee, and Slidell, a Louisiana politician, sailed to Havana in mid-October and transferred to the English mail steamer *Trent* for the Atlantic passage.

Captain Charles Wilkes, commanding the U.S.S. *San Jacinto,* learned that Mason and Slidell had boarded the *Trent* and sailed his vessel into the Old Bahama Channel to intercept the British ship. Wilkes was a sometime Antarctic explorer who hated the English because they had used some of his material on Antarctica without giving him credit. When the *Trent* came in sight, Wilkes fired two shots across her bows to convince her captain he meant business, then sent a boarding party to arrest the two Confederate envoys.

The *San Jacinto* made port at Fort Monroe, Virginia, on November 15 and put its prisoners ashore for transfer to Fort Warren in Boston. Washington and the rest of the North went wild with jubilation upon hearing the news of the capture, and the newspapers rang with editorial praises of Captain Wilkes, who was hailed as "the hero of the

Trent." At the British Legation, Lord Lyons' staff fluttered with disapproval, but Lyons himself remained calm. He sent off a long dispatch to the Foreign Office, then refused to make any statement to the American press.

"I suppose," Lyons wrote a friend, "I am the only man in America who has expressed no opinion whatever on the International Law question or on the course which our Government will take."

England reacted more vigorously and with no equivocation about the course the government should take. It was England's duty, declared an aroused citizenry, to bring the American pirates to their knees. More mildly, the Law Officers of the Crown opined that Wilkes had acted in violation of law by not seizing the *Trent* and bringing her into an American prize court for adjudication. Her Majesty's lawyers seemed to be saying that the insult to Britannica had not been serious enough.

Foreign Secretary Russell was delighted to find Secretary of State Seward on the wrong side of the law after having suffered through so many impertinent communications from this Yankee upstart. He drew up an ultimatum to the American government, demanding release of the Confederate envoys, an apology and reparations. Lord Lyons was told that if the demands were not met within seven days he was to leave Washington. On the advice of Albert, her Prince Consort, Queen Victoria modified the ultimatum to express the hope that Captain Wilkes had not acted under instructions. Meanwhile, Lord Palmerston ordered eight thousand British troops to Canada, and the Atlantic Fleet went on a war footing.

Here, with both British and American governments filling the air with war whoops, Lord Lyons and his soft-spoken horse sense took over. He called on Seward with the ultimatum on December 20 and found the Secretary of State much sobered and—as Seward later recounted —filled with memories of what the British had done to Washington in 1814. On his own, Lyons told Seward he was sure the Secretary could understand England's feelings, which were only those the United States would have in similar circumstances.

Lyons appealed to Seward's chauvinistic vanity, to what he knew was the Secretary's passion to have the United States recognized as England's peer. "Your country and mine are both powerful," he told Seward. "But they are also proud and sensitive. Let us neither be guilty of petty actions. This is a time for the United States to show

its acknowledged greatness by standing above pettifogging bickering."
Then he said he would leave the dispatch for Seward to study before
they began any formal discussions.

Seward was grateful for this opportunity to strike a noble pose.
He locked himself in his office and composed a reply notable for its
temperance and lofty thoughts. The United States, he said, would
continue to follow its high principles regarding the rights of neutrals,
principles for which it had always fought. Captain Wilkes' action was
disowned and the prisoners were ordered released. Lincoln was relieved. He called in Lord Lyons to praise him for his "courtesy and
understanding" and confided to intimates that he had known from the
start that "the traitors would be white elephants. We fought Great
Britain for insisting on the right to do precisely what Captain Wilkes
has done."

As an upper-class Briton of impeccably aristocratic background,
Lyons might have been excused—in that era—for looking down his
nose at Seward, the hard-fisted yet curiously idealistic New York politician. But Her Majesty's Minister refused to permit his feelings to
influence his dealings with the Secretary. He appreciated Seward's
shrewdness and driving force and knew he could not handle him
merely by that show of social superiority British diplomats employed
throughout the world. And he realized Seward's ambitions made him
a threat to Britain, as he revealed in a letter to Lord Russell on
January 7, 1861, two months before Lincoln took office.

"I cannot help feeling that he will be a dangerous Foreign Minister," wrote Lyons. "His view of the relations between the United
States and Great Britain has always been that they are a good material
to make political capital of . . . The temptation will be great for
Lincoln's party, if they be not actually engaged in a civil war, to
endeavour to divert the public excitement to a foreign quarrel. I do
not think Mr. Seward would contemplate actually going to war with
us, but he would be well disposed to play the old game of seeking
popularity here by displaying violence towards us . . ."

Lyons turned a kindlier eye on Lincoln, although throughout his
Washington stay he seemed always to be questioning whether this
strange-looking man could do the big job set out for him. He called
Lincoln "good-natured, kindly and honest," but added that a person
meeting the President "would not take him to be what in European
society is called a gentleman." Yet, said Lyons—with a kind of puzzled

admiration—even the most indifferent observer "would find it impossible to pass Mr. Lincoln in the street without notice."

At the State Department, described by the correspondent for *The Times* of London, William H. Russell, as "a dingy mansion, two stories high," Lyons conferred often with Seward, and was fascinated by the Secretary's aggressive air. Reporter Russell described this air as a "peculiar attitude . . . a well-formed and large head projects over the chest in an argumentative kind of way, as if the keen eyes were seeking for an adversary." Long before the age of psychiatry, Lyons wondered if this attitude were not "defensive."

Making his diplomatic rounds, Lyons also encountered some of the more colorful figures in the Washington bureaucracy, including the picturesque Kentucky Abolitionist, Cassius M. Clay, who became Lincoln's envoy to Russia. Clay regaled Lyons with tales of the numerous duels he had fought and gave the Britisher demonstrations in State Department corridors of his skill with the bowie knife. In Russia, Clay would meet the challenge of two Russian noblemen to a duel by landing a roughhouse on the jaw of one of his challengers and would not thereafter be harassed.

Then as now, the diplomatic corps was a clannish lot; the French Minister Mercier commented sardonically that he and his colleagues "huddled together for civilized warmth." Lyons, Mercier and the Russian Minister, Baron Edouard de Stoeckl, often pooled their expense accounts to hire a carriage together for White House parties, where Lyons exclaimed over the lavish hand of Mrs. Lincoln. At one soirée in December, 1861, Mrs. Lincoln was not content with the local caterers and engaged the famed Maillard of New York to feed her guests. Maillard showed up with a retinue of chefs, cooks and waiters and prepared a feast which Lyons found "Lucullan, with overtones of Caligula." The tables creaked under the load of a ton of turkeys, venison, pheasants, partridges, duck and hams, and there was a fountain supported by a group of water nymphs fashioned out of nougat. Both American whiskey and imported wines were available, plus a vast Japanese punchbowl brimming with ten gallons of champagne punch. Fort Pickens and the American ship *Union* were done in sugar. King George III, suggested Lyons, "little knew what he wrought," as he sampled a charlotte russe from a hive swarming with imitation bees.

By the time the new year 1862 dawned, Lyons had received the Grand Cross of the Bath for his work in what one historian called "doing everything possible to make the pill [of the *Trent* affair] as easy to swallow as possible" for the Americans. Yet the British continued to prepare for war against a change of mind by the flighty Seward. Seward baffled London by still another noble gesture when he offered to permit British troops to cross Maine by rail in order to avoid delays caused by the icebound St. Lawrence River. The British War Office was thrown into consternation by this turning of the other cheek, first refused to consider the offer, and then huffily agreed to ship its non-military supplies by train. In all, eighteen thousand troops were transported from England to Canada to keep the Yankees loose at the plate.

Lyons, meanwhile, tinkered with the job of playing both ends against the middle. He considered it his pragmatic, diplomatic duty to keep lines open to the Confederate capital in Richmond. Under Foreign Office orders, he instructed his Charleston consul, Bunch, to arrange "suitable" communications with Jefferson Davis' regime and to do his best to convey to the Confederate administration the assurance that England was keeping an open mind on recognition.

Bunch probably did no more than ordered, but he got caught. A dispatch bag he was sending to the Foreign Office fell into the hands of Union agents, and with it some two hundred private letters carried by the man to whom Bunch had given the official pouch for delivery. All the letters were from Southerners with relatives or friends in England, but one of them indiscreetly mentioned Bunch's negotiations in Richmond and revealed that Bunch had let it be known that England had taken "the first step of recognition."

Seward was furious. His slight, feeble frame quivered with nervous anger, and he summoned Lyons to his office for a tongue-lashing. Such a letter, he told Lyons, was "treasonable material" and very nearly constituted grounds for war. Lyons would admit later that he realized he was in deep trouble, but he kept his aplomb. Bunch, he said, was obeying instructions, but perhaps had overstepped his authority in an attempt to placate those Southern politicians who had been yammering for British recognition. If the report of Bunch's assurances in the letter was true, Lyons said, Bunch was being utterly unrealistic. Her Majesty's government had no plans to recognize Richmond. Lyons was speaking from instinct, but his instinct accurately reflected his government's official posture. Seward discovered the incident was a boon to the North when the American Ambassador to England, Charles Francis Adams, received a note from Foreign Secretary Russell declaring that "Her Majesty's Government have not recognized and are not prepared to recognize the so-called Confederate States as a separate and Independent State." It was Lyons who had planted this bug in Russell's ear.

England's attempts to play clandestine footsie with the South were partly due to the pressure maintained on Lord Palmerston, the Prime Minister, Foreign Secretary Russell and Lyons by that mouthpiece of English aristocracy and Big Business, *The Times*. From the very first, *The Times* had favored the Confederacy as a means to Britain's end of keeping the United States in its place—which was to say, well below Great Britain's lofty perch. Throughout the war, its editor, John Thadeus Delane, waged a war of vilification against the Lincoln administration and, with that maddening disregard for facts that characterizes certain editors all over the world, consistently maintained that slavery was not the issue, but states' rights. Delane apparently had not noticed that the development which sent the South plunging into secession was not any attempt by the Union to force its will on Dixie but the loss of a Constitutional election, legally conducted.

The New York *Herald*'s editor summed up the viewpoint of *The Times* and its well-heeled cronies:

"John Bull has so long been accustomed to look at the world through his commercial and manufacturing eyes that he can see nothing but huge granaries with which to replenish his coffers . . . True, he pays for all these luxuries, but he must have them, and if anything interferes with their production he is in a sad way, and sometimes he gets riled . . . He is so accustomed to have all his wishes obeyed—whether political or commercial—that he regrets times are not now as they were in the days when George the Third was king."

Lyons' comment was more wry. "The South has gentility and cotton fields," he wrote Lord Russell, "whereas the North has bombast and swagger. But I fear these are not yet valid reasons for backing what may turn out to be the wrong horse."

Meanwhile, France was edging closer to recognition of the Confederacy. Its cotton textile industry was hurting from the shortage of cotton in 1862 and Mercier, the French Minister in Washington, was bombarding Paris with recommendations for immediate recognition—in order, he implied, to steal a march on England and thus assure a better deal for French cotton buyers. With both England and France

thus looking south, Russia was the only major European power which
supported the Union cause. It was not that St. Petersburg had any
friendly thoughts about democracy—even the new and more liberal
Alexander II bolstered the absolutism of his monarchy—but that the
Russians were still angry at the French and British. The Crimean War
had ended less than ten years earlier, and the Russians were not about
to forgive the two perfidious Western powers which had fought on
Turkey's side.

Ambassador Cassius Clay's arrival in St. Petersburg coincided with
the dispatch by Foreign Minister Mikhailovich Gortchakoff of a long
letter proclaiming Russia's undying friendship for the Union. Wrote
Gortchakoff to Baron de Stoeckl in Washington: "The American
Union is . . . a nation to which our August Master and all Russia have
pledged the most friendly interests, for the two countries, placed at the
extremities of the two worlds . . . appear called to a natural community of interests and of sympathies . . . The American nation may
count upon the most cordial sympathy on the part of our August
Master during the important crisis which it is passing through."

Stoeckl dropped the hint to Seward that he might be able to get
permission from St. Petersburg to have the letter released to the general public. Lincoln was delighted with the suggestion; the letter, he
told Seward, would make good propaganda all over the world. Meanwhile, Stoeckl had revealed the contents of the letter to both Lyons
and Mercier, who were not pleased; they felt Russia was letting down
its own kind.

Shortly thereafter, the letter was published by newspapers all over
the world, including *The Times* in London, which adopted a surly
editorial tone seeming to imply that Alexander had betrayed his class.
Lyons found it ironic that an absolute monarchy should have words of
sympathy for the Union when England's constitutional monarchy remained silent. As a diplomat who preferred to have his own country
call every turn, Lyons felt—as he told the sly Mercier—that Russia
had been "spiteful."

Mercier, a slender dandy with finely-tonsured handlebar mustache
and sideburns, was bustling about Washington, his head full of
schemes. Mercier's Emperor Napoleon III had visions that would serve
both his imperialistic aims and his hopes of splitting the troublesome
United States permanently in half. When in April, 1862, England and
Spain withdrew from the tripartite occupation of Mexico, Napoleon

saw a clear path ahead. Mercier, then, was charged with arranging a personal meeting with Confederate leaders in Richmond in order to obtain assurances that the Confederacy would not interfere in any French move to take over Mexico.

Any doubts Mercier might have had about official Washington's reaction to his plan to visit Richmond were dispelled by the cunning Seward, who gave him the necessary pass despite Mercier's flimsy story that he was travelling south on business for French tobacco interests. "It'll do Mercier good to go to Richmond," Seward told Lincoln. "He believes the South will win this war, but a short stay in Richmond should convince him to the contrary."

Her Majesty's Minister Lyons was not so sanguine. In line with the policy of acting in concert with England, Mercier consulted Lyons about his visit, and Lyons smelled a rat. His suspicions about Napoleon's intentions concerning Mexico were vague, but he was convinced that France was trying to make a deal to get cheap cotton in return for recognizing the Richmond regime. Lyons could not object to the visit, of course. But he wrote Russell that Mercier was "up to something sly."

In Richmond, Mercier did most of his conferring with Secretary of State Judah P. Benjamin, whom he had known well when Benjamin sat in the Senate as a representative of Louisiana. Benjamin spoke fluent French, which no Union official ever encountered by Mercier could boast, and he had a suave, almost Caribbean charm. They talked about the possibility of an alliance between a French Mexico and the Confederacy that would break the Union power forever, and of the mutual prosperity that would accrue from an "arrangement" between industrial France and the agricultural South. Mexico was to be a sort of joint colony, to be exploited by both.

But the two men also discussed the course of the war, and Mercier returned to Washington convinced that the Confederacy would fight on to the last man and the last square inch of Southern soil. Avoiding the subject of Mexico, Mercier gave Lyons a fill-in on Benjamin's war talk, and Lyons reported the discussion deadpan to Lord Russell.

Mercier, he told the British Foreign Secretary, was convinced that recent events had increased the Confederacy's confidence and resolution. He quoted Mercier as saying that "If the Confederates are worsted anywhere they will still not surrender. They will destroy their stores of cotton and tobacco and all other property which they cannot remove. They will retire into the interior of their country and defy the North to follow them. Their unanimity and devotion to the cause are wonderful." Seward later told Lyons that Mercier had reported to him on conditions in Richmond and that as a result he (Seward) believed the Confederacy was about to launch its last effort. "I suppose," Lyons told Russell, "the truth lies somewhere between M. Mercier's views of the prospects of the South and Mr. Seward's."

At any rate, Mercier continued to connive with various Confederate leaders until the day in 1864 when Napoleon III installed the Hapsburg archduke, Maximilian, as Emperor of Mexico. With the war still on, Lincoln and Seward wisely decided to leave the Mexican situation to time and the aroused partisans of Benito Juarez. "Why should we gasconade about Mexico when we are in a struggle for our own life?" Seward wrote to John Bigelow in Paris. Three years later, Maximilian's French troops were defeated by a rebel force and he was shot, whereupon the flimsy fabric of Mexico's French "empire" collapsed.

The contrast between Mercier's grandiose dreams of empire and Lyons' hardheaded thinking was striking. An excellent judge of men, Lyons' reports on the military situation were almost as valuable as the thoughts he contributed on diplomatic matters. Lyons was much in favor of a move in Parliament in the spring of 1862 to arrange for mediation of the war by Britain, France and other European nations. Confederate sympathizers in England favored the move, too, for they saw as its result the division of the Union. But despite excellent advice from Lyons, which reflected his lack of confidence in the Union's heroic young general, George B. McClellan, the British government put off action because it believed McClellan would soon take Richmond.

Lyons had written Russell that McClellan would get to Richmond, all right, but wouldn't be able to capture the capital of the confederacy. Still, the British refused to move, especially after Robert E. Lee had replaced the wounded General Joe Johnston as commander of the Confederate armies in Virginia. Lee, said the British politicians, was untried. Lee, of course, promptly proceeded to push the indecisive McClellan around and save Richmond. The war, Lyons told Russell, "has become one of separation or subjugation." He added, "We have a very small chance of getting cotton from this country for a long time to come."

In the summer of 1863, when England was swept by a new wave of pro-Southern sentiment, and crusty peers in the House of Lords were bellowing demands that the country give military aid to the gallant South, Lyons once again offered cool and wise counsel. He was among those members of the Washington diplomatic corps who accepted Secretary Seward's invitation to tour New York State by private railroad car, and he was impressed by what he saw of the North's agricultural bounty and industrial might.

"The South's resources cannot compare with what I have seen," he wrote Lord Russell. "After more than two years of major warfare, the Union's production machinery is not only unimpaired, but its capacity has been mightily increased." Russell passed the word to some of the more obstreperous war hawks, and England resumed its policy of watchful neutrality.

On that tour, Seward hinted to Lyons that he would consider an invitation to visit England. Lyons found the idea amusing. He wrote Russell that if Seward "considered himself as returning the Prince of Wales's visit [before the war] the absurdity of the notion would alone prevent its being offensive . . . He has so much more vanity, personal and national, than tact, that he seldom makes a favourable impression at first. When one comes really to know him one is surprised to find much to estime and even to like in him."

Russell replied with amiable off-handedness that the time was not ripe for Seward to visit England—"I do not see my way to anything satisfactory."

By the autumn of 1864, both the war and Lord Lyons' brilliant tenure in Washington were drawing to a close. The Confederate armies were losing their men in battle and the Confederate dollar was losing its value in the international countinghouses. Lyons would be returning to London at the end of the year en route to his new post in Constantinople. But he still had one last, dramatic service to perform for his country—and for the United States.

During that autumn, the Confederacy launched a desperation campaign of terrorism, guerrilla warfare and sabotage from the sanctuary of Canada. Hit-and-run bushwackers burned river steamers in St. Louis, set fires in several Northern cities and robbed a number of banks. Then on October 18, a band of twenty men under the command of Bennett H. Young, a onetime Morgan raider, held up the town of St. Albans, Vermont, and took $200,000 from its three banks.

There was a shooting fight when the marauders set fire to several buildings, and a number of townspeople were wounded. The Confederates fled across the Canadian border, pursued by an irate posse, and after a tense confrontation with Canadian authorities, the posse was forced to withdraw while the Canadians took the raiders into custody.

Lyons was attending a dinner in New York at which a fiery general named John A. Dix was one of the principal speakers. During the dinner, Dix received a telegram telling him of the raid, and he immediately telegraphed orders to send a military force after the guerrillas and "if they cannot be found on this side, pursue them into Canada and destroy them." An uninhibited type, Dix announced the action he had taken to the dinner guests.

Lyons was appalled. England was already nervous about the North's massive military might, and London politicians tossed nightly on their beds at thoughts of a possible threat to Canada. Lyons knew that if an American military force crossed the Canadian border, war was all but certain. When Dix told him his orders had not been authorized by Washington, Lyons immediately left the dinner and telegraphed Seward, asking the Secretary of State if he was aware of the situation. Seward sat up in bed to dictate a telegram revoking Dix's order and sent a representative to Canada to talk over the contretemps.

Lyons undoubtedly was pleased by the commendation he received from Lord Russell for his quick thinking, but his comment on the matter to Baron de Stoeckl was typical of the young peer's pragmatic outlook.

"War is a business," said Lyons. "It should not be entered into in hot blood."

15

Black Tom

EARLY IN THE MORNING of Sunday, July 30, 1916, a soft southwest breeze stirred the sticky air which lay over Black Tom, a mile-long promontory jutting out into upper New York Harbor from the New Jersey shore south of and nearly opposite to the Statue of Liberty. All work had stopped at five o'clock on the evening before at the warehouses, piers and railroad track networks of this major transfer point for munitions and other supplies bound for the battlefields of Europe. Guards made their casual rounds.

Suddenly, at 2:08 A.M., the first of a series of mighty explosions rocked New York and Jersey City. A second terrific blast followed at 2:40, and for three hours thereafter the air was filled with a stream of high explosives and shells hurled skyward from a raging fire. Almost every window in Jersey City was shattered by the explosions, and thousands of heavy plate-glass windows in Manhattan and Brooklyn toppled into the streets. Buildings trembled for fifty miles around. Ellis Island was wrecked and scores of immigrants were evacuated. The blasts were heard in Camden and Philadelphia, nearly a hundred miles from the scene.

Black Tom was destroyed by the eruption of two million pounds of dynamite, and would not be restored until after the war. Three men and a child were killed. Damage was estimated at 14 million dollars. Black Tom was the latest, most horrifying and crippling blow delivered to the Allied war effort in America by an aristocratic German diplomat turned saboteur. Count Johann-Heinrich von Bernstorff,

Kaiser Wilhelm's Ambassador to the United States, member of an old Saxon family, certainly measured up to Theodore Roosevelt's definition of a diplomat: "A spy in a tail coat."

From the red brick embassy on Massachusetts Avenue, von Bernstorff masterminded a long succession of furtive attacks on America's role as an arsenal for the Allies, besides meddling outrageously in legislative affairs on Capitol Hill. Mysterious explosions destroyed ammunition dumps, powder plants, chemical installations and guncotton storehouses. Fires swept war plants. American ships bound for Europe with holds crammed with munitions caught fire and sank. In January, 1917, a shell assembly plant in Kingsland, New Jersey, went up in flames causing damage of 17 million dollars. Bernstorff's second-in-command, Dr. Heinrich Albert, the German Commercial Attaché, organized a munitions company under cover names which negotiated contracts that blocked off badly needed supplies from the Allies for more than a year. One of Bernstorff's agents dynamited the International Bridge linking the United States and Canada at Vanceboro, Maine. The agent was paid seven hundred dollars for the job. Meanwhile, Bernstorff had organized the German propaganda outfit, "Labor's National Peace Council," which offered generous benefits to members who went on strike in war plants and at port facilities. Two of the speakers at the Council's first meeting were members of Congress, Representatives Frank Buchanan and H. Robert Fowler of Illinois.

It is not recorded whether Bernstorff found these extracurricular activities distasteful, but the enthusiasm and efficiency with which he pursued them are perhaps revealing. At any rate, he was the instrument of a German policy decided upon by the Kaiser as a suitable last resort. At the outbreak of the war, Germany had only one part-time spy in the United States. When it became apparent that the war would be a long one, the Kaiser realized that United States shipments of supplies to the Allies were of enormous importance. Germany was cut off from the American market by British sea power, and it had too few submarines for diversion to American shipping lanes. Therefore, sabotage remained the only means of striking at America's war production effort.

For the United States, the Kaiser's decision marked a milestone in diplomatic relations. It was the first time a foreign power had made America the target for the activities of what has been called diplomacy's "Department of Dirty Tricks," an appellation which in a later day was pinned on America's Central Intelligence Agency. During all the other wars the United States had fought there had been desultory, sporadic acts of sabotage, but not until World War I was the Republic subjected to a major campaign of terrorism. By this time, too, the nation's ethnic complexion had changed. The country's population had climbed to 99,118,000, and its cities were filling up with immigrants from the Old World—Germans, Irish, Poles, Italians and the Latin-Slavic-Middle Eastern mixture of the Balkans. In the great masses of German-Americans and, to a lesser extent, the British-hating Irish, the Imperial German Government believed it had the material from which to mold an army of sympathizers which would aid and abet its strategy of subversion and sabotage.

Von Bernstorff arrived in the United States in August, 1914, with orders to do everything possible to cripple that war effort. He carried with him $150,000,000 in German treasury notes to finance his espionage and sabotage apparatus. With him, too, was Dr. Albert, who would operate out of offices in the Hamburg-American Building in New York. They came to an innocent and isolated country, unfamiliar with the intrigues of Europe and concerned only with trouble south of the Rio Grande and the domestic unrest caused by new and vigorous demands from labor unions.

In Washington, Bernstorff quickly set up his organization. Dr. Albert was the treasurer and would direct complex business manipulations. Albert was a tall, slender man with a face marked by duelling scars, polite and well-dressed to the point of foppishness. He was also an authority on economic conditions in the United States. After the war, Dr. Albert would be described by one American senator as "a Machiavelli . . . the mildest-mannered man that ever scuttled a ship or cut a throat." In charge of sabotage within the United States and Canada was Capt. Franz von Papen, the military attaché, a daring and arrogant opportunist who twenty years later would avert his fastidious nose and do Hitler's bidding as Ambassador to Austria and then Turkey. Von Papen then was a tall, broad-shouldered man with large bones and a thick military mustache. His speech was vigorous and often laced with sarcasm. He was a snob who had bolstered his status by marriage to the daughter of a wealthy Alsatian pottery tycoon, and a notorious womanizer. Finally, there was the naval attaché, Captain Karl Boy-Ed, who was responsible for the sabotage campaign against American shipping. Son of a German mother and a Turkish father, Boy-Ed was once addressed by an irreverent American journalist as "Eddie Boy." He was heavy-set and bull-necked, but polished and charming, and had a reputation as a propaganda expert.

Bernstorff's mission was clearly defined in a telegram received at the German Embassy on January 26, 1915, and many years later published by the German government. The telegram, from the General Staff via the Foreign Office, read:

For Military Attaché. You can obtain particulars as to persons suitable for carrying on sabotage in the United States and Canada from the following persons [three names listed] . . . One and two are absolutely reliable and discreet. Number three is reliable but not always discreet. These persons were indicated by Sir Roger Casement [the Irish patriot later convicted of treason by Great Britain]. In the U.S. sabotage can be carried out in every kind of factory for supplying munitions of war. Railway embankments and bridges must not be touched. Embassy must in no circumstances be compromised. Similar precautions must be taken in regard to Irish pro-German propaganda.

The telegram was signed by Arthur Zimmerman, at that time German Under Secretary for Foreign Affairs and later Secretary of State. In the latter post, he wrote the famous "Zimmerman Letter" which offered Mexico the states of Texas, Arizona and New Mexico in return for her entrance into an alliance with Germany.

The handsome von Bernstorff, with his immaculate grooming, his Kaiser mustache and his firm mouth which could melt into an ingratiating smile, was a great success in Washington, now a metropolis of 368,000 persons. He was much sought after by the town's rather dowdy hostesses and especially by a certain group of mentally-warped German-Americans dazzled by the glories of the Kaiser's empire. As an accredited ambassador, he had entrée to the White House, where Woodrow Wilson would find him "exquisite and authoritative . . . but with something that makes me feel uncomfortable." He sat regularly in the diplomatic galleries of the House and Senate and visited the cloak rooms, where he struck up a bantering friendship with the legislators. Democratic America still held the aristocrat of noble blood in wistful esteem.

Back at his embassy desk, however, Bernstorff was busy dirtying his hands with the affairs of his government. His first job was to open the way for the thousands of German reservists living in America to return home and rejoin the colors. To prevent such traffic, the Allies insisted that every traveler carry a passport, a document heretofore in very little use except by tourists seeking an official means of identification. Passports were examined at all Allied ports, and patrols stopped merchant vessels looking for suspects. Bernstorff therefore assigned Papen and Boy-Ed to the job of securing neutral passports for the Kaiser's returning soldiers.

Soon thereafter, an office was set up in New York staffed by a German reserve officer named Hans von Wedell, an American citizen who had practiced law and worked as a newspaper reporter in the city. Von Wedell roamed the German section of Yorkville and the New York and Jersey waterfronts buying neutral passports for from ten to twenty-five dollars each. During the first three months, Wedell sent more than three hundred reservists on their way. When the Justice Department got on his trail, Wedell fled to Cuba, but not before grooming a replacement, one Carl Ruroede, a senior clerk in the brokerage house of Oelrichs and Company. Ruroede did very well for a few months, until he was trapped while posing as a pro-German sailor with passports to sell by an agent of the Bureau of Investigation of the Justice Department (now known as the FBI). The authorities pounced, and Ruroede confessed and got three years in the Atlanta penitentiary. Subsequently, a wanted order went out for Wedell, and he was picked up by a British patrol boat from aboard the steamer *Bergensfjord*. At the time he was attempting to return to New York as Rosato Sprio, a Mexican. Two days later, the patrol boat struck a German mine and took Wedell to the bottom.

On balance, Bernstorff was satisfied with his little adventure in passport fraud. Nearly a thousand German reservists had been dispatched to the Fatherland, where their neutral passports were picked up and used by the Secret Service to send spies into England, France and Russia. But he was upset by a message from the Foreign Office which seemed to imply that he had compromised the Embassy. He hastened to reassure his superiors and to plead his own case by cablegram:

> In consequence of the instructions sent to me by private letter . . . to send home the largest possible number of German officers, it was necessary to furnish the latter with false passports . . . Details have unfortunately become known to public opinion and the American Government started an investigation, in the course of which there is no reason to fear that the Embassy will be compromised. State Department informed me definitely that this Government attached no importance to the rumors that the Embassy had been concerned . . ."

Berlin seemed quite satisfied with Bernstorff's performance, Zimmerman even agreed with him that Consul General Falcke in New York should be transferred to a South American post because he had raised what Bernstorff described as "pedantic objections" to the passport operation. At any rate, Berlin wanted Bernstorff to see what he could do about raising a little hell in Canada. Zimmerman had told him in one message that "the transportation of Japanese troops through Canada must be prevented at all costs if necessary by blowing up Canadian railways . . ."

There followed a comedy of errors which drove Bernstorff nearly to distraction and made him wonder, as he later noted in his diary, "whether there has been a deterioration of the superior German mind, caused by exposure to the New World." First the Foreign Office foisted upon him Horst von der Goltz, a German soldier of fortune who wanted to invade Canada through British Columbia with the aid of German warships in the Pacific and German-American guerrillas from the United States. Another von der Goltz brainchild—to blow up the Welland Canal—was abandoned because the Canal was found to be too well-guarded; besides, the agents lost their dynamite. One Werner Horn, a German reserve officer, blew up a section of the International Bridge in Vanceboro, Maine, but then pinned a German flag on his overcoat sleeve so he would be treated as a prisoner-of-war if he was arrested. He was arrested, all right, and spent the next several years in the Federal penitentiary in Atlanta. German agents planted bombs in a Canadian armory in Windsor and in an overall factory in Walkerville, but only the factory bomb exploded. A German-American in San Francisco agreed to blow up a Canadian Pacific Railroad tunnel near Vancouver for three thousand dollars, then spilled the plot to American and Canadian authorities and collected his fee when the Vancouver newspapers carried a faked story describing the "destruction" of the tunnel. A ship Bernstorff ordered chartered to carry arms to sympathizers in India became lost in the Pacific and after several wandering months finally put in at Hoquiam, Washington, where its $600,000 cargo was seized by American authorities.

But after these spectacularly comic failures, Bernstorff now went on to a series of sensational successes. He sent the amateurs packing and turned over the execution of his sabotage program to the experts. With the skillful assistance of such men as Franz von Rintelen, an international banker and confidence man, and Dr. Walter Scheele, a chemist whose specialty was explosives, Bernstorff from January 1,

1915 until America entered the war in April, 1917, presided over the destruction of more than 100 million dollars' worth of American ships, war plants and railroad freight yards. Bombs or incendiary devices were placed on forty-seven ships, and arson and explosions destroyed or partially damaged forty-three American factories. In addition, von Rintelen and the Commercial Attaché, Dr. Albert, set up dummy war production companies which negotiated government contracts enabling them to withhold from the allies more than five million dollars' worth of badly needed supplies.

Von Rintelen, a captain-lieutenant in the German Naval Reserve, had acquired his international banking experience in both London and New York. He was the scion of one of those aristocratic German families to whom the Kaiser was the Divine answer to their dreams of a world dominated by leaders with pure Teutonic blood lines. He had a trim figure and delicately nervous movements. In New York, he was a member of the New York Yacht Club. The only other German members were the Kaiser and his brother, Prince Heinrich.

When the war began, Rintelen was a director of the Deutsche Bank, and immediately was assigned to the staff of Admiral von Tirpitz, and soon thereafter arrived in New York via Norway with a $500,000 letter of credit and a forged Swiss passport which identified him as Emile V. Gaché, a Swiss citizen. Rintelen had promised his superiors action—by one means or another. "I'll buy up what I can and blow up what I can't," he boasted. He soon discovered there was not enough German money available to corner the munitions market, but he did what he could and in the meantime joined with Papen and Boy-Ed in a determination to blow up the rest.

On the side, Rintelen also acted as Bernstorff's agent in clandestinely seeing to the organization of the German-front Labor's National Peace Council. Later, Rintelen recalled the successful launching of the Council:

"The first thing I did was to hire a large hall and organize a meeting at which well-known men thundered against the export of munitions. Messrs. Buchanan and Fowler, members of Congress; Mr. Hannis Taylor, the former American Ambassador in Madrid . . . together with a number of university professors, theologians and labour leaders appeared and raised their voices. I sat unobtrusively in a corner and watched my plans fructifying. None of the speakers had the faintest suspicion that he was in the 'service' of a German officer sitting among the audience."

Papen offered Rintelen the aid of Dr. Scheele, the explosives expert. Scheele had spent several years in the United States doing chemical research and drawing fifteen hundred dollars a year as Germany's only prewar spy on American soil. At the war's outbreak, Scheele was president of the New Jersey Agricultural Chemical Company—and the inventor of an ingenious new bomb. It consisted of a lead pipe divided into two compartments by a copper disc. One compartment held potassium chlorate and the other sulphuric acid. The action of the acid on the copper disc took place at a uniform rate and thus determined how long it would take for the two chemicals to unite and produce an explosion.

By this time, Rintelen had set up E. V. Gibbons, Inc., a firm specializing in the export of war supplies to Europe. Shipments handled by Gibbons were sabotaged at Rintelen's convenience. He also had made friends with the captains of several of the ninety-odd German ships confined to New York and New Jersey ports by the vigilance of the British fleet. Rintelen now used both E. V. Gibbons and the interned S. S. *Friedrich der Grosse* to get Scheele into production on his bomb.

The ship was used as a workshop, with members of the crew as its technicians. Lead tubing, copper rods and chemicals were bought through E. V. Gibbons. At night, the bombs were carried over to Scheele's laboratory in Hoboken, where they were filled. Eventually, Rintelen's little workshop was manufacturing what he called his "cigars" at the rate of between fifty and sixty a day. Stevedores handpicked by a couple of captains from the Hamburg-American Line and the North German Lloyd Steamship Company stowed the bombs on designated American ships.

Meanwhile, Ambassador von Bernstorff had discovered Victoriano Huerta, former president of Mexico. Huerta had blamed American support of his enemies for his fall from power, and thus was anxious to be of service to Germany. Bernstorff conferred secretly with Huerta several times at the embassy in Washington and decided that if he could restore Huerta to power, the United States might be forced to intervene, and thus large quantities of munitions would be diverted to American forces fighting in Mexico.

"Make the financial arrangements," Bernstorff told Rintelen cryptically by telephone. "I hand this man over to you."

Rintelen was enthusiastic about the plan. He installed Huerta in a suite in a New York hotel, and the two spent their evenings there plotting. Rintelen gave Huerta $25,000 and promised the German government would back a revolution to the extent of another $100,000. But agents of Mexico's President Carranza got wind of the conspiracy and one of them bribed his way into a meeting of Huerta supporters in the Holland House. He promptly notified American authorities, and when Huerta tried to slip into Mexico he was nabbed by customs officers and tossed into jail on a smuggling charge.

Rintelen's days were numbered, too. New York detectives, headed by the brilliant Inspector Thomas J. Tunney, head of the Bomb Squad, nabbed five members of another of Bernstorff's bomb-manufacturing teams, and the prisoners talked enough to lead police to Karl von Kleist, a retired German merchant marine captain living in Hoboken. Von Kleist, it appeared, had a grievance against Dr. Scheele for holding out $117 in payment for some minor league spying Kleist had done. Police found Kleist's lack of discretion almost incredible, but even spies sometimes yield to the temptation to air their grievances, and Tunney's men forthwith went looking for Rintelen and Scheele.

Scheele already had flown the coop, Papen had given him $1800 and a steamship ticket to Cuba as soon as Kleist was arrested. Rintelen had had a quarrel with Papen and Boy-Ed over the $25,000 he gave to Huerta, and Papen had already arranged for his recall to Germany.

Bernstorff was annoyed at this development. Rintelen had been a human dynamo. But—this was before Kleist's arrest—he promised Rintelen he would pull strings to have him reassigned to the United States. "Von Papen is too dictatorial," Bernstorff told Rintelen. "But I will do some things behind his stiff back."

Thus, Rintelen was aboard the Dutch ship, S. S. *Noordam,* when Kleist was jailed. But British intelligence agents in London had been decoding cablegrams to him from Berlin, and it was no trick for British agents in New York and New York police to trace von Rintelen, as E. V. Gaché, to the *Noordam.* Rintelen was taken off the ship at Falmouth and interned as a prisoner of war. When America entered the war, he was extradited and drew four years in the Atlanta penitentiary on a charge of conspiracy to violate the Sherman Anti-Trust Act; the Espionage Act was not in existence at the time of Rintelen's activities.

Von Bernstorff, of course, was going his charming, terroristic way. Although some of the more fastidious hostesses barred him from their

Washington drawing rooms, he continued to be sought after by some segments of society. In turn, he entertained lavishly at fifteen-course dinners and champagne lunches and cozened politicians with gifts of vintage wines and fine cigars. He showed amazing skill in his softly-worded denials of any official German involvement in the wave of bombings and arson which swept the country. Even when the roof fell in on Papen and Boy-Ed, as it did in December, 1915, Bernstorff managed to convince an amazingly credulous State Department that his military and naval attachés, if indeed guilty of sabotage, had managed to execute their plots without his knowledge. "That man," Woodrow Wilson said after America entered the war, "would wiggle out of it if half of Washington saw him stealing the Washington Monument."

In a country in which the politicians must pay some attention to popular sentiment, little things often decide big issues. American newspapers, notably the Providence *Journal,* had been peppering their readers with stories alleging that Papen and Boy-Ed were involved in the sabotage of American war plants and shipping. In any other neutral country, this pair would have been shipped back to Germany long before. But Secretary of State Robert Lansing, uncle of the John Foster Dulles who would fill the same post under Dwight D. Eisenhower, could not seem to make up his mind what to do about Bernstorff's misbehaving boys. Lansing admired the British phlegm; he was wary of letting sophisticated Europe think of him as a wild-eyed Yankee who shied at espionage shadows.

Then on September 1, 1915, British police removed James J. Archibald from a ship being searched at Falmouth. Archibald was an American newspaper correspondent who, it turned out, was bearing dispatches from Austro-Hungarian Ambassador Dumba to his Foreign Office. One of these messages suggested a plan for fomenting strikes at the Bethlehem Steel Company plants. There was also a letter from Papen to his wife in which he wrote: " . . . how splendid on the Eastern Front! I always say to these idiotic Yankees that they should shut their mouths and better still be full of admiration for all that heroism."

There was a storm of public indignation in America. The State Department forced Dumba's recall, but took no action against von Papen. Lansing later explained he had agents collecting a dossier on Papen and Boy-Ed. In any event, the public forced Lansing's hand. A new wave of bombings of war plants and ship sinkings sent popular indignation soaring, and after three months of equivocation, the State Department on December 8 finally declared Papen and Boy-Ed *personae non grata* and demanded their recall.

Von Papen sailed for England and Holland on December 21, 1915, and on New Year's day was followed by Boy-Ed. Although Papen had been granted a "safe conduct" pass by the British, in accordance with diplomatic protocol, his baggage was searched by British officials at Falmouth on the grounds that the "safe conduct" referred to his person and not to his effects. Among other interesting documents, the British found Papen's check books, which showed he had received $3,102,000 from Dr. Albert to carry out his sabotage activities and which contained stubs linking him absolutely with such saboteurs as Werner Horn, von der Goltz and Scheele.

Papen went on to become postwar chancellor of Germany and, later, Hitler's diplomatic toady. But his work in America was carried on by a worthy successor, Papen's secretary, Wolf von Igel, whom Papen had been grooming for months. Bernstorff, who was repelled by Papen's frequent vulgarity, acknowledged that Igel lacked Papen's ability, but found consolation in a feeling that "von Igel is much easier to handle."

There was a jewel of consistency in Bernstorff's character. Despite bales of evidence tying him to German sabotage in America, he insisted in his post-war memoirs that he was a wooly lamb among wolves. In *My Three Years in America* he declared: "Whether the illegal acts of the secret agents sent to the United States by the Military authorities were committed in accordance with their orders or on their own initiative, I had no means of knowing at the time, nor have I been able to discover since my return home . . ."

But von Bernstorff never denied that he took personal charge of efforts to influence legislation on Capitol Hill. He saw such activities, quite properly from a diplomat's viewpoint, as consistent with his duties as the Kaiser's representative in the United States. Thus, he never disavowed cables such as the following, which he dispatched to Berlin in December, 1914:

In the Congress and House of Representatives [sic] the Hitchcock and Volmer resolutions respecting the export prohibition of arms, ammunition, etc., are under consideration. A strong agitation is being developed by the Germans and Irish with a view to carrying these resolutions. In view of the great importance of the matter, I considered myself authorized to assist the agitators financially and so I gave as a provisional measure the five thousand dollars for which I was asked by a trustworthy quarter.

Von Bernstorff received much aid and comfort from the National German-American Alliance, an organization of nearly three million members with a powerful lobby in Washington. He saw to it that his commercial attaché, Dr. Albert, supplied it with funds eventually amounting to more than $200,000. The Alliance also spent most of the $800,000 it collected for the German Red Cross for propaganda purposes. Bernstorff kept Berlin in touch with his dealings:

I request authority to pay up to fifty thousand dollars in order, as on former occasions, to influence Congress through the organization you know of, which perhaps can prevent war . . . In the above circumstances, a public official German declaration in favor of Ireland is highly desirable in order to gain the support of the Irish influence here.

Indisputably, Bernstorff was an operator of high caliber. Despite the compromising of several members of his staff and the arrest of several of his saboteurs, he managed to the very end to avoid a breach with the United States government. He even survived the comic accident which befell Dr. Albert on a New York elevated train, when that shrewd businessman-spy walked off the train at his station and left his briefcase behind. The briefcase was picked up by Frank Burke of the U.S. Secret Service, who had been tailing Albert, and was turned over to Secretary of the Treasury William Gibbs McAdoo.

Papers in the briefcase were covered with data relating to Albert's clandestine activities, including the operation of the Bridgeport Projectile Company, the firm Albert had set up in an attempt to corner the munitions market. McAdoo could not admit that one of his agents had made off with the briefcase, so he turned the documents over to the New York *World,* which gleefully splashed their contents all over Page One.

But von Bernstorff stayed on in Washington until the United States declared war on Germany in April, 1917. Until almost the very end, he claimed to have believed he could avoid hostilities between his country and the United States by preventing the American government from finding an incident that could be considered a *casus belli.* He saw his sabotage activities as a means of impressing on the United States that it was futile for America to supply large amounts of aid to the Allied cause. But the decision by German war hawks to pursue a campaign of unrestricted submarine warfare ended all his hopes. As he sailed homeward, Bernstorff perhaps found consolation in a record which showed he had fought unceasingly against the submarine policy —and that he had never once fallen from the diplomatic tightrope he walked for more than three years.

16

Hirohito's Amateur Typist

S H O R T L Y A F T E R his indictment as a war criminal, Shigenori Togo had an informal chat with General Bonner Fellers, aide to General Douglas MacArthur, during which he delivered a blistering attack on Japanese diplomats that would have done credit to those Congressmen who regularly denounce America's diplomats as a collection of casual playboys. Togo, who was Japan's Foreign Minister at the time of Pearl Harbor, had two words to describe the staff of the Japanese Embassy in Washington during the hours immediately preceding the sneak attack of December 7, 1941:

"Drunkards!" snarled Togo. "Dilettantes!"

Togo was not trying to apologize for the attack on Pearl Harbor. Rather he was explaining why the Japanese warning of an imminent severing of relations with the United States was not delivered in time to conform with the provisions of the Hague Convention. In Togo's curious world, apparently, his country did not lose face by its furtive action against the American naval base in Hawaii, but by the failure of its diplomats in Washington to serve proper notice that such an action was to be expected. To Togo, Japan stood indicted of discourtesy before the world because its representatives in Washington had not seen to their duties.

Those duties, on the evening of December 6 and the morning of December 7, entailed the decoding and typing up of a fourteen-part note for transmission to Secretary of State Cordell Hull. The note represented one of the few concessions wrung from the Japanese ruling military clique by Emperor Hirohito and Togo, since its text gave the United States what the Japanese Chiefs of Staff felt was "due" warning of what was to come. However, the Chiefs' interpretation of the word "due" was not quite applicable under the circumstances. After first agreeing to give Washington an hour's warning, they discovered that the Hague Convention mentioned no specific time limit and reduced it to thirty minutes. Probably the Chiefs congratulated themselves on the fact that it would take Hull at least fifteen minutes to read the note, thus further diminishing its effectiveness. But it was legal; it complied with the fine print.

In any event, Tokyo took no chances on the contents of the note leaking out in advance of the delivery time decided upon. The first thirteen parts were not dispatched from the Tokyo Central Telegraph Office until the morning of Saturday, December 6 (Washington time) between the hours of 6:30 and 10:20 A.M. The fourteenth part was cabled between 3:00 A.M. and 4:00 A.M. on December 7, only some nine and a half hours before the first bombs were dropped on Pearl Harbor. This was of more than ordinary significance, since the fourteenth part announced the formal breaking off of negotiations.

Still, Togo felt he was proceeding with the utmost propriety. Before dispatching the first thirteen parts of the note, he cabled the Washington Embassy that as soon as the whole note arrived every "preparation" should be made so that the note could be delivered to Hull at any time "upon receipt of further instructions." By preparation, of course, he meant decoding and typing.

But although Japan was, in effect, represented by two ambassadors in Washington—Admiral Kitchisaburo Nomura and Saburo Kurusu—authority in the Massachusetts Avenue Embassy was so divided that discipline was a sometime thing. The first thirteen parts of the note arrived during the early evening of Saturday, December 6, and were carried down to the code room for deciphering. By one of those coincidences which complicate if not influence the course of history, there was a party at the embassy that night for a staff member departing for a new post. The code clerks had finished decoding only the first nine parts when they decided it was time to adjourn and join in merrymaking.

Nomura dropped in at the party, a Nipponese lord of the manor among his fiefs, but Kurusu was dining at "Evermay," at the Georgetown mansion belonging to Ferdinand Lammot Belin, a multimillion-

aire industrial prince who had once served as American Ambassador to
Poland. Kurusu had been pressed to break bread with Belin by
Ferdinand L. Mayer, a career American diplomat who had known
Kurusu when both men were serving in Peru eleven years before.
During a call upon Kurusu that morning, Mayer had become convinced that Kurusu was trying to give warning of a momentary attack
by the Japanese on an American installation. At the Belin home,
both the host and Mayer pressed Kurusu for more information, but
finally would conclude that the envoy had not been made privy to
the details of the attack. Kurusu stayed late at Belin's, but even had
he been on the scene at the Embassy it is unlikely he would have
interfered with the staff's wholesale defection to the sake bowl. As a
"special envoy" charged with handling matters of high policy, Kurusu
left the housekeeping chores to Nomura. Meanwhile, he did nothing
to dispel the staff's impression that he was the real boss.

In diplomatic drawing rooms all over the world, it is agreed that the
Japanese is a notoriously poor drinker; with a knowing shake of their
heads, his peers from other countries will explain that it has something
to do with his body chemistry. At any rate, the Japanese code clerks
got rousingly drunk in the process of lifting an interminable series of
toasts to their departing colleague, and did not go back to work until
shortly after 10:00 P.M. Helped along by strong draughts of tea, they
managed to finish decoding the first thirteen parts of the note by 1:00
A.M. December 7, then staggered off to bed.

Still, neither Nomura nor Kurusu troubled himself to see to the
"preparation" of the note with the dispatch urged upon them by
Togo's cable. No typists with the necessary top security clearance were
summoned to transcribe the thirteen parts as they came in; the sections
were merely put aside as they were decoded while the clerks waited for
the fourteenth part to arrive. That fourteenth part did not arrive
until 7:00 A.M. Sunday morning, with only a duty officer on hand.
This worthy promptly alerted the other clerks and they went back to
work, bleary-eyed and with aching heads.

Meanwhile, a cable arrived from Togo instructing Nomura and
Kurusu to present the note to Secretary Hull at 1:00 P.M. Washington time. Casually, at about 10:00 A.M., Kurusu telephoned the State
Department and arranged for the appointment with Hull three hours
later. Then he ordered that "someone" prepare a clean typed copy of
the note.

At this point, panic struck. There were no typists with top security clearance to be found. The two comely females usually assigned to work of a classified nature were spending the weekend in New York City. Reluctantly, the job was assumed by a junior secretary named Katsuzo Okumura, who would tell a war crimes interrogator after the war that he felt "unworthy" of the duty. His feelings were understandable. Okumura was strictly a hunt-and-peck typist, and there were more than four thousand words in the first thirteen parts of the note. He sat down to the typewriter and laboriously began his search of the keys.

When Okumura finished typing the first thirteen parts at about noon, he decided to type over some of the pages he considered to be slightly less than perfect. In addition, he had to constantly revise his work to conform with additions and corrections sent into him from the code room. At 12:30 P.M., one of Kurusu's aides telephoned Hull's office that his boss would be late for his appointment. Okumura got the fourteenth part from the code clerks at 1:30 P.M., ten minutes before the attack on Pearl Harbor began. Kurusu and Nomura left the Japanese Embassy at 1:55 P.M. by limousine and were ushered into the diplomatic waiting room at the State Department at approximately 2:05 P.M. Secretary Hull was still on the telephone with President Roosevelt, who had just informed him in a voice Hull later described as "steady but clipped," that the White House had a report that the Japanese had attacked Pearl Harbor.

If Pearl Harbor marked the beginning of an era in which the United States became the Number One world power, it also signalized a change in attitude among the plain citizens of the world, and especially in the United States, toward the world of diplomacy. Nomura and Kurusu became the symbols of what was suddenly regarded as a corrupt and sinister calling, represented also by rascals such as von Ribbentrop and von Papen of Germany, whose function was to undermine and betray the governments to which they were accredited. Later, new names from the Soviet Union and other Iron Curtain countries would be added to this Hall of Infamy. And yet, unlike the Ribbentrops, Nomura and Kurusu were not wicked men, but merely diplomats serving the established policy of their government. For pragmatic reasons, both men regretted their country's determination to wage war on the United States, and both sought privately in their talks with Americans to persuade Washington to find a way for the Tokyo militarists to save face and thus avert a resort to force by either side.

This is not to say that Nomura and Kurusu were men the average American Ivy Leaguer, risen to both pecuniary and social affluence, would welcome to his club. They were diplomats in the old, Bismarckian iron mold, untroubled by the venality of their bosses for the simple reason that they had their own careers to worry about. Besides, like most Japanese of any prestige and power, they believed in their nation's destiny as eventual ruler over the less progressive areas of the Orient. Their attitude was not unlike that of the millionaire Midwestern feed merchant toward the emerging African countries. Kurusu was shrewd and tough; he had assimilated some of the less attractive traits of the Nazi politicians with whom he associated during his tenure as Ambassador to Berlin, where he had signed the Tri-Partite Pact. Nomura was inclined to be lazy, and he was not very bright. But, after all, neither of them violated the rule set down by François de Callières, an adviser to King Louis XIV of France, who decreed that in executing his country's policies an ambassador is not required to sin "against the laws of God and Justice," by which he meant no diplomat is expected to commit assassination.

Nomura was appointed Ambassador to Washington in February, 1941, a few weeks after Franklin D. Roosevelt had asked Congress for a half-billion-dollar expansion to provide for a "two-ocean fleet." His apparent sincerity impressed Hull at the very outset. "This is a Japanese I think we can trust," Hull said of Nomura after their first meeting. Nomura played poker and drank whiskey. Perhaps it was what correspondents called his "Western outlook" that helped him to find favor with the crusty and ailing former House member from Tennessee. Hull was not overly fond of foreigners, and if this seems a curious quirk in a Secretary of State, it must be remembered that the State Department before Pearl Harbor was not the powerful and sophisticated principality it has since become. Hull's staff was small enough so that in 1939 its group picture could be taken on the steps of the Old State Building next to the White House. Unlike Dean Rusk in 1967, Cordell Hull found no reason in 1941 to be particularly interested in, say, the economic stability of Indochina.

Nomura could be suspect because he was a retired admiral, but he had acquired a patina of drawing room respectability as head of the "Peers' School," which taught good manners and culture to Japan's noble youth. He was fond of remarking that there were no problems two "civilized" nations could not settle by negotiation, and he was even on friendly terms with the terrible-tempered Admiral Kelly Turner, Chief of War Plans. He and Turner visited frequently, and Nomura listened politely to Turner's warnings that the United States would fight if Japan should attack Russia, an eventuality of which Turner was convinced. When he got a word in edgewise, Nomura assured Turner that Tokyo and Washington would work together to avert war.

Turner found himself irritated by Nomura's elegant blandness. He also believed that Nomura's successes at poker were due more to luck than to any skill or knowledge of the game. But he soon learned not to press this theory too hard. One night, when Nomura was a heavy winner and began to talk about having to arise early the next morning, Turner insisted that the Japanese stay on "for a few more hands." At 5:30 A.M., Nomura had trebled his winnings and Turner quit.

There were indications, however, that Nomura was sadly lacking in the purely technical aspects of an ambassador's job. In July, 1941, Japan had forced the Vichy Government of France to agree to Japanese occupation of French Indochina in order to secure a base from which to attack China and Malaya. By this time, United States experts had broken the Japanese code and President Roosevelt knew about the Japanese plans almost as soon as they were formulated. He called in Nomura and gave him a message for transmission to Prince Fumimaro Konoye, the Japanese Prime Minister, in which he offered to guarantee the neutralization of Indochina from occupation by any power—British, American, Gaullist or Chinese. This was an offer that merited Tokyo's careful consideration.

But Nomura must have flunked diplomatic English somewhere along his path to the eminent pedagog's chair he filled at the Peers' School, for his translation of the message into Japanese produced a gibberish that Prince Konoye found unintelligible. By the time Joseph Grew, the American Ambassador to Japan, explained the President's offer to Foreign Minister Teijiro Toyoda, the Japanese government had announced its intention of occupying Indochina and could not retreat lest it lose face. Nomura's ham-handed handling of Roosevelt's message undoubtedly cost thousands of Allied lives which were lost in the fighting in Southeast Asia. Clearly, Nomura was more perceptive at the poker table than he was when poring over a state document.

In the years that have passed since Pearl Harbor, some historians have suggested that Nomura purposely fouled up the Roosevelt message because he saw it as a possible deterrent to Japan's pursuit of its manifest destiny. But the consensus of men who knew him best in both America and Japan refuses to accept Nomura in such a Machiavellian role. "His word was good," Hull said, "but his intelligence was third-rate." Prince Konoye dismissed Nomura more cavalierly. "Nomura," said His Highness, "was a stupid man."

Prince Konoye, as a matter of fact, was interested in rapprochement with the United States for a variety of reasons, chief of which was his feeling of guilt for having led his country to the brink of war by his sometime belligerence and his toadying to the military. He had made the former Foreign Minister, Yosuke Matsuoka, the fall guy for Japan's dilemma—to fight or lose face—but he could not shirk his own responsibility. Moreover, Emperor Hirohito had warned Konoye that under no circumstances was he to get Japan into a war with either the United States or Great Britain. Konoye yearned for an opportunity to wiggle out of his predicament. And, again, Nomura would mishandle his assignment.

For some time Konoye had been toying with the idea of going to America to talk personally with President Roosevelt and arrange a harmonious agreement which would end the threat of war. Foreign Minister Toyoda presented the proposal formally to Ambassador Grew on August 18, 1941.

Grew liked the idea. He noted in his diary that Konoye's proposal shattered all precedent: "For a Prime Minister of Japan . . . to wish to come hat in hand, so to speak, to meet the President of the United States on American soil, is a gauge of the determination of the Government to undo the vast harm already accomplished in alienating our powerful and progressively angry country."

Because Konoye feared an angry reaction from the Germans and Italians, every effort was made to keep the prince's proposal a secret. But for one of the few times in his professional life, White House Press Secretary Steve Early was slumbering at the switch. He announced that Nomura had an appointment with President Roosevelt, instead of taking Nomura in a back door, and when the meeting was over, Nomura emerged to compound the felony by confiding to reporters that he had just delivered a message from his Prime Minister to the President.

Predictably, the Axis powers were indignant at what their spokesmen described as Konoye's "truckling to the Americans and the British." In Berlin, Adolf Hitler was "pained and angry" at the news. In Washington, the German Embassy inquired through a second secretary (a diplomatic snub) whether Konoye was "losing his mind." Nomura ignored the German inquiry while he tried to figure out what he'd done wrong. He had thought it "greatly exhilarating" to announce publicly a new contact between his government and the President. In Tokyo, Konoye was less than exhilarated by several threats of assassination obviously inspired by the military clique.

Both Hull and Roosevelt were disinclined toward a meeting with Konoye, but Roosevelt might have strung the prince along and perhaps eventually agreed on a confrontation had Nomura not let the cat out of the basket. Once the news was out, however, a decision had to be made and it was negative. Roosevelt did not put it in so many words, but he instructed Hull to summon Nomura and tell him that before any meeting could be arranged between Konoye and the President, Japan would be required to renounce the Tri-Partite Pact with Germany and Italy and indicate her willingness to withdraw her troops from China. These were terms Japan could not accept, of course, and so there was no meeting.

Nomura, who had been "ecstatic" at the prospects of the Konoye visit—partially because it offered the opportunity to polish Japan's image and its status as an equal among the great powers—was crushed by the Roosevelt-Hull rejection. He considered that the "American politicians" had thrown away a real chance of averting war, and he became convinced that Roosevelt was determined to enter World War II by the "back door"—that is, by forcing Japan to provoke hostilities so that he could get on with the job of helping England in Europe.

Indeed, Roosevelt's recalcitrance was ammunition for those Americans who were saying the same thing. Both the President and Hull took refuge behind the assertion that the Konoye visit would be a waste of time. Hull later said he estimated that "there was not one chance . . . in twenty or one in fifty or one in a hundred" of such a meeting producing any results. For men sworn to investigate any avenue that might lead to peace, Roosevelt and Hull seemed suddenly to be possessed of closed minds. They stood on the argument that existing treaties were sufficient to avert war, provided that Japan lived up to them. Nomura sought in vain to convince them that at that point the treaties were irrelevant, that having gone so far on the path of belligerence, Konoye

wanted an excuse to make a detour over the opposition of the militarists. And, indeed, the Japanese brass hats had gone along with
Konoye's proposal, with a time limit. Nevertheless, Roosevelt was convinced from what he had seen of the messages between Tokyo and the
Japanese Embassy—which the American code-breakers transmitted to
the White House almost hourly—that Tokyo was committed to war.
He believed that any agreement he might reach with Konoye would be
repudiated by the generals, and that therefore the time had come to
prepare the nation for the inevitable conflict.

Konoye's abortive, and face-losing, attempt to get Roosevelt to invite him to drop around to the White House undoubtedly was one of
the major contributing factors to the fall of his cabinet in October.
But the military was breathing down his neck, and in any event he
would not have been in power for long—unless, of course, he had
succeeded in wangling concessions from Roosevelt. When the Konoye
government fell, the government press service announced merely that
"The Cabinet found it difficult to reach an agreement of views concerning the manner of executing national policy."

The military, of course, was furious at Konoye for hesitating at the
brink of war after supinely going along with its policy of escorting it to
that jumping-off point. Despite some foot-dragging by the Japanese
Navy, which feared it would not have enough oil to fight the United
States, the Army generals successfully pushed through the nomination
of Lieutenant General Hideki Tojo as the new Prime Minister. Curiously, the pacifist Hirohito apparently had no objection to awarding
the portfolio to his War Minister, a hardboiled saber-rattler known as
the "Razor Blade," who had commanded the Kwantung Army in
China and had been chief of the ruthless and barbaric Japanese
national gendarmerie. Surely, the Emperor expected no peace over-
tures from this descendant of Samurai warriors who roared that Japan
should fight China and Russia at the same time.

Tojo, however, seemed determined to assume the posture of the
warrior elevated to statesmanship and thus newly absorbed with the
olive branch. In November, Saburo Kurusu was dispatched as a special
envoy to Washington to assist the downhearted Nomura, who was
constantly begging to be called home, and to carry to Roosevelt a
"new offer." In fact, there was nothing new about the offer except that
some of the language employed was softer. Japan still wanted America's oil and trade embargoes lifted and the right to maintain "police"

units in China. After the war, Foreign Minister Togo would insist that the offer left room for bargaining, "as Washington should have understood." But the words were those of an ultimatum.

The man who delivered this "offer" to Washington was a veteran politician and diplomat with an American wife and a son with American citizenship. Saburo Kurusu had married his Chicago-born secretary and had gained a reputation as a regular fellow among American diplomats in various foreign posts. His wife did not accompany him on his mission to America, but stayed behind to be with their only son, Ryo. Later, a Japanese newspaper would quote her as saying that a newsreel film showing the Japanese attack on Pearl Harbor was "quite thrilling," and adding that "I hope Ryo will be able to do the same thing." Ryo, an aeronautical engineer, was killed in an air raid near Tokyo.

Had the United States Navy not been torn by fratricidal strife, fed by personal ambitions, Washington might have been able to do some undercover business with Kurusu while he was en route to the capital. Captain Ellis M. Zacharias, skipper of the heavy cruiser *Salt Lake City*, was in Honolulu when Kurusu stopped off there and he pleaded with the headquarters of the Commander in Chief, Pacific, to be permitted to have a "little chat" with the special envoy. Zacharias, a former intelligence officer, had met Kurusu several times previously and had pried a good deal of information out of him over a bottle of whiskey, including a tidbit that led Zacharias to a job of research on Japanese spies in Hawaii.

But CINCPAC found other things for Zacharias to do—aboard his ship—just as the Navy had been finding other duties for him since he was removed from the post of intelligence officer of the Eleventh Naval District in San Diego in November, 1940. Zacharias spoke Japanese fluently and had had twenty-five years of experience in intelligence, but he was too outspoken and controversial, especially about what he called "those goddam malingerers" in Intelligence. There had been something of a flap, also, when his superiors discovered that Zacharias had given a cocktail party in Washington and invited the Japanese naval attaché so that "some of my sailors" could ransack the attaché's apartment.

Kurusu said later that he would have "enjoyed" a talk with Captain Zacharias. "Perhaps," said Kurusu, "my friend Zach and I could have had a discussion which would have been of assistance to me in explain-

ing to Secretary Hull and the President the real situation in Japan."
From his later conversation with another friend, the former diplomat,
Ferdinand Mayer, it does not seem utterly unreasonable to speculate
that Kurusu might have told Zacharias of his fears of a sneak Japanese
attack on the United States. Zacharias was a good host, with a well-
stocked bar.

But Kurusu went on to Washington, where he and Ambassador
Nomura were received by President Roosevelt and Secretary Hull on
November 17, 1941. The Bobbsey Twins, as some irreverent Washington journalists called them, had sought permission from Tokyo to
soften the terms of the "offer," but Foreign Minister Togo had blistered Kurusu with an abusive cable for daring to question Togo's
authority, and when they went to the White House the tough language was intact.

Hull confided to his memoirs that he disliked Kurusu at first sight.
"Neither his appearance [Kurusu was short and squat, whereas
Nomura was tall and with an elegance of carriage] nor his attitude
commanded confidence or respect," Hull wrote. "Knowing what I did
from the intercepts [of Japanese coded messages] it did not seem possible to me that he did not know he was to lull us with talk until the
moment Japan got ready to strike."

At any rate, on November 27 the United States replied to the Japanese "ultimatum" with an ultimatum of its own, which among other
things demanded that Japan evacuate China and Indochina, agree to
renounce extraterritorial rights in China and recognize the government of Chiang Kai-shek in Chungking. Roosevelt and Hull had read
enough in the intercepts to persuade them to gird the nation's loins
for war.

Specifically, they had learned from transcripts of tapped telephone
conversations between Tokyo and the Japanese Embassy that the
Japanese Army was not interested in considering any possible American concessions. These conversations were in a rather simple code that
was easily broken, and they featured self-conscious performances by
Nomura and Kurusu, who behaved like amateur actors who had not
quite learned their lines. Their negotiations with Washington were
referred to as "the marriage proposal," President Roosevelt was "Miss
Kimiko," and the Japanese Army as "Mr. Tokugawa." Any new turn
in the crisis was conveyed in the phrase "a baby is born," concessions
had either side climbing up a mountain, and a firm attitude was ex-

pressed by reporting that one party or the other was coming down the mountain. Thus:

TOKYO: Is Miss Kimiko likely to come down the mountain?

KURUSU AND NOMURA: No. She is having a baby. What about Mr. Tokugawa?

TOKYO: He wants nothing more to do with the marriage proposal.

KURUSU AND NOMURA: Is there any chance of Mr. Tokugawa coming down the mountain?

TOKYO: None whatsoever. But please continue to discuss the marriage proposal.

Meanwhile, during the first week of December, 1941, American intelligence intercepted an order from Tokyo to the Japanese Embassy to destroy all but one of their coding machines and all but one of their code books. An FBI man watched Embassy personnel tending a bonfire in their backyard the same day the order was intercepted.

By this time, Washington knew that the Japanese fleet was at sea and presumed that it was on attack course, but no one in authority seemed to think it was headed for Pearl Harbor. Eleven months earlier, in January, Ambassador Grew had predicted an attack on the Hawaii base, and Captain Zacharias was forever warning his indifferent superiors to extend their patrols in that neighborhood, but neither the White House nor the War Department seemed to have any idea what was afoot.

They should have got a broad hint, at least, from a telephone conversation transcribed by the FBI in Honolulu. It was between Mrs. Motokazu Mori, wife of a Japanese dentist, who claimed she was a correspondent for the Tokyo newspaper, *Yomiuri Shimbun,* and the newspaper itself. The phone conversation was loaded with material any competent intelligence officer would have found suspicious. Mrs. Mori and her Japanese caller spent two hundred dollars of the newspaper's money saying things like:

TOKYO: Hello, is this Mori?

MORI: Hello, this is Mori.

TOKYO: I would like to have your impressions on the conditions you are observing at present. Are airplanes flying daily?

MORI: Yes, lots of them fly around.

TOKYO: Are they large planes?

MORI: Yes, they are quite big.

TOKYO: I hear there are many sailors there, is that right?

MORI: There aren't so many now. There were more in the beginning part of this year and the ending part of last year.

TOKYO: Are any Japanese people there holding meetings to discuss U.S.—Japanese negotiations being conducted presently?

MORI: No, not particularly. The Japanese are getting along harmoniously with the Americans. We are not hated or despised. The soldiers here and we get along very well.

TOKYO: Are there many big factories there?

MORI: No, there are no factories, but a lot of small buildings of various kinds are being constructed.

TOKYO: What about searchlights?

MORI: Well, not much to talk about.

TOKYO: Do they put searchlights on when planes fly about at night?

MORI: No.

TOKYO: What kind of an impression did Mr. Kurusu make in Honolulu?

MORI: A very good one. Mr. Kurusu understands the American mind, and he was very adept at answering queries of the press.

TOKYO: Do you know anything about the United States fleet?

MORI: The fleet here seems small. I don't know if all the fleet has done this, but it seems that the fleet has left here.

This conversation was tapped on Saturday, December 6. But when it was shown to General Walter Campbell Short, commander of the Hawaiian Department, he spent only ten minutes considering it before deciding that "no one of us can figure out what it possibly means." Short also suggested that Lieutenant Colonel George Bicknell, the Army intelligence officer who had brought the transcript to him, was "a little too intelligence-conscious." Then General Short, who had been frequently glancing at his watch, went off to a dinner party at Schofield Barracks.

It was, of course, Ambassador Nomura who had recommended Mrs. Mori to *Yomiuri Shimbun* as both a competent correspondent and "a Japanese citizen highly regarded by the government." Military dinner parties, as the late General George S. Patton once remarked, "have lost more wars than shortages of ammunition."

At just about this time, a relatively obscure functionary at the Japanese Embassy made his bid for a hero's role. Hidenari Terasaki, the Second Secretary, was a pacifist who had enjoyed cordial relations with American foreign service personnel as head of the American Section of the Japanese Foreign Office. He invariably accompanied Nomura and Kurusu to their meetings with Hull, and the Secretary of State liked and trusted him. That Terasaki had an American wife seemed to impress Hull favorably, although the Secretary had not been similarly moved by a consideration of Kurusu's Chicago spouse.

Terasaki had been urging Kurusu to double-cross the Foreign Office by telling the Americans on his own authority that Japan would get out of China. He argued that once the militarists were confronted with the knowledge that their ambassador had taken such a step they might be forced to honor their treaties. Besides, Terasaki told Kurusu, it would offer the generals "a way out."

When Kurusu did nothing, Terasaki took another route. He called upon Doctor E. Stanley Jones, a Wesleyan clergyman who was on friendly terms with Roosevelt, and asked Jones to introduce him to the President so that he could explain Japan's "psychological" position. Roosevelt hadn't time to see Terasaki, but he told Jones to have Terasaki write him a letter setting forth his case and that he would read it. In the letter, Terasaki urged Roosevelt to "help us from a war mentality to a peace mentality. Don't compel us to do things, but make it possible for us to do them. If you treat us this way, we will meet you more than halfway."

A few days later, Roosevelt called Kurusu in for a discussion of the letter. Apparently, it was the nudge Kurusu needed to risk unilateral action that could lose him both his professional and physical head. He told Terasaki, "You have suggested that I be a national traitor. How about being one yourself? I think we should approach the President . . . and suggest he send a cable directly to the Emperor appealing for peace." Then he added that he had already asked Tojo's permission to do this and had been rebuked for exceeding his authority. Therefore, the cable would have to be sent "over Tojo's head."

Delighted, Terasaki put the proposition to Jones, who carried it to the White House on December 3. He informed Roosevelt that the suggestion was Kurusu's and that therefore the President need not feel he was snubbing the "people here" should he decide to send the peace message. Roosevelt agreed to "send the cable," but when Jones urged him not to send it "through channels," the President smiled wryly. "I can't just go down to the cable office and tell them: 'I want to send a cable from the President of the United States to the Emperor of Japan,' can I?"

Subsequently, the President decided to send the cable through Ambassador Grew, who had the right to have an audience with the head of the state. Hull objected on the grounds the Emperor was merely a figurehead and that the militarists would regard the message as a sign of weakness on Washington's part, but Roosevelt overruled him. The cable went off on Saturday, December 6. Briefly, the note urged the Emperor to use his influence to encourage a withdrawal of Japanese troops from both China and Indochina, in return for which he offered an American guarantee against any Western interference in those areas.

Had Hirohito received the cable in time, there is no doubt he would at least have insisted on postponing the Japanese attack on Pearl Harbor. There were built-in recall messages in the attack orders of the fleets then on their way to Honolulu, the Philippines and Malaya. But when the President's cable was received in Tokyo, it was held up by Army censorship and then by the Army High Command and Foreign Minister Togo for fourteen hours. Grew did not get to see the Emperor until twenty minutes before the first bomb was released on Pearl Harbor.

Hirohito has since indicated to Jones that "if I had received the cablegram from Roosevelt a day sooner I would have stopped the attack." He was the only one in authority in Tokyo with such an inclination. When H. R. Baukhage, the radio commentator, visited the Japanese Embassy Saturday afternoon for an interview with Kurusu, he noted a flurry of activity among staff members and employees; they were carrying cardboard cartons and wastebaskets crammed with papers out of various rooms to the back of the house. Baukhage didn't know it, but there was a bonfire in the garden in which the staff was burning codes and secret documents.

Baukhage found Kurusu less communicative and candid than in past meetings, but judged strictly by his other activities, Kurusu was still trying to save the peace. This was the day when he spent frantic moments trying to persuade the two former American diplomats, Ferdinand Mayer and Ferdinand Belin, that war still could be averted if Roosevelt would provide the Japanese military junta with a face-saving "way out." Dinner had just been served at Belin's Georgetown home when Kurusu was called to the telephone at 8:30 P.M. to receive a message from the Embassy that the President had transmitted a personal appeal to Hirohito. "This is a very clever move on the part of the United States," Kurusu told Belin and Mayer. "The Emperor can hardly say a flat 'no' or 'yes,' and so there shall have to be some more thinking in Tokyo, and that will give us all more time." But Kurusu was so indefinite in his information that the Japanese planned a surprise attack that when the dinner broke up Belin concluded it would not be worthwhile waking Secretary Hull to tell him about it.

By that time, anyway, both Hull and Roosevelt knew more about Tokyo's plans than Kurusu did. Naval Intelligence had intercepted and decoded the first thirteen parts of the Foreign Office's message to the Embassy breaking off negotiations, and the message was brought to the White House at about 9:30 Saturday night by Lieutenant Commander Alwin D. Kramer, attached to the Far East Section of Naval Intelligence. He left the folder containing the message with Lieutenant Lester Schulz, Annapolis '34, a member of the White House Naval Aide's staff, who had reported to his post only two days earlier. Schulz took the folder to the Oval Room, where Roosevelt was chatting with his special assistant, Harry Hopkins, and stood there while Roosevelt read and re-read the message.

"This means war," Roosevelt told Hopkins.

It did indeed. The next afternoon—Sunday, December 7—Admiral Leigh Noyes, the Navy's Chief of Communications, was sitting in his office at the Navy Department studying the fourteenth part of Japan's curious declaration of war. The telephone rang at about 1:35 P.M. and Noyes picked it up to hear the voice of a radioman from the communications watch. He told Noyes the Navy installation at Mare Island in San Francisco Bay had picked up a local transmission between the Navy Yard in Honolulu and headquarters of the Commander in Chief, Pacific Fleet. It read: "Enemy Air Raid—Not Drill."

Noyes ran down the hall to the office of Secretary of Navy Frank Knox, who was conferring with the Chief of Naval Operations, Admiral Harold R. Stark, and Admiral Kelly Turner.

"My God!" exclaimed Knox. "This can't be true! This must mean the Philippines!"

Stark's voice was soft. "No sir, this is Pearl."

Knox called Roosevelt on his direct line to the White House. In turn, Roosevelt called Secretary of War Henry L. Stimson, who was at lunch. As he put down the phone, Stimson recalled later, he said to himself, "Well, that is an excitement indeed."

The President phoned a number of other people, including Press

Secretary Steve Early, before calling Secretary Hull. He dictated a statement for the press to Early, and told him to hold it up for final confirmation, "probably in the next few minutes." Then he got on the phone to Hull, just as Kurusu and Nomura were walking down the corridor to Hull's office in the State Department.

Hull's voice was raspy. He said he had a good mind not to see the Japanese envoys. He paused, then added that he might as well go ahead and see them, that there was "one chance out of a hundred that the news of the attack isn't true."

When Nomura and Kurusu finally were admitted to Hull's office it was 2:20 P.M. and Pearl Harbor was in flames. They were not invited to sit down, and so they stood like sheepish schoolboys in front of Hull's mahogany desk, with Andrew Jackson glaring at their backs from a steel engraving on the wall.

The Secretary asked why Tokyo had instructed the envoys to deliver the note "at precisely one o'clock," and why they had arrived so late. Diffidently, Nomura explained that there had been a delay in decoding the message. Hull cut Nomura off as he then started to answer the first question. The Secretary was in a cold fury.

"I must say that in all my conversations with you during the last nine months I have never uttered one word of untruth," he rasped. "This is borne out absolutely by the record. In all my fifty years of public service I have never seen a document that was more crowded with infamous falsehoods and distortions—infamous falsehoods and distortions on a scale so huge that I never imagined until today that any government on this planet was capable of uttering them."

"It was frightening," Nomura would recall on a later day. "I was dreadfully upset that I should have caused this man to descend to such anger."

Nomura started to say something, but Hull held up his hand. Then he waved the two envoys to the door. Heads down, Nomura and Kurusu walked out of the office. It was 2:32 P.M. Five minutes before, Steve Early had dictated the President's statement simultaneously to the three wire news services.

Among the millions of Americans who heard about Pearl Harbor on their radios that Sunday afternoon were Representative Lyndon Baines Johnson of Texas, alone in his apartment (Mrs. Johnson was in Texas); a twenty-eight-year-old Los Angeles lawyer named Richard Milhous Nixon; George Romney, thirty-four-year-old Detroit manager of the Automobile Manufacturers Association; and Robert Kennedy, a sixteen-year-old student at the Portsmouth Priory School in Portsmouth, Rhode Island.

A few hours later, Assistant Secretary of State Adolf Berle took custody of Nomura and Kurusu and moved them to a hotel, where they were put under a twenty-four-hour "protective" guard. Berle rejected Nomura's request that his Samurai sword be dispatched to him from the embassy so that he could commit suicide. Kurusu sent down for a bottle of Johnny Walker Black Label Scotch and turned on the radio.

A Summing Up

17

Is Embassy Row Obsolete?

HAULED BACK to a recollection of the sorry performances of Tokyo's Nomura and Kurusu and the corresponding opaqueness of Franklin D. Roosevelt's foreign policy advisers in the months preceding Pearl Harbor, the diplomat today will hustle forward with the assurance that diplomacy has changed since that casual era. The implication is that the average foreign office is smarter and so are its diplomatic minions. This is pure goldbrick salesmanship.

Certainly, diplomacy has changed. It has changed since the American Revolution and even since the assassination of John Kennedy. But it has changed without any substantial improvement. A better way of putting it would be that, while the need for expert diplomacy is greater, the human material entrusted with that diplomacy is no better than, and may even be inferior to, that of 1790, when Thomas Jefferson became the first Secretary of State.

Indeed, so far as the sticky chore of handling matters of serious substance is concerned, the traditional ambassador with his rich trappings is all but outmoded. The so-called summit meeting was unheard of until after World War II. But when a head of state wants to get something done nowadays, he arranges a face-to-face encounter with his opposite number of the government concerned. The reason is that, for the most part, ambassadors are not competent to conduct important conversations. Few of them come to Washington with an adequate grounding in the new international politics, and fewer still have done their homework on the United States. Also, the ambassador is

233

forced to handle too much trivia and thus hasn't the time to become
conversant with the complicated personality of the country to which
he is accredited. Many of them have socially ambitious wives who are a
double-barreled nuisance. They waste their husbands' time and energy
on party-going and they make enemies with their social aggressive-
ness.

One result of this turgid situation has been the abdication by many
ambassadors and ministers of their traditional chore of gathering
information about their host country. Increasingly over the years, this
job has been turned over, largely by default, to the various Departments of Dirty Tricks within the embassies—the military attachés and
other espionage experts planted by the intelligence services back home.
It is no accident that more than forty per cent of Soviet ambassadors
serving abroad have prior intelligence experience and connections. In
the case of the Soviet Union, the ambassador usually is the embassy's
top spy. But other embassies, including those of our Western Allies,
are also well sprinkled with professional intelligence agents, as are
American embassies abroad. It is no longer surprising to discover that
the labor attaché of the Italian Embassy in Washington is a career
employee of Rome's Secret Service, nor that the agricultural attaché of
the American Embassy in Paris is on the payroll of the Central Intelligence Agency. That's the way the ball has bounced.

There is an expedient reason for all this cloak-and-dagger activity. It
is that the Cold War and the Age of Space have made the propaganda
campaign a major vital part of every nation's national security program.
Or, as Laszlo Szabo, a former major in the Hungarian intelligence service, put it: "Propaganda is the big front in the secret war." Consequently, it became official policy to infiltrate U.S. diplomacy with youth
and labor groups financed with CIA money in order to put muscle into
America's efforts in foreign influence-peddling.

To admit such tactics are necessary in such times, however, is not
to say that the authentic diplomat should abandon himself to a succession of cocktail parties and wreath-layings. After subversion's dirty
work is done, there still remains the job of tidying up, an assignment
which earlier generations of diplomats performed with considerable
finesse and expertise. Lord Lyons' effectiveness during the Civil War
in avoiding a break between Great Britain and the United States
would be beyond the capability of most of today's residents of Embassy
Row. So would the part another Briton, Lord Harlech—then Sir

David Ormsby-Gore—played during the Cuban missile crisis of 1962.

Moreover, the decline in diplomatic quality, compounded by the unwillingness or inability of a handful of ambassadors from important countries to perform more vigorously their role as negotiators and spokesmen for their governments, has helped give the trade a bad name since World War II. It is not only that a President named Johnson should refuse upon first assuming office to take the diplomatic colony seriously, but that embassies so often have been mixed up in so many unsavory adventures.

The sordid maneuverings during the Suez crisis of 1956, for example, seriously undermined the confidence and trust of the American government in the governments of Great Britain, France and Israel. Not only were the three governments taking serious military steps behind our back, they were lying to our face and even contriving elaborate ploys to lead us further astray. These tactics were a betrayal of one of the cardinal concepts of relations among allies—that if circumstances render honesty temporarily inexpedient, no red herrings should be dragged across the path. Lyndon Johnson's successful deception of the Viet Cong and North Vietnamese regime in the months preceding the South Vietnam election was another thing entirely. In this instance, the United States was misleading an enemy with whom American troops were engaged. The British, French and Israelis were playing dirty tricks on a friend.

This is not to say that the United States has been blameless. Washington has played its role in the perversion of the ancient art of diplomacy with its tapping of telephone wires, notably those of the Dominican and Indian embassies. It has also fought fire with fire by planting false information with certain embassies after discovering those embassies were passing on intelligence to both Moscow and Peking. But it is a fact, unfortunate from the viewpoint of national security, that the United States has been more sinned against than sinning, more spied upon than spying. Even after dismissing the spy plots of the Soviet Union and its satellites as the normal activities of ideological enemies, there remains the fact that for the first time in its history the United States has been forced to mount a surveillance of friendly embassies sheltering diplomats strongly suspected of political trading with its enemies.

In short, a strong argument can be made that diplomacy has slipped back, quietly and comfortably, into the Age of Machiavelli. In the

United States, foreign governments pay lobbyists fat fees to persuade Congress to pass legislation favorable to their interests and to plant propaganda with the national media. Military and cultural attachés, scientific and educational experts on embassy staffs, steal or buy every piece of secret information they can unearth. Abroad, the United States in turn stacks its embassies with similar agents, bribes officials of unfriendly governments to defect, subverts and even overthrows other governments, and seeks to take over international organizations whose influence is deemed important to the Republic's foreign policy.

Unfortunately, the more frantic domestic critics of America's adventures in thus mixing espionage with diplomacy seem determined to avoid facing the facts of modern international life. An example is the curious fuss raised over the financial subsides provided by the Central Intelligence Agency to the National Student Association and other presumably simon-pure groups over the past decade. The outcries have been so hysterical as to raise the question of whether the United States deserves to survive the Cold War. Certainly, the nation seems to have bred a frighteningly large number of naïve and rather silly fools.

In the real world of geopolitics, there can be only amusement over the demands of some Americans that the CIA repent its wicked ways, accept only archbishops and Eagle Scouts into its house, and devote its energies to helping old ladies across the street. Americans generally just cannot seem to grasp the reality that employees of the nation's spy shop are necessarily commanded and paid to do things which would be considered untidy and coarse if practiced by members of the Ladies Aid Society of Turnip Green, Alabama.

This is curious, because the same citizens casually take for granted the machinations of the various espionage *apparati* of the Communist world and exult when the FBI catches one of the Reds with his cloak awry. In this regard, there is at least the tacit admission that the United States is engaged in a Cold War. And yet Americans always seem surprised to learn that their government has been taking countermeasures.

The fact that four Presidents—starting with Harry S Truman—believed it necessary for the CIA to infiltrate these organizations with money and counsel should lend the strategy a touch of respectability. Moreover, the record shows that the CIA's financial assistance to the students' group achieved some sound results.

In at least one instance, an American student unwittingly and off-handedly passed along some information which he believed to be superficial, but which enabled the CIA to complete its evaluation of a new Soviet missile. Of lesser but still vital significance was the information picked up in such student-rally cities as Prague, Warsaw and Moscow by CIA's willing and unwilling tools. In point of fact, the American delegates carried on only limited intelligence work of the kind any American tourist might casually undertake, but in addition they also were able to provide the CIA with important information on Communist youth representatives who might be persuaded to defect. For its money, the CIA also acquired bales of secret information on the composition and aims of various foreign organizations at world youth rallies. Purloined Communist documents in the hands of American officials show that beginning in 1955, NSA representatives attended various youth festivals and student rallies dominated by Communist delegations and managed to prevent the Reds from taking over these meetings.

There is, of course, no pat reply to those who complain that the CIA's infiltration of these American groups was immoral, except to suggest that all wars are immoral, whether they are hot or cold. And the United States was faced with the reality that the Communist regimes, and especially the Soviet Union, were spending millions of dollars a year to influence student groups, labor union leaders, Western politicians and world publications. The thought that the CIA should have sat back and done nothing seems preposterous, although the Bobbsey Twin mystique of the American politician, especially in Congress, regularly threatens legislation which would force the CIA to do just that.

Without passing moral judgment on all this hanky-panky—on all sides—it is yet important to point out that the hanky-panky makes it increasingly difficult for any embassy of any country to do its proper job of convincing by persuasion. An ambassador whose counsel is constantly bypassed by his government in favor of that of some secret intelligence operative carried on his staff as a fisheries expert will begin to have second thoughts about his own effectiveness. Eventually the ambassador will decide that there is no longer any point in trying to talk Lyndon Johnson into shifting policy just enough to give his country an advantage over an aggressive neighbor. The result of such continuing frustration is predictable—men of lesser talent wind up with ambassadorships, and the process of deterioration is quickened.

President Kennedy was often portrayed as frustrated by the inadequacies of his own State Department, but he took some comfort in the knowledge that, as he once confided to an aide, "I can tell those jokers to get off their hams and do a day's work." Certain ambassadors left Kennedy with a feeling of impotent defeat. On one gray occasion he remarked bitterly to Averell Harriman, the famed peripatetic trouble shooter, that "At least half the ambassadors in this town would have a tough job telling you the time of day."

There is every reason to believe that Kennedy was giving the Washington diplomatic colony the benefit of the doubt. The consensus of State Department officials and diplomatic journalists produced by a wide range of interviews is that over the past decade there have been only three first-rate ambassadors assigned to Washington. Two of these were from Communist governments, Soviet Ambassador Anatoly Dobrynin and the late Polish Ambassador Edward Drozniak. The other was Ormsby-Gore. Two others, Britain's Sir Patrick Dean and France's Charles Lucet, were rated as competent men whose effectiveness was greatly reduced by circumstances peculiar to their assignments.

As an effective diplomat, Dobrynin often has been compared with Ormsby-Gore, who was British Ambassador during the Kennedy years and for a short while after Lyndon Johnson took office. But the point could be made that Dobrynin rates higher marks because he came to Washington as a stranger, whereas Ormsby-Gore was an old and valued friend of President Kennedy.

At any rate, Dobrynin is held in the highest respect by both Washington officialdom and journalists who cover the diplomatic scene. He is a polished technician, a professional in a field not oversupplied with professionals, and as such he is on cordial terms with President Johnson and Secretary of State Rusk. Llewellyn Thompson, American Ambassador to Moscow, has called Dobrynin one of the five really first-rate diplomats he has ever encountered. As a good ambassador should, Dobrynin conducts important conversations and he is capable of great frankness. He has a ready smile and his English is impeccable; newsmen have discovered that he is never at a loss for an answer, no matter how tough the question. Most important, he correctly represents not only his government's viewpoint but, in turn, the American viewpoint to his bosses. He never softens an American response in an attempt to make himself look good, as, for example, Spain's Merry del Val is inclined to do. And he has a competent and reasonable-minded backstop in the Embassy's Number Two man, Minister Counselor Alexander Zinchuk.

Drozniak was in the same mold as Dobrynin, a diplomat who not only persisted in his optimism but who constantly worked to justify it. He came to Washington in 1961, during one of the many crises over Berlin, and he never had a really easy time of it until the Cold War began to thaw in 1965. But he hammered away at his theme that "as human beings" the world's peoples could not accept the possibility of a war which would mean their complete destruction. Drozniak enjoyed cordial relations with both Kennedy and Lyndon Johnson, both of whom interceded in his behalf when Congress threatened to withdraw reciprocal tariff concessions to Poland. When he died, in November, 1966, there were tributes from President Johnson and Dean Rusk to this diplomat whom the Washington *Post* described as "a most attractive man."

Britain's Ambassador Dean is also a professional, but a lackluster one. He is an able backroom man and has a massive integrity, but he has no impact on official Washington. He came to the United States from the post of head of the Foreign Office's Secret Service, and he came reluctantly since he had hoped to be named Under Secretary of the Foreign Office. Newspapermen come away from meetings with him feeling he doesn't really like his job, except for the opportunity it affords him to chum around with his old friend, Allen Dulles, former director of the Central Intelligence Agency.

France's Lucet has been dismissed by journalists Ted Weintal and Charles Bartlett, a couple of experts on the care and feeding of ambassadors, as nothing more than a cultural attaché. This seems an overly harsh appraisal. Lucet, a career man, would do better under someone other than Charles de Gaulle. Le Grand Charles is so much his own government that neither Lucet nor any other French ambassador is permitted much leeway or independence of action. Nevertheless, Lucet is popular with both Americans and his Embassy Row colleagues; he is a highly civilized human animal who seems to enjoy meeting people even at some of the more tedious "cultural" shindigs which are regular fare at the French Embassy.

The rest of the ambassadors range from ordinary to strictly ornamental. President Johnson is fond of German Ambassador Heinrich Knappstein, possibly because Knappstein stands still for Johnson's hearty Texas jollying and seems unembarrassed when Johnson plants

a ten-gallon hat on his head. But Knappstein has little influence either
with the State Department or with other ambassadors. Although he
works hard and subjects his staff to a Prussian discipline, he is dull and
unimaginative. Whatever is accomplished of any significance is the
work of Knappstein's Number One aide, Georg von Lilienfeld, although Lilienfeld is capable of raising American hackles by his glorifi-
cation of German politicians.

Spain's Merry del Val is window dressing for Franco's police state.
The Belgian Ambassador, Baron Louis Scheyven, is a pleasant fellow
who is lost in any discussion of substantive political matters. Talat Al-
Ghoussein, Ambassador of oil-rich Kuwait, does little more than enjoy
the gay life with his beautiful wife and defend the status quo of his
medieval sheikdom. A story passed around by newsmen purports to
offer Al-Ghoussein's reaction when he suffered a heart attack while
dictating to his secretary. "Don't just sit there," he told her, "go out
and buy me a hospital." American officials have trouble convincing
Pakistan Ambassador Ghulam Ahmed that the U.S. government is
serious in trying to persuade his government to spend more of its
American aid dollars to improve the lot of its citizens and less on
military hardware.

Of those ambassadors who have come and gone, Ormsby-Gore was
by far the most intelligent, the most competent and the most effective.
His rapport with Kennedy was a big help, of course, but he would
have been outstanding under any circumstances. He had the kind of
modern approach to world problems—including a willingness to accept Great Britain's fall from international eminence—that at once
burnished his idealism and sharpened his realism. Former Russian
Ambassador Mikhail Menshikov—"Smiling Mike"—skipped about
town like a song and dance man, but as a diplomat he was vastly
overrated. Unlike Dobrynin, he hadn't the imagination or the talent
to do more than parrot his government's official mouthings.

For the most part, the Latin-American, African and Arab diplomats
are a poor lot. The Latin Americans are too frivolous, the Africans too
sensitive and unsophisticated, and the Arabs too inflexible and dis-
trustful. In the past, South America had distinguished diplomats in
Colombia's Carlos Sanz de Santamaria and Bolivia's Victor Andrade,
both of whom showed a deep concern for Latin America-United States
relations and an awareness of the necessity for social reform in their
own countries. They were particular favorites of President Kennedy.

But as a whole, the Latin-American embassies are little more than country clubs for their hedonistic staffs; a German diplomat once dismissed the entire South American contingent as "those clowns."

Far more fascinating for an American, however, is the rating given various United States officials by the diplomatic colony. Since most of the ambassadors are men of high sophistication, it is not surprising that most of them took a rather cool view of Washington's assembled talent in the foreign affairs field. Equally unsurprising, perhaps, is that those who knew John Kennedy unamimously gave him exceedingly high marks as both a personality and a statesman. They found Kennedy intelligent and witty, knowledgeable and charming, courteous— and, of course, touched with style and grace.

Lyndon Johnson gets mixed reviews. Almost all foreign diplomats pay tribute to his sincerity, his dedication to his job and his capacity for hard work. Curiously, while some diplomats complain that he is abrupt and sometimes discourteous, just as many others point approvingly to his good manners. Some find him too complex, others complain that he tends to oversimplify. One diplomat summed him up for the majority when he remarked that "Mr. Johnson is an efficient President who does not give sufficient consideration to the fact that there are points of view other than his own."

Most diplomats like Secretary of State Dean Rusk, but feel he defers too much to President Johnson in making policy, especially in Vietnam. Rusk is regarded by some European ambassadors as too much of a hawk. These same men speak approvingly of Defense Secretary McNamara's "reasonableness." Ambassador-at-Large Averell Harriman and Llewllyn Thompson, former Ambassador-at-Large and present Ambassador to the Soviet Union, are rated the two ablest diplomats in the American stable. Both are cited for their frankness and their ability to grasp the problems of other governments. Several ambassadors, however, find Harriman's fabled no-nonsense approach unattractive. To them, it is unnecessary rudeness.

Former Under Secretary of State George Ball is missed by many ambassadors because he listened patiently to their problems, a part of Ball's role as devil's advocate within the Administration. But many of them find Ball's successor, Nicholas deB. Katzenbach, the former Attorney General, a trifle impatient. Most of them were sorry when Alexis Johnson, an old Far East hand, left his post as Deputy Under Secretary for Political Affairs to become Ambassador to Japan. As a career foreign officer, Johnson had a special rapport with foreign diplomats. They also have praise for William P. Bundy, Assistant Secretary of State for Far Eastern Affairs, as a professional, but very little for Bundy's brother, McGeorge, former national security affairs adviser to Kennedy, who is described by most of the diplomatic set as having been too brusque and imperious. Several ambassadors make a point of saying a good word for William B. Macomber Jr., a former Ambassador to Jordan and former assistant administrator of the Agency for International Development, who in February, 1967, was named Assistant Secretary of State for Congressional Relations. They had hoped Macomber would get a post in which he would have more contact with the diplomatic colony.

Understandably, the typical ambassador to Washington is largely preoccupied with the works and pomps of Dean Rusk, since it is the Secretary of State who sets the tone of the relationship between the State Department and Embassy Row. Even those diplomats who criticize Rusk as a Secretary of State like him as a person, and it is ironic that the quality these elegant personages most admire in the Secretary is his naturalness and lack of side. Almost to a man, Embassy Row agrees that he is an easy man to talk to and that his company is always pleasant.

Rusk is admired most for his negotiating skill, his ability to remain calm under the most trying circumstances. Two of his chief boosters in this regard, oddly enough, are Soviet Foreign Minister Andrei Gromyko and Soviet Ambassador Dobrynin, who have frequently carried praise of this facet of Rusk's competence to President Johnson. "I have tried," Gromyko told Johnson, "and I cannot force Secretary Rusk to lose his temper." Dobrynin has said that Rusk "argues like a civilized man should, with words that have meaning." Most diplomats also are impressed by what they call Rusk's "dedication" and his easygoing but firm determination to achieve what Rusk calls "a period of boredom—that is to say, peace." They go along with Rusk's belief that tensions will decrease if international relations can be kept in the background.

Nevertheless, the diplomatic colony as a whole is not, on balance, happy with Dean Rusk. Aside from the contention that Rusk should make more foreign policy, as Dean Acheson did under Harry Truman and John Foster Dulles did under Dwight D. Eisenhower, ambassadors complain that Rusk keeps them too much in the dark, that they seldom know what he's thinking.

They attribute Rusk's reticence to one of his self-imposed commandments of office—that he should communicate his views only, and privately, to the President. This, they say, makes it impossible for them to provide their foreign offices with anything but a series of expert guesses on the future direction of American foreign policy. Some blame the situation on Lyndon Johnson and his continuing campaign against leaking information, but generally the diplomats feel Rusk should convince Johnson that dropping hints is a vital part of a Secretary of State's job.

"Dean Rusk is afraid of Johnson," says one Latin-American ambassador. "He'll do anything to hold his job."

Most diplomats agree that Rusk suffers from a paucity of ideas and an unwillingness to take the initiative in the maneuvering with the Communist bloc. They say he has never suggested any ideas for a new policy toward Communist China, despite a change in the American climate which seemingly would make the public more receptive to a change in direction. He is also accused of having dilly-dallied on the problem of reorganizing NATO, with the result that De Gaulle seized the initiative and set about trying to dissolve the alliance. The Secretary is derided as a bureaucrat who lacks enterprise and, worse, as unreceptive to the ideas pressed upon him by the diplomatic colony.

Rusk is anti-European, say the Europeans, a Secretary who wastes too much of his time trying to placate Latin America. He is anti-Latin America, say Latin Americans, a Secretary who divides his time between worrying about Vietnam and calling down curses on De Gaulle. Some compare Rusk unfavorably with Arthur Goldberg, American Ambassador to the United Nations, who delights them because he gives the impression of always suggesting some new and adventurous innovation in American policy. Most ambassadors also criticize Rusk for the deterioration of relations between Washington and UN Secretary General U Thant; they claim Rusk is permitting a personal dislike of Thant to influence his appraisal of the Secretary General's peace proposals for Vietnam. And yet in all these complaints there is little bitterness or indignation. Embassy Row's attitude toward Rusk and, indeed, toward the entire American diplomatic establishment, is more professorial than cynical, more sorrowful than angry—an attitude that falls just short of being patronizing, because of its underlying note of sympathy.

Thus in their rating of Dean Rusk and other American officials concerned with foreign policy, members of the diplomatic colony are most correct in pointing out that at least some of the deficiencies they note should be attributed to the circumstance that the United States is "still a young country." They speak as diplomats. They are not recalling that the United States was born in the late year 1776, but that until shortly before World War II it was a diplomatic nonentity. In their opinion, it takes centuries to build a really sophisticated foreign service, and in that context the United States is only a little more than a quarter of a century old.

The diplomats have something there. Despite its involvements— with England in the War of 1812, with Mexico in the 1840's, with England again during the Civil War, with Spain in 1898 and with the Central Powers in 1917—the United States remained almost purely isolationist until 1939. Indeed, in that year the Congress ignored what was happening in Europe and passed the Neutrality Act which tied a knot in the cord of America's isolation. It was not until almost a year later that Washington sent arms to China to further its war against Japan and transferred fifty over-age destroyers to Great Britain to help fight the German U-boats. From its role as the Arsenal of Democracy, America went on to dispatch troops to the front lines after Pearl Harbor, and then, after the surrender of Germany and Japan, to take Britain's place as the political leader of what came to be known somewhat euphemistically as the Free World. Thus, when President Kennedy sent the first troops to Vietnam in 1962, the United States had been building its modern diplomatic establishment for only twenty-three years.

Therein may lie the cause of the general air of ineffectuality that surrounds the relationship between foreign-policy Washington and Embassy Row. It perhaps also explains why so many otherwise competent and poised State Department staffers still stand in awe of the elegant representatives of nations which have been on familiar terms with power for long centuries. In terms of diplomacy, the United States is still too young, and the Old World, especially that part which has its roots in Europe, unfortunately has grown too old. Too old, and too tired.

Index

247

A Note About the Author

Andrew Tully was born in Southbridge, Massachusetts. After graduation from high school, he went to work for the Southbridge *Evening News* and the now defunct Worcester (Mass.) *Evening Post*. At the age of 23 he took over the Southbridge *Press* and became the youngest newspaper publisher of his time. During World War II the Boston *Traveler* sent him to Europe to cover Patton's Third Army; he was the first American correspondent to enter the city of Berlin. In 1955 he was awarded the Ernie Pyle Award and the Headliners' Award for a series about the Soviet Union. Mr. Tully has covered Washington for 20 years. He writes the popular newspaper column "National Whirligig" for the Bell-McClure Syndicate. He is the author of *The Time of the Hawk, The FBI's Most Famous Cases, CIA: The Inside Story, Capitol Hill.*